OVER THE BATTLEFIELD

OPERATION EPSOM

IAN DAGLISH

Pen & Sword
MILITARY

This book is dedicated to the Argyll & Sutherland Highlanders: past, present, and future; by an author who is proud to tell the tale of their 2nd Battalion (Reconstituted); proud also that his father, when serving with the Bishopton Home Guard, wore the badge of the regiment.

CONTENTS

ACKNOWLEDGEMENTS

This book has been several years in the planning. In that time, the author has been privileged to establish friendships in many places. Furthest apart, and yet most closely connected, have been Stirling Castle, spiritual home of the Argyll & Sutherland Highlanders, and the village of Gavrus, where the reputation of the Argylls' 2nd Battalion (Reconstituted) was forged in fire. The fight for Gavrus thus became a worthy addition to the annals of the Old 93rd, the 'Thin Red Line' of the Crimea. A high point in the author's research came in 2004, when he accompanied a party of Argylls on their return to Gavrus. On a memorable sunny afternoon in late June, as the band played in the grounds of the Gavrus château, the Jocks sat and told their stories to admiring young folk from the village. Walking down across the bridges, the antitank gunners revisited the spots where their six-pounders were sited, sixty years before.

Scottish soldiers feature prominently in this story, and the author is grateful to Rod MacKenzie at Stirling Castle and Sandy Leishman at the 518 Sauchiehall Street museum for access to the archives (respectively) of the Argyll & Sutherland Highlanders and the Royal Highland Fusiliers. Others deserving of the author's thanks include David Fletcher, Historian at The Tank Museum, Bovington, who supplements the valuable archive in his care with a vast store of knowledge freely shared. Historians of the Second World War should applaud the continuing efforts of Allan Williams, Air Photo Archive Manager at The Aerial Reconnaissance Archive (TARA) at Keele University, to ensure the preservation in accessible form of this important national archive. Though the British 'Public Record Office' at Kew has now lost its unique brand identity to become yet another generic 'National Archives', nevertheless its outstanding service continues to do justice to a national treasure.

The author thanks the distinguished Normandy historian Jean-Claude Perrigault for his gracious offers of documents and advice, and Charles Markuss for freely sharing his comprehensive knowledge of the German Army as well as assisting with German nomenclature and advising on many technical matters. Both Charles Markuss and Stephen King contributed valuable documents relating to the Royal Artillery. Further help has come from a growing body of keen historians striving to solve the remaining puzzles of the Normandy campaign, especially such 'historiens passionnés' as Philippe Caffarel of Gavrus, Gérard Ghewy of Tourmauville, and Jean-Marc Lesueur, who welcomes visiting veterans and their families, and whose family tend the graves of so many British soldiers, including the three Argylls who lie in Tourville.

Very special thanks go to two friends who have assisted this project. Kevin Baverstock, cartographer and Normandy historian, has continued to offer encouragement and given freely both of his Normandy archives and of his remarkable image-processing expertise. Annick Bittle of Gavrus is thanked for unfailing hospitality to a weary historian returning to the village after long days spent tramping the Odon valley with notebook and camera under June sun and (as in 1944) the occasional 'orage'.

The author is grateful to the late Monsieur Raoul Caraboeuf for battlefield photographs taken shortly after EPSOM, and to John Roberts for archive material in the care of the 43rd Light Infantry. The Library and Archives of Canada, Ottawa, made available records of photo reconnaissance carried out by 400 Squadron, RCAF. Images © Crown Copyright 1944/MOD are reproduced with the permission of the Controller of Her Majesty's Stationery Office.

INTRODUCTION

'Some battles are easy to describe, others difficult, a few impossible.'

So wrote a historian of the Normandy campaign, who placed Operation EPSOM squarely in the last category. Alexander McKee went on to depict the battle as 'impossible to describe in any connected narrative.'[1] Perhaps this is one reason why EPSOM has been neglected by history, passed over as yet another of Montgomery's attempts to take the city of Caen. Yet this book is more than a response to the gauntlet thrown down by McKee. This author believes that EPSOM has importance and interest on several levels. Strategically, this was the battle during which the German army in Normandy lost the strategic initiative. As a tactical study, this Normandy battle is almost unique in offering glimpses of the contestants' key formations in both attack and defence, since the roles became reversed half-way through.

This study was originally inspired by the 2nd Argyll & Sutherland Highlanders' defence of a little French village in the Odon valley. Were the story of Operation EPSOM simply a matter of ground taken and lost, the Argylls' isolated action might seem almost an irrelevance to the 'big picture'. However, since one of the key themes of this book is the way in which inexperienced British troops stood up against some of Germany's best, the example of Gavrus becomes very much relevant. The author is pleased to recount the story in unprecedented detail, with a chapter to itself. It is a tale worth telling.

The author hopes that the use of maps, diagrams, and a grouping of key events into discrete passages will bring to life the story of a complex battle. Whether or not the result succeeds as a 'connected narrative', you the reader may judge.

Ian Daglish
Alderley Edge
2007

Three Argyll & Sutherland Highlanders lie in Tourville churchyard.

Private Charlton
A Coy, aged 27

Private Morrison
A Coy, aged 21

Private Brittlebank
C Coy, aged 24

VERSON – La Gare

Today the A84 Autoroute replaces the former railway. Looking east from Grainville towards Colleville, this sector of the single-track line ran in a deep cutting.

NOTES ON CONTENT AND TERMINOLOGY

1.

Like the author's previous work, Above the Battlefield: Operation GOODWOOD, this is the story of a battle. Once again, rather than burden the story with overmuch technical detail, a quantity of background information is presented in chapter-end reference notes and in separate appendices, organized by topic, into which the reader may dip at will. As certain appendices in the GOODWOOD study are applicable also to EPSOM, it was felt best to avoid repetition and instead offer complementary information. For example: whereas the earlier work presented appendices detailing British armour organization and tactics, this volume presents details of British infantry organization, antitank tactics, and tank-infantry coordination, all more relevant to the EPSOM battle. However, one short appendix dealing with map interpretation is repeated herein for the reader's convenience.

2.

Wherever possible, direct quotations are presented verbatim, with original spelling, punctuation, and abbreviation. In the case of military terminology, the author hopes that the reader will be able to decipher (for example) such standard forms as 'pl' for platoon, 'coy' for company, or 'ATk' for antitank from the context in which they appear. In a similar vein, units of measurement are generally reported in terms appropriate to the nationality. The Allies referred to guns by weight of shell (6 pounder, 25 pounder) and calibre in millimetres (75mm, 'eighty-eight'); whereas the German nomenclature favoured centimetres (7.5cm, 8.8cm; note however that the point is used rather than the German comma for decimals). Both imperial and metric measures of distance are used, as appropriate. For example, if a British unit advanced on a front estimated as 'two hundred yards', it would be misleading to record the measure as 200m, yet otiose to give it as 182.88m. One further point should be made about British terminology. In other armies, the 'regiment' was a fighting unit composed of integrated battalions. As explained in Appendix II, British brigades were composed of battalion-strength units, whether tanks or infantry, each with its own, proudly held regimental affiliations, and it was not at all unusual for such an individual battalion to refer to themselves as 'the regiment'. So was maintained 'the British practice of adopting the most confusing nomenclature possible.'[2]

3.

Two important line features traversed the EPSOM battlefield north of, and roughly parallel with, the River Odon. In 1944, the main highway between Caen and Villers-Bocage was the Route Nationale 175, running through Mouen, Tourville, and le Valtru. A few hundred metres to the north ran a single-track railway, its cuttings and embankments representing a major obstacle to north-south traffic. Today, the old road has been reclassified as the D 675; and its replacement, the RN 175 (recently renamed A84), is a major highway built over (and sadly obscuring) the former rail bed.

The spelling of French place names is often found to vary, even in French-language publications. For consistency (apart from verbatim quotations - see above), modern names are used. The single exception to this rule is the little hamlet known in 1944 as 'le Haut-du-Bosq' (or to the Seaforth Highlanders, HANT de BOSQUE). Today the name has fallen out of use, modern maps referring to the cluster of buildings south of Cheux simply as 'le Bosq'.

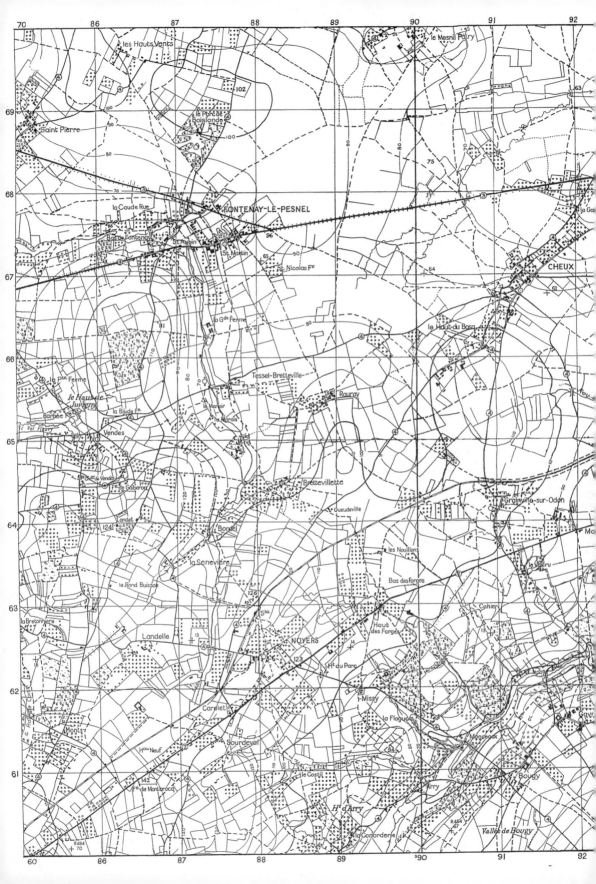

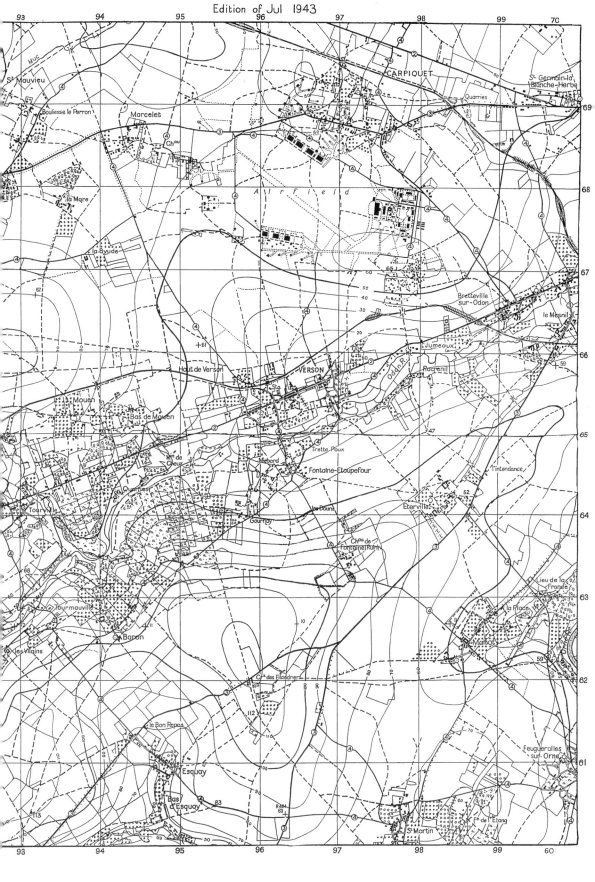

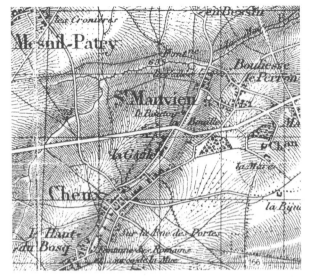

But the earlier name figures in so many wartime accounts that to change it would be needlessly confusing. Otherwise, place names are presented as they appear – including hyphenation - on modern maps of the French Institut Géographique National (IGN). Hence the village often referred to by the British as 'Saint Mauvieu' appears in its modern form of 'St-Manvieu', and the nearby stream dubiously known as the 'Muc' assumes its more decorous modern appellation of 'Mue'. As to pronunciation, readers are left to their own devices, like the men of 1944 who, confronted with 'le Mesnil-Patry' quickly settled on 'mess-in-the-pantry'. As for 'Cheux', while some Argylls favoured 'shair', the Glasgow Highlanders 'decided to call it "CHEWKS", and it has been known as that in the Unit ever since.'

4.

English-language history often anglicizes German terms. As a general rule, names of German units, ranks, weapons systems, etc. will herein be presented in German form (again, verbatim quotes excepted). There are several reasons for this. Recent years have seen a 'creeping' of German terms (*Panzer, Schwerpunkt, Panzerfaust,* and even *Auftragstaktik*) into English-language texts. Adopted piecemeal, this can result in grammatical absurdities (e.g., *'panzers'* or *'panzerfausts'* in place of the correct plural forms *Panzer* and *Panzerfäuste*). At a time when increasing use is being made of German sources, by translators writing in numerous languages, it seems all the more inappropriate to translate original terminology into a confusing muddle of pidgin-German terms. The author hopes that the reader will feel flattered rather than inconvenienced by these attempts at precision.

References

(1) 'Caen, Anvil of Victory', Alexander McKee, p 153-155

(2) 'Firepower', Bidwell & Graham, p 197

Chapter 1

MID JUNE:
DAYS OF FRUSTRATION

The invasion had succeeded. On 6 June, over 150,000 troops were landed in Normandy. Within a week, a single Allied bridgehead stretched from the River Orne to the eastern coast of the Cotentin peninsula. The *Kriegsmarine* was contained. Successive attacks by destroyers, U-boats, and E-boats were driven off; RAF Bomber Command would shortly take the fight to their bases to complete the neutralization of the sea-borne threat to the vital shipping lanes. The enemy threat from the air failed to match expectations. Though *Luftwaffe* sorties over the crowded Normandy beachhead would be a continuing irritant for weeks to come, the impact of these was marginal; the elaborate anti-aircraft precautions of the invasion plan proved largely superfluous. But command of the sea and of the air was not matched on the ground in Normandy. As days turned to weeks, the armies' progress fell increasingly behind plan. Frustration set in.

STRATEGY AND TACTICS

The invasion planning was awesome in its detail. Rather less detailed, and certainly less specific, were the plans for what the armies would do once ashore. This was perhaps to be expected. Detailed planning covered every aspect of the delivery of the invasion forces to the Normandy beaches, their reinforcement, and their sustenance. The major unknown factor was the weather, and even that might be accommodated by some flexibility in timing. Conversely, once the invaders were landed, the responses of the enemy were unpredictable. Tactically, would the *Panzer* reserves be released early or held back? Strategically, would Allied deception plans persuade the defenders to retain forces in the Pas de Calais, against the threat of a further invasion force landing there?

The general idea was that the Allied forces should strike out aggressively. To the west, the Americans would concentrate on sealing off the Cotentin peninsula, preparatory to freeing the port of Cherbourg and breaking out towards Brittany. In the east, the British would hold Caen and, more importantly, the high ground east of the Orne River. This defensive bulwark would then cover the left flank of forces pushing rapidly towards the line Vire – Falaise.

There was concern that the pattern of previous amphibious operations should not be repeated. The landing at Salerno in September 1943 had come worryingly close to being forced back into the sea, until Kesselring ordered his defending forces to withdraw north. More recently, in January 1944 an American corps had landed unopposed behind German lines at Anzio. There, the painstakingly slow build-up of the beachhead and Kesselring's energetic response in sealing it off had combined to reduce the strategic value of the operation. From Churchill downwards, determination was expressed that OVERLORD should not be 'another Anzio'. This factor influenced Montgomery's strategy for the ground battle.

From the outset, on assuming command of 21st Army Group in January, Montgomery was determined to deny Rommel the strategic initiative in Normandy. His earliest intervention in the OVERLORD planning was to demand what others had seen as ideal but ambitious: a substantial expansion of the initial assault from three to five divisional beachheads. This achieved, he went on to insist that the flanks of the amphibious force be covered by three full airborne divisions, insurance against early reinforcement of the defenders. And the emphasis once ashore would be on rapid exploitation. *'Fairly powerful armoured force thrusts on the afternoon of D-Day… to wait till D plus 1 would be to lose the opportunity, and also to lose the initiative.'* The tone was aggressive. *'Armoured thrusts must force their way inland'* in order to establish *'firm bases well in advance of our own main bodies'* which *'the enemy will be unable to by-pass.'* Risks were to be taken. *'I am prepared to accept almost any risk in order to carry out these tactics. I would accept even the total loss of the armoured brigade groups.'*[1] (Perhaps regretting the enormity of this last statement, though characteristically unwilling to retract it, Montgomery went on to add that the eventuality was 'not really possible'.)

There can be little doubt that Montgomery's expectation of penetrating the crust of German defences and sending armour *'cracking about'* in the defenders' rear was genuine. The tone was to be set by the very first wheeled vehicles to cross the Normandy beaches. 'Bingforce' was a reinforced squadron of the Inns of Court (a Royal Armoured Corps armoured car regiment). 140 cavalry and engineer personnel in half-tracks and scout cars (as many as could be crammed into the two LCTs available) were to land on Juno beach immediately behind the Canadian assault troops and press inland before the defenders were awake to the invasion. According to the plan, the cars were to race inland, destroying key bridges *behind* them before 'holing up' to **Inns of Court.** await relief.[2]

On a still larger scale, 7th Armoured Division was to land as quickly as possible following the establishment of a beachhead. The division's arrival was delayed by continuing poor weather conditions. Meanwhile, hopes for bold forays 'cracking about' behind German lines dwindled as a defensive line stiffened. Having failed to take Caen on 6 June, the following days saw British 3rd Division unable to break the German line to the north of the city. To either side, the fighting swung to and fro. East of Caen, paratroops and Scots strove for a lodgement on the high ground of the Bois de Bavent. To the west, Canadians and SS commenced a blood feud astride the Caen-Bayeux highway. But the net result was a front line considerably closer to the beaches

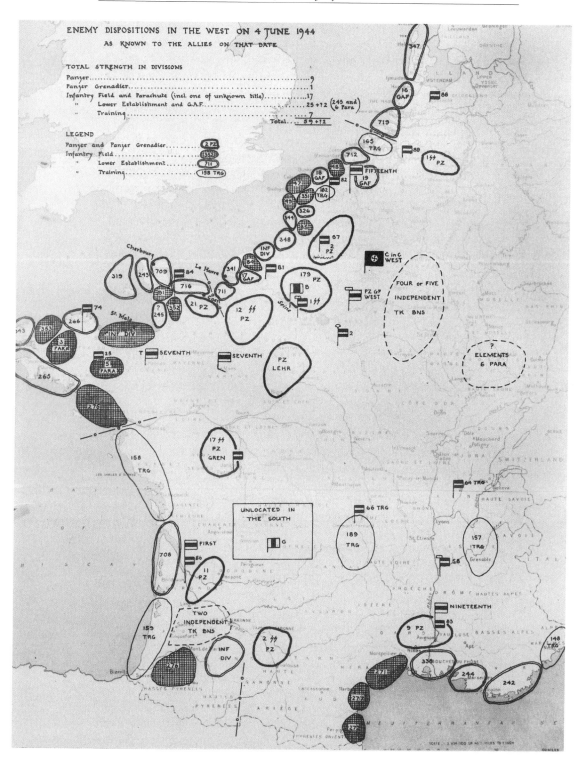

than planned. 2nd Army commander Dempsey's fear that the campaign might 'congeal' if early advances were not achieved seemed increasingly likely to be realised. To unglue the situation, he and Montgomery were fully prepared to land the British 1st Airborne Division behind Caen: the Airborne were put on standby, though Air Marshall Leigh-Mallory refused to approve the operation.

Leigh-Mallory had been similarly pessimistic about the 6 June landings, pressing Eisenhower that the proposed drop of two American airborne divisions would result in disastrous casualties. Eisenhower later confessed that approving that drop had caused him more anxiety even than authorizing the sea-borne invasion.[3] In the latter case, he had only to accept the findings of the meteorologists; the former decision meant overruling his air Commander-in-Chief. In the event, even though widely dispersed by weather conditions, the American drop was a strategic success. Whatever his motives, Leigh-Mallory's misgivings were not entirely unfounded. Earlier airborne operations, in particular over Sicily, had come close to disaster. In mid-June the full extent of the disruption caused to the Germans in Normandy by the American airborne assaults had yet to be assessed, yet their dispersal far beyond the target Drop Zones was recognised only too clearly. Undaunted, Dempsey continued planning a further drop well into June.[4] Once 7th Armoured Division was ashore – the first full British armoured division to take the field in Normandy – Montgomery's hopes of some *'cracking about'* were rekindled. Ever fond of cricket analogy, he was going to *'hit the Germans for six'*; to achieve this, his 'best batsmen' would be called to the crease. The formations selected to envelop Caen were two divisions that had served him well in North Africa: 51st Highland, whose divisional signs marking the route of Montgomery's advances led him to call them his 'Highway Decorators'; and 7th Armoured, Monty's 'Desert Rats'. The

7th Armoured Division – The Deset Rats.

highlanders would bludgeon their way around the south east of Caen, there to form the anvil against which, paratroops or no paratroops, the Desert Rats would strike the hammer blow. To achieve this, the armour would loop far to the west, by-passing strongholds bitterly disputed by the *Panzer-Lehr* division: Tilly, Audrieu, and Cristot. Exploiting an identified weak point in the German line, 7th Armoured would descend on the market town of Villers-Bocage, and thence strike east to complete the envelopment of Caen.

The plan failed. 51st Highland Division proved unable to break out of the bridgehead east of the Orne River, their attempt beaten back with heavy loss. 7th Armoured also fell short of Montgomery's expectations. Tactics honed in the wide open spaces of North Africa proved impossible to replicate in the close country of Normandy. After advancing

51st (Highland) Infantry Division.

along narrow country lanes, sometimes on a single-vehicle front, 22nd Armoured Brigade was famously ambushed at Villers-Bocage. And so, on 13 June, D+7, the expected envelopment of Caen faltered with its hammer and anvil still thirty kilometres apart. For the time being, there would be no *'cracking about'*.[5] With his star batsmen in disgrace, Montgomery would have to turn to less experienced players, further down the batting order. And for them there would be an entirely different battle plan.

THE FOLLOW-UP CORPS

If the strategic planners experienced a level of frustration in the early days of the Normandy campaign, so too did many of those 'waiting the call' in England. Numerous personal accounts reveal the feelings of those left behind by the events of 6 June. Whether driven by patriotic fervour, by the discomforts and inconveniences of the transit camps that ringed the southern coasts of England, or simply by a desire to 'get it over with', many of these looked forward with keen anticipation to embarking for France. In this, the attitudes of inexperienced follow-up formations contrasted sharply with some of the experienced divisions chosen to spearhead the invasion. Divisions brought back from North Africa and Italy to breach the Normandy defences included many who harboured bitter resentment against *'Fling 'em in Monty'*.[6]

As Montgomery and Dempsey reconsidered their plans for developing the Normandy campaign, a key factor would be the 'follow-up' divisions of VIII Corps. The Corps had evolved slowly since its birth, at Aldershot in the troubled summer of 1940, and its principal components were now the three divisions: Guards Armoured, 11th Armoured, and 15th Scottish.

Forming an armoured division from the Brigade of Guards had been a somewhat revolutionary idea. When senior guardsmen were first told that they would be responsible for programmes of mechanical, gunnery, and wireless training, *'None of the assembled officers knew anything about tanks and they left the room feeling slightly dazed.*[7] By tradition, the regiments of Foot Guards held themselves to be the best infantry in the world (a role to which they would speedily revert after the war). But in tanks? Doubts notwithstanding, the situation in mid-1941 remained desperate; armour rather than infantry now appeared the decisive arm; and His Majesty the King gave approval.

11th Armoured Division had a less controversial genesis. In its embryonic form it followed 1940 thinking in having two brigades of tanks, 29th and 30th. By mid 1942 the trend was towards a more balanced structure, and the division exchanged 30th Armoured for a brigade of infantry from the Welsh border shires. 159 Brigade's three infantry battalions thus became *'motorized'* (not armoured, but assured of soft-skin transport to enhance their mobility), alongside the single, armoured, 'motor' infantry battalion of 29th Armoured Brigade. That brigade's three tank regiments came from different corners of the Kingdom. Still, the 23rd Hussars and 24th Lancers, the 2nd Northamptonshire Yeomanry, and the 2nd Fife and Forfarshire Yeomanry all shared the traditions of shire yeomanry: peacetime volunteers, officered by country gentlemen and members of the shire town professions. The training the division underwent was relentless and serious, especially during the period from March 1941 to September 1942 when it was commanded by the armour visionary, Percy Hobart. *'Up hill and down dale, both literally and figuratively, he chased his men, from Brigadiers downwards; yet all respected his remarkable talents.'*[8] Training apparently complete, the division was looking forward to deployment to North Africa when sailing was cancelled at short notice. (The Casablanca conference identified infantry, not armoured, formations as the priority; adding insult to injury, drafts of men already embarked were not returned to the division.) So, through 1943, though 11th Armoured considered itself fully trained and battle-ready, its components still lacked combat experience.

This state of affairs changed in two vital aspects at the end of the year. The 24th Lancers left, to be replaced by 3rd Battalion, The Royal Tank Regiment. The contrast was marked. Three regiments of armoured cavalry, 'donkey wallopers' leading armoured 'sabre squadrons', were now joined by Tank Corps professionals, some of whom had experienced four years of armoured warfare, from France to the Middle East. And with the appointment of a new commander, fresh from the North Africa campaign, 11th Armoured Division gained the youngest general officer in the British army. At the age of thirty seven, Major-General G P B ('Pip') Roberts had already gained more experience in the turret of a tank than any officer of comparable rank.

15th (Scottish) was the infantry division in this tank-heavy corps. Yet it had not always been so. Raised in haste and confusion in September 1939, the nascent division was long starved of equipment, selections of its manpower frequently drafted to fill-out other formations. Then, in 1943 came the order that the 15th Scottish was to become one of the newly-conceived 'mixed' divisions: one of its three infantry brigades to be replaced by a brigade of tanks. The new Order of Battle proved temporary. Before the end of the year, 6th Guards Tank Brigade moved on, replaced by a brigade of Highland infantry. But the intervening opportunity for exercises in infantry-tank cooperation had been put to good use, as later experience was to show.[9]

Rather than return the lost 45 Brigade, the War Office saw fit to assign 227 (Highland) Brigade to the division. For one of this brigade's battalions, the 10th Highland Light Infantry, the assignment was actually a return to the 15th Division. The other two infantry battalions of the brigade were Regulars, something new to the 15th, whose infantry units had hitherto been strictly Territorial: *'richly endowed… with the Territorial Army's spirit of voluntary service to country and pride in regiment.'*[10] However, while Regular Army in title, the 2nd Gordon Highlanders and 2nd Argyll and Sutherland Highlanders in equal measure had their roots in the Territorial Army. Each had been promoted in status (respectively, from the parent regiments' 11th and 15th battalions) when the decision was made to 'reconstitute' battalions lost at the fall of Singapore. The material impact of the change was slight, but for both battalions the honour was significant. For example, the 2nd Argylls proudly

Guards Armoured Division.

11th Armoured Division.

15th Scottish Division.

assumed the mantle of the 93rd of Foot – the famed *'thin red line'* of Balaclava.

And so, 15th (Scottish) Division reverted to an organisation similar to that of its illustrious predecessor of the First World War: a triangular formation of three infantry brigades, each with its three battalions of infantry. The men carried on their shoulders the 'O' badge of their forbears ('O' being the fifteenth letter of the alphabet), albeit now with the addition, sanctioned by His Majesty, of the red Lion Rampant, the Royal Emblem of Scotland. And, as the sole infantry division of VIII Corps, the 15th could expect to play a leading part. According to the accepted wisdom of the British Army, it was the infantry who breached the enemy's lines for the cavalry (or latterly the armour) to sweep through. So, by 1944, in the words of the divisional historian, *'the 15th Scottish was a Division second to none and trained to the moment – though most of its fine soldiers still lacked fighting experience and asked themselves, as soldiers will, what that unknown experience would bring.'*[11] Or, as the history of the divisional reconnaissance regiment recounts, *'The regiment awaited its own D Day like the batsman who has proved his eye and strokes at the nets, yet has a certain feeling of the stomach mingled with his impatience and his curiosity about the bowling as he awaits his innings.'*[12]

In truth, the respective divisions of VIII Corps were as ready as the available training could make them. Indeed, some units may have been over-trained. Since the make-do-and-mend days of 1940 and 1941, by 1944 equipment was flowing freely. In a Britain where everyday life was overshadowed by rationing and shortages, Army equipment and supplies were now arriving with unparalleled bounty. Training exercises were laid on in profusion. At this time were seen the largest military manoeuvres ever to take place on British soil.[13] But how successful was the training? This was a time when the development of Battle Schools for officers was a relative novelty, and standardised Battle Drill for soldiers was viewed with considerable disquiet by elements within the Army. Given the peculiarly regimental structure and traditions of the British Army, the nature and content of training remained very much a regimental matter. Some vital aspects of warfare were simply not covered. Much training revolved around weapons skills (learning by rote, including the notorious 'naming of parts') rather than battle tactics. A highly respected infantry leader of the Normandy campaign later stated that, *'The British infantry platoons and companies were over-trained and bored stiff with basic infantry tactics.'*[14] Training was further complicated by lack of awareness of what was being trained for. Even though 11th Armoured Division was finally permitted to extend its manoeuvres over and through the rich farmland of the Yorkshire Wolds, this open, gently undulating landscape of crop and pasture bore little resemblance to the dense bocage that awaited in the Normandy hedgerow country. And as for the opposition, *'For most who trained us, what we could expect from the enemy was a closed book.'*

VIII Corps insignia.

What would be the task of the Corps as a whole? Only in April did divisional commanders and above attend Montgomery's exposition of the Normandy plan at St Paul's School. For the rest, the move of VIII Corps to the south of England clearly heralded a destination somewhere in northwest Europe. And the fervent activity of waterproofing vehicles which was to occupy so much of that spring indicated the imminence of departure. But only with the momentous events of 6 June did the 'follow-up' role of VIII Corps become clear. And even then, as Pip Roberts revealed at an 11th Armoured Division conference held at 10.00 hours on 7 June, the task was undefined.

'The general plan of the Battle of Normandy was made known… There were three possibilities for our employment on landing,

(1) to join the 7th Armoured Division in a chase for Falaise;

(2) to concentrate on the bridgehead for the first big thrust;

(3) to fight on the beaches if things had not gone as well as expected.'[15]

Hardly a sound basis for detailed battle plans.

THE *SS-PANZERKORPS*

The formations which were to lie in the direct path of VIII Corps' first attack, and the later arrivals which were to threaten the British gains, were the four *SS-Panzer* divisions of the first and second *SS-Panzerkorps*. These too had experienced frustrations in the course of the first half of 1944.

The 'senior partner' in the *SS-Panzerkorps, 1. SS-Panzerdivision* proudly bore the name *'Leibstandarte'*, harking back to early days when the unit served as Hitler's personal lifeguard unit. Evolving from honour guard (mocked by the army as 'asphalt soldiers') into battle hardened veterans, the *Leibstandarte* fought through Poland, France, Greece, and Russia. Only in 1942 did the division enjoy a brief opportunity to rest and refit in the south of France. Then, following the cataclysmic disaster of the loss of *6. Armee* at Stalingrad, in early 1943 the *Leibstandarte* was sent from the OKH Reserve in occupied France back east to the Russian front. There, flanked by its sister *2. SS-Panzer* (*'Das Reich'*) and *3. SS-Panzer* (*'Totenkopf'*) divisions, the division took part in the great battles for Kharkov and the Kursk salient.

Back in the west, urgent steps were taken to fill the void left by the departed reserves. Contrary to the wishes of the *Waffen SS* (whose high loss rates led them to prefer reinforcement of existing divisions over proliferation) two new formations were raised, which ultimately became the *9. SS-Panzer* (*'Hohenstaufen'*) and *10.SS-Panzer* (*'Frundsberg'*) divisions. And shortly after began the creation of yet another. This was the division destined to stand in

1. SS
Panzerdivision
Leibstandarte.

12. SS
Panzerdivision
Hitlerjugend.

9. SS
Panzerdivision
Hohenstaufen.

10. SS
Panzerdivision
Frundsberg.

the path of VIII Corps: *12. SS-Panzerdivision*, its title of *'Hitlerjugend'* inspired by the youth movement which provided much of its rank and file.

Though a great deal has been written about the uniqueness of the *Hitlerjugend* division as a fighting formation, the impression can be misleading. In some respects, the division even bore certain similarities to its future opponent of 15th Scottish. Each had been formed in a time of hardships and shortages around a cadre extracted from a 'parent' division (15th Scottish from 52nd Lowland; *Hitlerjugend* from the *Leibstandarte*). Each had experienced changes in role: the Scots briefly becoming one of the 'New Model' divisions incorporating a tank brigade; *Hitlerjugend* being initially conceived as a *Panzergrenadier* rather than a *Panzer* division. Each had experienced trials and tribulations in sourcing the equipment needed. In 1940, 15th Scottish scavenged so heterogeneous a collection of antique artillery pieces that Mons Meg (a 15th Century cannon) was daily rumoured to be on her way to the division from Edinburgh Castle. In its brief and hasty period of formation, *Hitlerjugend* had to make do with Russian antitank guns, Italian trucks (many merely light vans, lacking cross-country capability) and Moto-Guzzi motor-cycles for the dispatch riders, as well as various other non-standard items.[16]

Nor was the age difference so great as is sometimes supposed. *Hitlerjugend* was recruited largely from seventeen year-olds of the 1925-1926 age-class. By 1944, two thirds of its members were eighteen years old, most of the rest older, an age profile not dissimilar to the *Hohenstaufen* and the *Frundsberg* divisions. While the average age within 15th Scottish was higher, this was largely because the division had been forming and training for four years, and it too was not without its share of recently-joined eighteen year olds (and younger, as many a Normandy headstone will attest).[17]

In the coming clash between British VIII Corps and the two *SS-Panzer* corps, the differences that really mattered were not so much age as attitude, training, and experience. For all the difficulties of its hasty recruitment, the *Hitlerjugend* enjoyed a proportion of battle-hardened leaders. Many of these were from the parent *Leibstandarte*, some like Wilhelm Mohnke literally battle scarred (after losing his foot in 1941 he was relieved from combat duties until recalled to command the new *26. SS-Panzergrenadier-Regiment*). The young men who made up the Other Ranks were receptive to the veterans' training. Though not of itself military, *'The "boy scout" aspect of Hitler Youth training*

Wilhelm Mohnke.

made them especially suitable as soldiers from the fieldcraft point of view, and the "political" indoctrination, such as it was, had given them not merely a "cause" and a "hero", but more important, a belief in the "destiny of youth" which resulted in a conscious feeling of superiority amounting to arrogance, no bad armour against the unspeakable shock of war.'[18]

Whereas certain aspects of the training received by the infantry and tanks of the British VIII Corps were of questionable utility, veteran officers and NCOs who had served with the *Leibstandarte* had a very clear idea of what was needed. The priorities were recorded by a divisional staff officer. First: physical fitness (many of the recruits were malnourished and in poor physical condition). Second: 'character development' (many were orphaned; many had suffered either directly from bombing or from evacuation from the cities). And third came combat preparation. This was not the *'naming of parts'* so beloved of the British. In a departure from pre-war German policy, it was decreed that, *'It is not reasonable to teach the recruit, during long lectures on the science of ballistics… all the technical details… since nearly all these matters present themselves in a significantly different manner later on the field of battle.'[19]* The emphasis was squarely on getting the recruits out of the classroom, away from the barrack-square, onto the simulated battlefield. Introductory use of blank rounds was to be minimized. The discipline and responsibility of live firing was introduced early. While British junior officers might engage in sand-table exercises and classroom TEWTS ('tactical exercises without troops'), their German equivalents would be expected to deliver their solution to a tactical problem in the form of a 'frag' order, shouted to their classmates and straight afterwards implemented in the field.[20]

Drill was abandoned. Indeed, in the similarly trained *9. SS 'Hohenstaufen'*, divisional commander Bittrich found to his dismay in January 1944 that an honour guard would be required for a visit by *Generalfeldmarschall* von Rundstedt. But his *Panzergrenadiere* had no training in presenting arms! Fortunately, it was found that the ceremony was still practised in the divisional *Wirtschafts-Bataillon*, and so the visiting *Befehlshaber West* was greeted by an honour guard of butchers and bakers.[21] In further contrast to British policy, camaraderie between officers and men was actively promoted, even to the extent of using first names (though such informality should not blind one to the extremely harsh discipline characteristic of the German ground forces).

And to this ultra-practical training was added the final ingredient: real action. In early June, while the formations of VIII Corps were awaiting passage to Normandy, the *Hitlerjugend*, training and equipping barely complete, was flung into battle. Losses were heavy. Armour tactics which the

Waffen SS troops learning their trade on the eastern front.

division's leaders had developed against the Russians proved less effective against Canadians supported by the Royal Artillery.[22] NCOs accustomed to the savagery of the eastern front allowed young soldiers to commit acts of barbarism which led to an escalation of reprisals.[23] Inexperienced young *Panzer* men and *Panzergrenadiere* quickly learned lessons of ruthlessness and survival. Meanwhile by 11 June, when the decision was made to recall *Hohenstaufen* and *Frundsberg* to Normandy, the young soldiers of those divisions had experienced two full months of bitter combat on the Russian front. In knee-deep snow and through glutinous muddy thaw, they had repeatedly prevailed against superior numbers. They had experienced heavy losses and recovered bodies of comrades brutally tortured. Such were the opponents gathering to oppose the men of VIII Corps.

WEATHER

In the first week of June, the Allies had been doubly fortunate. Fortunate both in forecasting an improvement in the unseasonably bad weather that might permit the invasion to go ahead as planned, and in having leadership with the courage to trust the forecast and commit to the assault. (The German defenders, conversely, lacked the ability to monitor Atlantic weather conditions[24], and missing the signs of improvement were lulled into a false sense of security.) Had the invasion been postponed more than twenty four hours, the next date when moon and tide served would have been a fortnight away. Quite apart from the disruption to plans and risks to security, launching an invasion in the third week of June would have proved disastrous if not impossible, due to still worse weather. (Omar Bradley later pointed out that had the invasion been postponed yet further, i.e., to July, *'it would have been August before we could count on quality tonnage through Cherbourg, September before we broke out. Instead of wintering on the Siegfried Line, we would have been lucky to have reached the Seine. And France rather than the Rhineland would have been ravaged... even Paris might have been reduced by artillery and air bombardment.'*)[25]

The invaders' good fortune did not last. The 6 June landings succeeded in spite of the worst early-June weather in recent memory, but still worse was to come. Following 6 June, fresh to strong winds and rough seas greatly hampered the build up of the bridgehead and occasionally threatened air operations. Anxiety turned to dismay on 19 June as unexpectedly strong northerly winds set in, growing in strength. By the end of the day, an onshore wind exceeding thirty knots was making the operation of small craft over the landing areas impossible. Troops already embarked for the short cross-channel voyage were left having to ride out the storm in their vessels, often

inadequately equipped for the ordeal.

The unforeseen 'Great Storm' raged for three full days. By the time it abated on 22 June, the Normandy coastline was strewn with the wreckage. In addition to eight hundred craft of all sizes washed up on shore, in various stages of disrepair, severe damage had been done to the 'Mulberry' harbours so energetically sponsored by Winston Churchill. Indeed, the American

'Mulberry A', virtually complete in the waters off Omaha Beach, was considered irreparable. As its designer found, '*I visited the devastation at Omaha beach where I saw bombardons whirling about in the water, numerous vessels drifting ashore and three small landing craft piled on top of each other on the beach. It was a tragic sight.*'[26]

The build-up phase was critical. Even as the forces engaged on 6 June grappled with one another, the rush to reinforce them got under way. Both sides faced logistical difficulties. Every Allied soldier, every piece of equipment, every drop of fuel had to be transported from England. On the other hand, German reinforcements were found by stripping sectors already under threat. Largely dependent on rail transport for their mobility, German armoured formations struggled to make progress over a French railway network ravaged by Allied airpower. Infantry divisions from Brittany and further afield made slow progress by bus and bicycle, in farm carts and on foot. Yet on they came, divisions which could perhaps form a defensive cordon around the beachhead and allow the Panzer divisions to be withdrawn into strategic reserve.

Montgomery wrote on 20 June. *'This weather is the very devil. A gale all day yesterday; the same today. Nothing can be unloaded. Lying in ships off the beaches is everything I need to resume the offensive with a bang.'* [27] His frustration was palpable. Two weeks after invasion, the Allies' progress was slow. In the British sector there seemed real risk of the situation 'gluing up'. The D Day objective of Caen still stood rock-like in defiance of the Allied tide. The offensive was in danger of stalling and the threat of a German counter-strike loomed.

References

(1) letter to Army commanders, 14 April, 1944, quoted in D'Este, *Decision in Normandy*, p 80-81

(2) This story deserves to be told at length. Suffice here to say that the plan began to come apart at the water's edge, and reached its conclusion at the Jerusalem crossroads south of Bayeux, when the last survivors of this daring exploit were strafed by American aircraft.

(3) *Victory in the West*, L. F. Ellis, p 138-139.

(4) In May, 2002, the author visited Montgomery's proposed 1st Airborne landing area around Esquay with two officers of 6th Airborne Division, veterans of the 6 June landings. Viewing the open, gently rolling high ground between hills 112 and 113, their reaction was *'What a marvellous DZ!'* In fact, such a descent onto open ground, miles beyond friendly lines and ringed by alert German armoured forces, would most probably have resulted in an unparalleled disaster dwarfing the later Arnhem operation.

(5) Recent studies have suggested that the British assault divisions selected for D Day were allowed to believe that simply getting ashore was the main hurdle. Also, systemic shortcomings in the experience and training of British armour meant that armoured brigades accompanying the invaders *'never started to fulfil Montgomery's idea'* since they were not *'trained to "crack about" in the enemy rear but to support infantry'*. (*Against Odds*, Dominic Graham, p 153; see also *Military Training in the British Army 1940-44 From Dunkirk to D-Day*, Timothy Harrison Place

(6) 7th Armoured and 51st Highland divisions failed in Normandy to live up to Montgomery's expectations. 50th (Northumbrian) had experienced near mutiny in the Mediterranean, and high absentee rates continued in its New Forest encampments. During one of Monty's morale-raising lectures to one of that division's brigades, *'he was not well received. Some of those troops were not too keen to be told that as a reward for their past bravery they were now going to be allowed to undertake special risks. There were rumblings of discontent.'* (*Accidental Warrior*, Geoffrey Picot, p 35; see also Dominic Graham, Chapter 12.)

(7) *The Story of the Guards Armoured Division*, Rosse & Hill, p 17-18. In his *Reflections 1939-1945*, Charles Farrell reflects with pride on the achievements of his 3rd Tank Battalion, The Scots Guards, but now feels that *'the move to armour was, on balance, a mistake,'* and that it would have been better *'if a Guards Infantry Division had been formed.'* (p 42)

(8) *The Proud Trooper*, W Steel Brownlie, p 345

(9) The VIII Corps historian later recorded that *'The long period of cooperation and mutual training, however, had established between 15 (Scottish) Division and 6 Guards Tank Brigade a trust and confidence seldom achieved by different arms of the service.'* (*Operations of Eighth Corps*, G S Jackson, p 7.) Sadly, as will be seen, such levels of trust and confidence between armour and infantry were not achieved during EPSOM.

(10) *The Fifteenth Scottish Division*, H G Martin, p 2

(11) Martin, p 25

(12) *The Scottish Lion on Patrol: the Story of the 15th Scottish Reconnaissance Regiment 1943-1946*, W Kemsley and M R Riesco

(13) *Military Training in the British Army, 1940-44*, Timothy Harrison Place, p 18-19. This valuable work is a comprehensive account of the strengths and weaknesses of British preparation for the

campaign for north western Europe. Note in particular page 3: *'The formation under which British troops fought the campaign, 21st Army Group, cannot be compared to Kitchener's New Armies, thrown into battle virtually untrained in 1916… Their successors of June 1944 might have been unblooded, but there was no excuse if they were untrained.'*

(14) *18 Platoon*, Sydney Jary, p 18-19

(15) *A Short History of the Ayrshire Yeomanry (Earl of Carrick's Own), 151st Field Regiment, RA*, Young & Gray, p 13

(16) In one respect at least, non-standard equipment was to stand the tank crews of *Hitlerjugend* in good stead. Leather suits acquired from Italian naval stores were to prove a useful protection against fire when abandoning a burning tank.

(17) In his account of life in a British infantry regiment, Robert Woolcombe recalls Montgomery's pre-invasion morale-boosting visit to the 6th King's Own Scottish Borderers. *'In the same instant he has asked the Colonel a question- "What's the average age of your battalion?" "Twenty-five, sir" promptly. "Twenty-five? A good age, twenty-five." The tones were keen edged and very alert. As thin and wiry as the man. They repeated the age musingly…'* (*Lion Rampant'*, p 17)

The colonel's instant response was quite likely accurate, since 6th KOSB as other units of 15th (Scottish) had been embodied since 1939, the ages of its more recent recruits balanced by the older men, who often gravitated to the more specialised roles within Support Company.

(18) McKee, p 84

(19) *SS-Panzer-Grenadier-Division "Hitlerjugend" Guidelines for Combat-like Basic Rifle Training*, 30 October 1943, in *The History of 12. SS-Panzerdivision*, Hubert Meyer, p 346

(20) *'During TEWTs, for example, German infantry officers were given only a few minutes to propose a solution to the tactical problems they were set. Their British counterparts were usually given a whole hour.'* From *Raising Churchill's Army*, David French, p 174.

(21) *Im Feuersturm Letzter Kriegsjahre*, Wilhelm Tieke, p 21-22 (English edition p 6-7)

(22) *'The tactic of surprise, using mobile, fast infantry and Panzers… had often been practiced and proven in Russia. This tactic, however, had not resulted in the expected success here.'* The divisional Operations Officer was reflecting on failed attacks on 8 June. Hubert Meyer, p 57.

(23) The origins of the blood feud conducted between Canadian and SS soldiers on the approaches to Caen are unclear. By mid-June, both sides were openly killing prisoners. After reviewing impassioned claims from both sides, this author doubts whether the question of *'who started it'* will ever be resolved. Besides, whatever the judgment of hindsight, both sets of combatants at the time truly believed their enemies to be in the wrong.

(24) At this time, three German submarines were assigned to meteorological patrol in the North Atlantic, among them the U-534, now raised and preserved in Birkenhead, England. The diversion of these vessels from combat to reporting the weather indicates the value placed on such information.

(25) *A Soldier's Story*, Omar Bradley, p 265

(26) Personal account by Sir Bruce White, KBE, Director of Ports and Inland Water Transport at the War Office from 1941 to 1945. White and others concluded that the British had been more painstaking in the construction of their 'Mulberry B' and that although unfinished at the time of the storm, and severely damaged, it was both capable and worthy of being completed. Certainly, the British 'Gooseberry' breakwaters had enabled some hundreds of craft to survive off Juno beach, and some eighteen LSTs had actually unloaded there during the storm.

(27) *Monty: The Making of a General*, Nigel Hamilton, 1981, quoted in *The Forgotten Victor*, J Baynes, p 188

Chapter 2

LATE JUNE: PLANS AND PREPARATIONS

Montgomery's hopes of 'cracking about' in order to 'peg out claims inland' had been disappointed on D-Day, and continued unrealised in the days following invasion. But the strategy was not entirely abandoned. It would be wrong to imagine a sudden switch from 'breakthrough' aspirations to a strategy of attrition. True, the EPSOM plan that evolved in late June was methodical rather than opportunistic. Montgomery's insistence on manpower and logistical build-up prior to the operation was reminiscent of his famous preparation for Alamein, and foreshadowed future 'colossal cracks' to be delivered against the Germans in Normandy.[1] But Montgomery still believed it possible to break free of the Normandy beachhead before the month's end. Intelligence suggested that the German front in the British sector between Caen and Caumont was thinly stretched, as indeed it was. Even so, while Montgomery's eyes were on the open country beyond Caen and the Falaise road, so too were the German defenders of Normandy planning for the decisive counterstroke which would drive the Allies back to the beaches.

THE BRITISH GENERALS

Prior to his arrival in Normandy, Lieutenant-General Sir Richard O'Connor, newly-appointed commander of VIII Corps, had spent much time in 'contemplation and reflection' over a 'beautiful sand model' of the proposed invasion area.[2] Occasionally sharing the contemplation of the model was 1st Airborne Division commander Major-General Robert Urquhart. The focus of Urquhart's interest was the Falaise road, south east of Caen, where his division was tentatively slated to drop in the general area of Bretteville-sur-Laize, there to await the arrival of forces advancing around both the east and west of Caen.

Lieutenant-General Sir Richard O'Connor.

O'Connor crossed to Normandy on 10 June, to be joined the following day by his headquarters staff (who then took a wrong turning and blundered into a battle being fought in the vicinity of Pegasus Bridge). On 13 June, VIII Corps headquarters was established in the woods around the Manneville Château outside Lantheuil, a mile from Montgomery's own headquarters at Creully. (The château had previously served as home to the headquarters of the German *716. Division*; the reception of the British by the count in residence was 'decidedly cool', he being a Vichy French naval officer who had suffered bombardment by the British at Toulon in 1940 and the Americans at Oran in 1942.)

As the divisions of VIII Corps completed their cross-channel journey to Normandy, O'Connor discussed plans with Montgomery. By now, the idea of simultaneously enveloping Caen from both east and west had been dropped in favour of a single flanking manoeuvre around the east. Operation DREADNOUGHT envisaged an VIII Corps advance through the bridgehead east of the Orne River, yet still intended to link with a 1st Airborne Division drop astride the Falaise road. Possibly mindful of the congestion he had witnessed around Pegasus Bridge, O'Connor rejected this plan. The logistical difficulties of bringing his entire corps into action through the narrow bridgehead were altogether too problematic. Montgomery the logistician concurred. On 19 June, he wrote to O'Connor, '*I am very grateful for the clear exposition on the problems of the attack from the existing bridge-head east of the Orne, and considered the problem after leaving you and told Bimbo [General Dempsey] to chuck it; 8 Corps instead to deliver its blow on the EVRECY flank.*'[3] The EPSOM plan was born.

THE GERMAN GENERALS

On 19 June, in a meeting at Cully, 2nd British Army commander Dempsey announced that the '*Allied foothold... was now firm enough to withstand any attack the enemy might choose to launch against it.*'

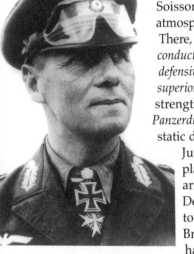

The planners of *Heeresgruppe B* saw the matter differently. Two days before, Hitler had held a conference at Margival, near Soissons (his final visit to France, conducted in an atmosphere 'somewhere between confusion and chaos').[4] There, the *Führer* had directed that, '*It is out of the question to conduct the fighting at the bridgehead Caen-Carentan only in a defensive manner since the enemy would smash everything with his superior deployment of materiel.*'[5] The assessment of Allied strength was well made; equally, it was true that the *Panzerdivisionen* were not designed to hold the front line in static defence. Consequently, two days later, on that same 19 June, *Generalfeldmarschall* Rommel's Army Group planners were presenting options for a multi-division armoured counterstroke designed to achieve just what Dempsey had ruled unfeasible. The plan was to drive toward the beaches, striking the boundary between the British and American armies; to separate the Allies, and halt the progress of the invasion. At least for the six weeks demanded by Hitler before his 'new bomber weapon' could be deployed against the beachheads.[6]

Generalfeldmarschall **Erwin Rommel.**

Infantry divisions were trudging their way to Normandy to take their place in line. The first elements of *2. SS-Panzerdivision, 'Das Reich'* were arriving after their difficult journey from the south. And the powerful (and now combat-proven) *II. SS-Panzerkorps* was on its way back from Galicia. The plan appeared feasible, on paper at least. The prospect of eight armoured divisions (*1. SS, 2. SS, 9. SS, 10. SS,* and *12. SS*; plus *2., 21.,* and *Lehr*) bursting

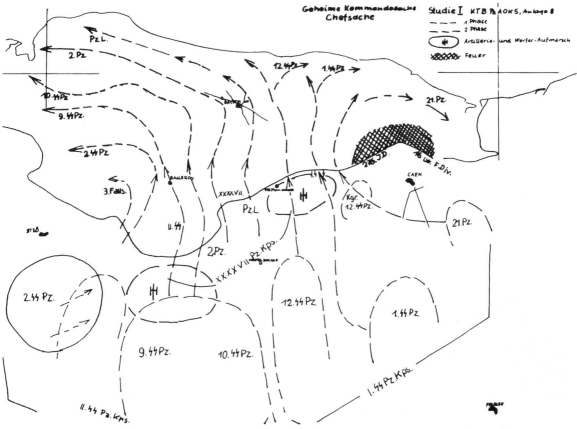

One plan to assemble eight Panzer divisions for a decisive counterblow.

out amidst the invaders had great appeal. Critics and cynics might point out that those divisions already in the line were somewhat worn down by combat; that the terrain favoured the defence, and along with Allied air and artillery superiority ruled out the effective coordination of large-scale armoured formations. But critics and cynics did not get very far with Hitler. And the distance to be covered to the beaches seemed so very slight on the map. Besides, the German talent for organization and improvisation in the face of adversity was capable of achieving a great deal, as outnumbered German forces in Russia had repeatedly shown, and as events in the West in September and December 1944 were to confirm.

Rommel cautiously declined to give a start date for his promised counteroffensive, vaguely suggesting early July. Moreover, he covered himself with the clause that everything depended on Hitler's assurance (verbal, apparently given at Soissons) that British naval artillery would be neutralized – an evident impossibility, though not a factor for which the army could be held responsible. But preparations began in earnest. The race was on to be first to assemble the necessary force for a potentially decisive battle.

THE EPSOM PLAN

As Dempsey was expressing his confidence in resisting any German offensive, so too on 19 June Montgomery was describing to Dempsey and Bradley his new plan to attack around the west of Caen. Moving through a sector bitterly contested by the 3rd Canadian Division, O'Connor's VIII Corps would be tasked with passing over the Odon River and the high ground beyond, to seize the Orne River crossings and surround Caen.

In his accounts of the Normandy campaign, Montgomery maintained that he never departed from an original strategy of drawing the German armoured formations on to the British front to permit an ultimate American breakthrough. It is now generally accepted that these accounts contain a large dose of post-rationalization. Indeed, many feel that Montgomery would have served his own interests better by confessing the considerable degree of flexibility he employed in his handling of the campaign. After all, the Normandy campaign was one of his notable successes. In the case of EPSOM, it is clear that Montgomery intended both to retain the strategic initiative, pre-empting any German counter-stroke, and to attempt the decisive breakthrough on the Second Army front which he truly believed was possible.

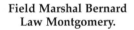

Field Marshal Bernard Law Montgomery.

On 19 June, Montgomery's goal was the Orne River, *'and gaining a position on the high ground north-east of Bretteville-sur-Laize, dominating the exits from Caen.'*[7] To reach this goal, the Odon crossings and the (ultimately notorious) Hill 112 were mere waypoints. (Though as will be revealed, British and German plans were asymmetrical: this hill which the British regarded simply as a means to an end, the Germans saw as a vital bastion, to be held at all costs.)

In fact, not just one but three British corps would be involved, though as Dempsey put it, 'not as a coordinated Army operation'. East of Caen and the Orne, I Corps would attempt a left-flank pincer movement, around and into Caen; though without reinforcement its chances of achieving much more than it had in the preceding weeks were slim. West of Caen, XXX Corps would step off a day before VIII Corps, with the dual intention of seizing ground to cover the right flank of VIII Corps' advance, and of drawing the defenders off balance. This was to begin on 22 June, in preparation for the main assault by VIII Corps the following day.

Gerneral Miles Dempsey.

If Montgomery experienced frustration during the great storm of 19 to 22 June, many of the soldiers summoned for EPSOM suffered more immediate discomfort. Men of the Argyll & Sutherland Highlanders were among those

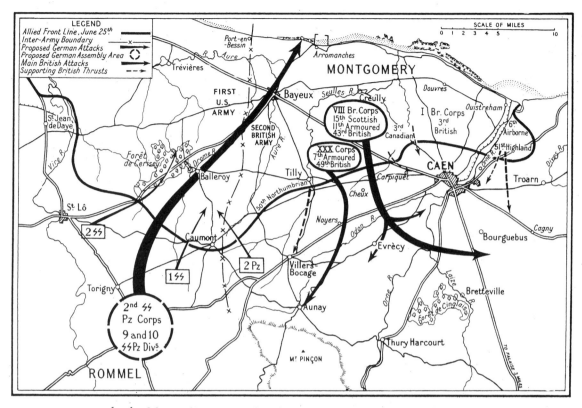

who had been disappointed to be passed-over on June 6, then annoyed at being held at the docks awaiting embarkation for six long days. Once aboard, matters hardly improved. An antitank gunner boarding with the vehicles at Tilbury recalled, *'We sailed on the 19th June on a Liberty ship. As shipbuilders, we didn't think much of it, and thought even less when we had to spend five days on it instead of the expected five hours. It wasn't, as the Navy would say, "victualled". There was no food or water and we survived on our emergency rations.'*[8] The foot soldiers of the battalion travelling from Newhaven fared little better. They found themselves *'rolling about in the grey of a Channel gale, unable to land; and there for two days and two nights they lay at anchor, except during the occasional enterprising attempts by the captains to enter the Mulberry harbour – operations which involved a great deal more rolling about and were a nightmare to the seasick.'*[9] At least the foot men disembarked on 21 June; the vehicles remained at sea even longer.

So, as the storm raged, the developing plan had to be modified. Timings were put back, with the XXX Corps battle (Operation MARTLET) now to begin on 25 June, and VIII Corps' Operation EPSOM on 26 June. Even so, timing was tight. 15th Scottish Division, assigned to lead the way through the German lines, would barely be in time for the start, and opportunities to liaise with the supporting 31st Tank Brigade were minimal. (The two formations had never worked together; only last-minute officers' sand-table exercises and TEWTs had been possible in the pre-invasion concentration areas.)[10]

11th Armoured Division was assigned to support and 'follow through' the Scots' penetration of the German line, supported themselves by the relatively experienced 4th Armoured Brigade, effectively doubling the division's tank strength, though with the restriction that once across the Odon, the 4th Brigade was to *'remain in the area between the two rivers* [i.e., the Odon and the Orne] *as flank protection.'*

Guards Armoured Division was not going to arrive in time. Even its advance party only managed to land at Courseulles-sur-Mer on 22 June; the infantry brigade came ashore on 22 and 23 June; the tank brigade would arrive between 28 and 29 June. In place of the Guards, 43rd (Wessex) Infantry Division was attached to VIII Corps to provide a 'firm base' for the forthcoming operation. (And even the 43rd was not itself complete: half its reconnaissance regiment was lost on 24 June when a magnetic mine sank the *Derry Cunihy* transport, and it was July before the reorganized regiment could get into action.)

MARTLET

If VIII Corps' EPSOM advance was to reach the Odon River crossings leading to the Orne, it would have to present its right flank to the 'heights of Rauray'. Dempsey and O'Connor alike were convinced that the success of EPSOM would require a preliminary assault led by 49th Division to seize those heights: Operation MARTLET.

Visitors to the 'heights' of Rauray are frequently bemused to find no towering cliffs, no steep slopes, nor even tightly packed contours. In fact, the area from Fontenay-le-Pesnel all the way to the outskirts of Caen is characterized by broad, open fields with only the most subtle changes of elevation. The ground does indeed rise to the south of Fontenay, reaching its highest point roughly half-way to Grainville-sur-Odon around the tiny hamlet of Rauray. This low ridge hardly deserves its title of 'heights' or of 'Rauray spur'. From its high point, the ground falls away barely ten metres per kilometre, in all directions. In fact, the tactical significance of this location depends entirely on the smooth contours

of the landscape to the east. Today, following the little country road that leads south out of Fontenay towards Rauray, past the 49th Division monument, one has little sense of gaining elevation. But gaze to the east, past the tranquil, tree-lined British cemetery carefully tended by the Commonwealth War Graves Commission, and the importance of the ground becomes clear. One can see all the way to Caen. And guns emplaced here could enfilade the flank of the VIII Corps advance. As the *Hitlerjugend* divisional historian recorded, *'This view would make the Panzer men, who have found their way painfully through the broken terrain up to here, heave a sigh of relief.'*[11]

Nevertheless, the German line was stretched thin. *12. SS-Panzerdivision* was still holding a line running from Fontenay-le-Pesnel all the way to Epron, north of Caen, a concave front line of almost fifteen kilometres held by two depleted *Panzergrenadier* regiments. This was not the classic, multi-layered defence-in-depth favoured by German tacticians. The only depth in the defence was afforded by the division's second tank battalion, four depleted companies of *Panzer IV* emplaced in carefully selected spots behind the line, and further back the divisional artillery.[12] Behind this artillery stood only the anti-aircraft regiments of *III. Flakkorps*, their batteries strung out in a line from Aunay-sur-Odon to St-André-sur-Orne. The only reserves available to the *Hitlerjugend* were its first (*Panther*-equipped) tank battalion and the reconnaissance battalion, both held behind the left flank, where *Hitlerjugend* abutted the *Panzer-Lehr-Division*. Holding the front line to the west, the *Panzer-Lehr* was similarly stretched. After prolonged heavy fighting, by 25 June only 66 of its 190 tanks remained operational.

A major new British offensive was expected daily. When the barrage began in the small hours of 25 June, its scale left the German defenders in no doubt that this was it. The brunt of the XXX Corps attack fell on the westernmost battalion in the *Hitlerjugend* line: *SS-Sturmbannführer* Olboeter's *III/26. Panzergrenadiere*. The little town of Fontenay had been prepared. Though lacking wire and mines, the *Pioniere* had assisted the *Panzergrenadiere* to turn every defended locality into a strongpoint. Heavy weapons were emplaced and camouflaged, machine guns carefully sited and lines of fire cleared. In the town, the rubbled remains of buildings were utilized wherever possible, but the entire front line running roughly along the line of the Fontenay-Caen road (the modern D9) was covered by entrenched forward observation posts, gun emplacements, and command bunkers.

Shortly after 04.00 hours on 25 June, the 49th (West Riding) Infantry Division set off southwards in the direction of Fontenay-le-Pesnel. Behind a barrage put down by nine field and four medium artillery regiments, the advance commenced on a three-battalion front, with tanks of 8th Armoured Brigade in close support. Moving downhill, the leading units found themselves enveloped in a dense mist, thickened still further by fumes and smoke from the artillery bombardment. With visibility virtually nil, platoons lost their direction and the advance slowed. Nor did matters greatly improve when the rising sun finally burned through the fog. The defenders had been subjected to an ordeal worse than any previously experienced but the survivors recovered quickly. As soon as the barrage passed overhead, the infantry emerged. A nearby tank commander watched the young grenadiers: *'They came out of their foxholes as if lifted by ghostly hands and, like moles, machine guns and steel helmets, with almost indiscernible faces below, pushed toward the enemy... then, when the figures with the flat helmets* [i.e., the British] *were moving about in the chaos of the houses and streets, many almost at touching distance, well-aimed machine gun salvoes whipped out of the German foxholes... a few of these were generally sufficient.'*[13]

Silos of grain factory by Fontenay road.

It was a day of close-range fighting, sometimes hand-to-hand in the rubble of Fontenay. If the British were confused by the mist and smoke, so were the German defenders handicapped by their loss of communications. Forward observation posts had been obliterated. With radios malfunctioning and field telephone wires cut by the barrage, companies were isolated from one another and fought on alone until runners could brave the torrent of fire to pass on reports and return with orders. Still, the defenders were fighting on their own ground. By the end of the day, in spite of heroic efforts against determined opposition, the 49th Division had not even secured all of Fontenay. It had fallen well short of its assigned objective, the hamlet of Rauray.[14]

SS-Obergruppenführer **Sepp Dietrich was convinced that Operation MARTLET was the main Allied offensive.**

Although failing in its primary aim, the first day of MARTLET had not been a total failure. At least in its secondary objective of diverting German attention from EPSOM, it had succeeded. Companies of *Hitlerjugend* tanks had been stripped from their positions behind the line (where Operation EPSOM was due to begin) and sent westward to reinforce the action around Fontenay. The sheer weight of the assault on Fontenay convinced Sepp Dietrich that this was the principal axis of Montgomery's offensive. At the end of the day, his *I. SS-Panzerkorps* staff were horrified by the gap blown open between the *Hitlerjugend* and *Panzer-Lehr*. Although isolated pockets of resistance were still holding out in Fontenay, the loss of the town was agreed to be inevitable. The priority for 26 June would be a counter-attack by a *12. SS-Panzerregiment* battle-group to plug the gap in the line. In order to prevent a breakthrough, the defenders' attention was to remain focused on this area even after the start of EPSOM.

THE BEGINNING OF EPSOM

Neither the failure of XXX Corps to take Rauray on 25 June, nor the worsening

Caen

The 'heights' of Rauray. The view from east of the 49th Division monument, over the tranquil Commonwealth War Graves Commission cemetery towards Caen.

weather could be allowed to delay the EPSOM plan. Montgomery had already waited far longer than he wished. He had to get in his blow before a German counter-strike upset his careful planning. By the morning of 24 June, he possessed confirmation from ULTRA decrypts that trains bearing elements of *II. SS-Panzerkorps* had arrived in France from Russia on 18 June. Later that morning came news of seventy-eight trains bearing *9. SS* and sixty-two with *10. SS-Panzerdivision* unloaded in France on 21 June.[15] Montgomery dared wait no longer.

After dark on 24 June, the guns that were to support EPSOM were moved forward to their allocated Gun Areas, to lie up under concealment all the next day. The artillery barrage due to open up at 07.30 hours would startle and impress the inexperienced Jocks setting off for their Start Lines. Though in fact it was not of a scale comparable to later Operations, when artillery ammunition became even more plentiful.[16]

And more serious still was the absence of the air strikes planned for 26 June. Deteriorating weather led to the cancellation of the heavy bombers due over Verson and the waves of mediums scheduled to hit Carpiquet and Bretteville-sur-Odon. Fifteen fighter-bomber squadrons were on call, but the prospects for their involvement in the ground battle were slim.

During the night of 24-25 June, the infantry battalions which were to lead the way advanced to the Assembly Areas which their advance parties had previously reconnoitred. There had been little enough for them to see. Guided forward by wary Canadians, who by now knew every ruse to hide from German observers, warned that any visible movement would bring down German mortar bombs, the recce groups could make out little of interest or value. To the right, 46th Highland Brigade would be starting from the narrow sunken lanes of le Mesnil-Patry, a low ridge blocking the view south. To the left, viewed from Norrey-en-Bessin, 44th Brigade's initial objective of St-Manvieu was hidden in the valley of the Mue; only the top of its church tower

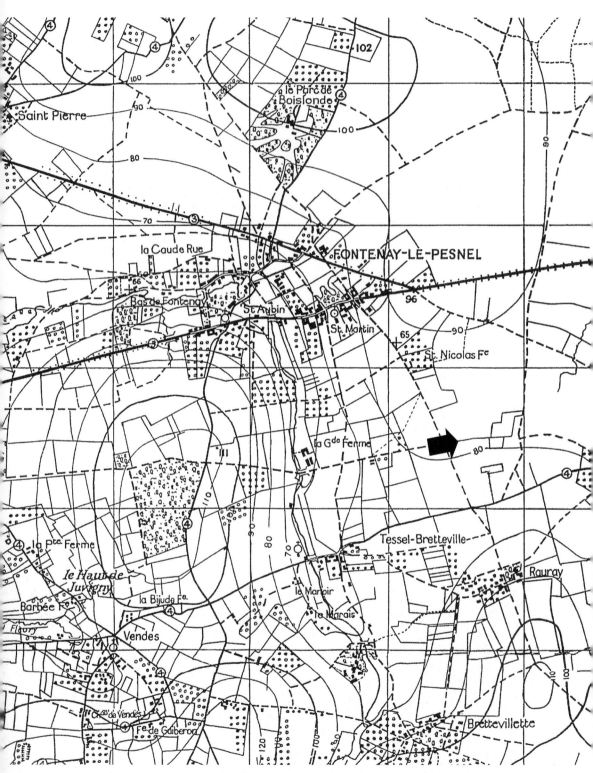

The MARTLET battleground (arrow indicates viewpoint of page 37 photograph).

showing through the trees.

For 15th Scottish, it was a day of apprehension and discomfort. A typical battalion *'began the approach march to the assembly area on the 25th June in sultry heat and stifling dust. Sweat poured down and caked the dust.'*[17] Time hung heavy in the Forward Assembly Areas. Men wrote letters home (some of these being precautionary letters of farewell to be left with personal effects). It was Sunday, and Church services were held. (With the prospect of battle looming, Confirmation Schools had been so well attended that a series of three were conducted, leading over a thousand men of the division to join either the Church of England or of Scotland.) The General gave a briefing for all officers in the division, down to company commanders; later regimental commanders held their own O (orders) Groups. At last, as the sun set, the companies were formed and began to move out of their FAAs to the Forming Up Places. The warm, dusty evening was punctuated by the tramp of marching feet. All were apprehensive. For some at least, apprehension was mixed with relief at 'getting it over with', and some even felt a glow of pride. A junior officer recalled, *'The troops in amazing spirits. For here was the Second Front. We were upon the rostrum of the world… These were wonderful moments.'*[18]

References

(1) Though the phrase 'colossal cracks' was Montgomery's own, this author wishes to acknowledge Stephen Ashley Hart's pivotal study, *'Montgomery and "Colossal Cracks": The 21st Army Group in Northwest Europe'*
(2) Jackson, p 13
(3) O'Connor Papers, quoted in Baynes, p 187
(4) Speidel, quoted in *Ultra in the West*, Ralph Bennett, p 82
(5) War Diary *Heeresgruppe B*, quoted in Meyer, p 91
(6) Presumably an optimistic expectation of V1 missiles.
(7) *Normandy to the Baltic*, Field Marshall Montgomery, p 65
(8) Corporal James Campbell, interviews with the author.
(9) *History of the Argyll & Sutherland Highlanders*, McElwee, p 16
(10) The reasons for this unsatisfactory state of affairs are discussed in Appendix VII.
(11) Meyer, p 94

(12) The division was missing its antitank and *Nebelwerfer* battalions, which were still forming. The role of the reconnaissance battalion in this battle, in line with German practice, would include reinforcing the line with its infantry. So too would the *Pioniere*, the assault engineer battalion, fight in the line, having done their professional best before the battle to fortify the divisional positions.

(13) Hans Siegel, recorded in Meyer, p 99

(14) For a detailed account of Operation MARTLET and the exploits of 49th Division up to 1 July, the reader is strongly recommended to consult the authoritative and highly detailed *Breaking the Panzers: the Bloody Battle for Rauray*, Kevin Baverstock

(15) Bennett, p 81-82

(16) By the crude measure of guns-per-kilometre of front, EPSOM enjoyed just 64, versus 98 for TOTALIZE, 105 for VERITABLE, and 259 for GOODWOOD – though the front at GOODWOOD was rather small for comparison! French, p 255.

(17) Memoirs of Sergeant Hugh Green, Intelligence Section, 10th HLI, the archives of The Royal Highland Fusiliers, Sauchiehall Street, Glasgow

(18) *Lion Rampant*, Woolcombe, p 39

Chapter 3

MONDAY 26 JUNE: BREAK IN

The men of 15th Scottish Division waited in their Assembly Areas. From midnight, a light drizzle became more constant. Some managed to sleep. Others just waited: on edge, apprehensive. *'We spent that night huddled under some bushes in steady drizzle, cold, tired and feeling sorry for ourselves.'*[1] A young officer of the KOSB woke around 05.30 hours and joined his fellow officers in the barn where the flare of a petrol stove heralded breakfast. *'We ate and said little… exchanged trivialities without a word about the battle.'* And after, *'One performed Nature's duty in an adjacent cabbage patch. It struck me as oddly unnecessary.'* The company commander *'came across to do likewise. "Perhaps they won't start shelling until the barrage opens?" I asked him. For the enemy were quiet. He raised his eyebrows. How the hell could he say?'*[2]

For those 'in the know', the failure of 49th Division to hold the Rauray spur was not encouraging. With the dawn, the rain slackened but the clouds remained, and the damp summer-morning air was milky with mist. The promise of 'the whole Tactical Air Force' grew less comforting. Nothing much would be flying from England today. Still, the artillery was on cue. At 07.29 hours, the loudspeakers crackled into life over the waiting gun lines with the one-minute standby, then thirty seconds, twenty, ten, 5, 4, 3, 2, 1, FIRE! Six hundred and thirty artillery pieces were joined by a battleship and two cruisers, the morning stillness shattered as the shells passed overhead. *'It was the moment for which the 15th Scottish Division had been preparing for five years.'*[3]

FORMATION

15th Scottish and all its supporting arms advanced on a front of little over two miles. Yet few of these twenty thousand men were actually in the front line.

The infantry division was to attack with two of its three brigades 'up': 44th Lowland to the left, 46th Highland to the right, and 227th Highland in reserve (its three battalions likewise allocated 'left', 'right' and 'reserve' roles). Each of the two lead brigades went forward with two of its battalions in front and one in reserve. And each of those four leading battalions placed only two rifle companies in front, their other two rifle companies held in reserve with Headquarters and the Support Company platoons somewhere behind. In other words, each fresh battalion still at full strength with around 850 officers and men entered its first battle with two 115-man rifle companies leading the way. The entire VIII Corps assault was spearheaded by eight rifle companies and their supporting armour.

This total of less than a thousand should definitely not be imagined as a single line of men strung out at ten foot intervals. The leading rifle companies generally formed with two platoons in front, the third platoon and company headquarters following some distance to the rear. And within a platoon, two sections would lead, each with seven or eight rifles and one Bren gun, followed in turn by platoon headquarters and a third section.

So, on that wet morning of 26 June, the lead element of VIII Corps was actually just thirty-two groups of nine or ten men advancing at intervals of a hundred yards or more. They walked forward at a steady pace over mostly open ground, wet fields of waist- and even shoulder-high grain. In his classic account of the Normandy campaign, Keegan preferred to view the scene at platoon rather than section level, citing '24 groups of 30 riflemen' (arguably, it was sixteen not twenty-four platoons that led the first wave).[4] This author prefers to focus on the section: the fundamental building-block of the infantry and the essential focus of the individual soldier's loyalty. Also, while some liken the advance of 26 June to that on the Somme on 1 July, 1916, there were differences. The sections of 1944 moved simultaneously but independently; the Kitchener units of 1916 advanced *en-masse* in battalion lines; many of them not even subdivided into formal platoons.[5]

Unlike their German opponents who were trained to advance in bounds, from cover to cover, seeking gaps through which to infiltrate and outflank, the foremost sections of 15th Scottish were choreographed to advance more-or-less in unison and to a strict timetable: a timetable set by the Royal Artillery. The impressive

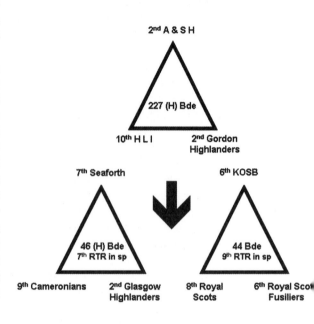

15th (Scottish) Division

31st Tank Bde in support

"2 up" attack formation 26 June

2nd A & S H

227 (H) Bde

10th H L I   2nd Gordon Highlanders

7th Seaforth   6th KOSB

46 (H) Bde   44 Bde
7th RTR in sp   9th RTR in sp

9th Cameronians   2nd Glasgow   8th Royal   6th Royal Scots
                    Highlanders   Scots   Fusiliers

Platoon Assault Formation
Extended Line – Open Ground

sections at full strength
not to scale
assume five+ yards spacing between men

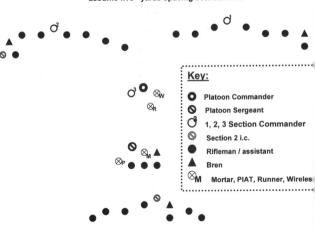

Key:

○ Platoon Commander

◐ Platoon Sergeant

♂ 1, 2, 3 Section Commander

◓ Section 2 i.c.

● Rifleman / assistant

▲ Bren

⊗M Mortar, PIAT, Runner, Wireless

barrage was to pound its start line for ten minutes while the leading rifle sections closed up. Then it would lift: one hundred yards every three minutes. So, in theory, 'all' the little bands of infantrymen had to do was stay closed-up to the preceding barrage while moving forward at a little over one mile-per-hour. In theory, this was to continue until the leading companies reached the first objective. After a mile and a half, the east-west road from Caen to Fontenay was an ideal landmark on which the advance was to pause. The barrage would halt for fifteen minutes while the two leading companies of each battalion secured the ground and the following two companies were passed-through, ready to take the lead in their turn when the artillery barrage again moved on.

Throughout their training – and sometimes with live ammunition involved – the infantry had been exhorted to keep up with the artillery, to 'lean on the barrage.' This meant walking towards the long line of shellbursts, up to five hundred yards deep, no further distant than two hundred yards from the nearest impacts and sometimes as close as fifty. This was not easy. At such close ranges, even though most of the shards of metal flew forward from the points of impact, the concussions from the blasts radiated outwards as body-blows, physical as well as psychological obstacles to the advancing men.[6] But remaining close made good sense. Lessons learned since the Somme in 1916 and reinforced in theatres of war from 1940 to 1943 indicated that enemy positions overrun immediately as the barrage passed over had a much better chance of being taken than those given even brief seconds for men to emerge from cover and man guns. Doctrine coldly maintained that losses caused by rounds falling short would be acceptably lower than those inflicted by alert defenders. In April, the battalions of 15th Scottish had their opportunity to experience this in training: moving up close to artillery concentrations 'thickened up' by their own three-inch mortars. The 2nd Argylls recorded that, *'The exercise was a great success and of real value. All ranks were impressed by the accuracy and devastating effect of Arty. They were also impressed by their ability to get so close up to it in absolute safety.'*[7] Absolute safety was perhaps overdoing it. There were real risks, as the men would learn when advancing under a barrage fired by guns whose barrels were worn from extensive use. But the system worked. It was the professionalism developed by the Royal Artillery which, together with airpower, enabled inexperienced divisions of civilian soldiers to prevail, in attack and in defence. Crude though they might seem, these tactics underpinned Montgomery's strategy in Normandy.

The system was not without its flaws. For it to run smoothly, 'all' the men had to do was advance at a steady pace. But on 26 June, fear of approaching the barrage ahead and casualties caused by 'short' rounds were not the only obstacles to progress.

THE LEFT: 44th BRIGADE

The 44th (Lowland) Brigade selected two battalions of 'Royals' to lead the assault. Their first objectives lay in an arc within two miles of the Start Line. On the extreme left of 15th Scottish, the 6th Royal Scots Fusiliers were to seize

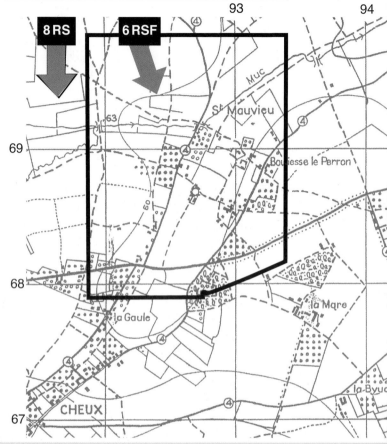

The assault of 44 Brigade. (St Manvieu detailed opposite.)

8 RS

6 RSF

93

94

St Mauvieu

Muc

63

69

Boussesse le Perron

68

la Mare

la Gaule

CHEUX

la Byuc

67

Below: Norrey-en-Bessin: the church steeple was never completely reconstructed.

6 RSF Start Line

6 RSF advance

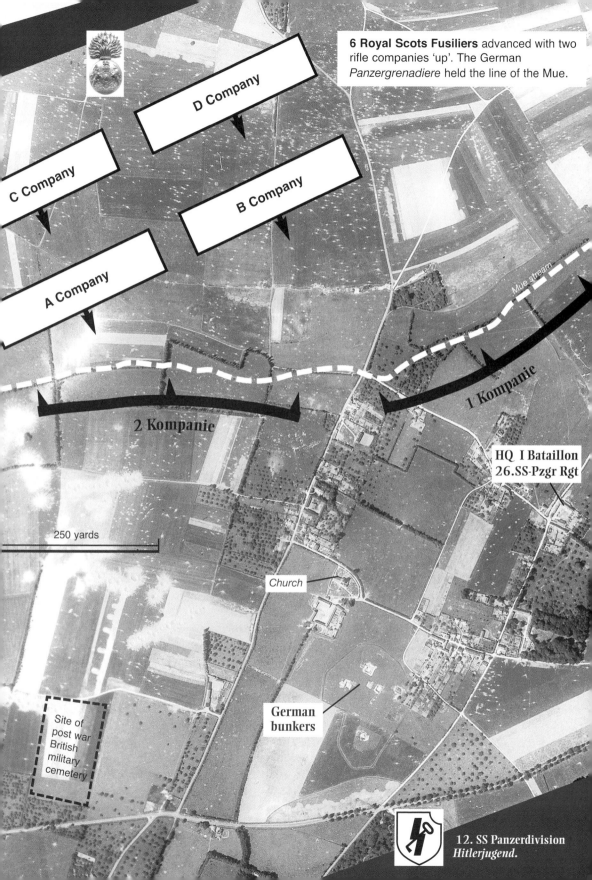

6 Royal Scots Fusiliers advanced with two rifle companies 'up'. The German *Panzergrenadiere* held the line of the Mue.

D Company

C Company

B Company

A Company

Mue stream

2 Kompanie

1 Kompanie

HQ I Bataillon
26. SS-Pzgr Rgt

250 yards

Church

Site of
post war
British
military
cemetery

German
bunkers

12. SS Panzerdivision
Hitlerjugend.

the little village of St-Manvieu which had so long defied the Canadians. To their right, 8th Royal Scots (the 'First of Foot') were charged with advancing to the Fontenay-Caen main road (the modern D9, for EPSOM codenamed 'Cassino'), then passing fresh companies through to secure the cluster of buildings known as la Gaule at map reference 920675, and the little wood between la Gaule and St-Manvieu at 928680.[8]

The first difficulty encountered by 6th RSF was their Start Line. To avoid disasters, it was always best to select a physical feature as the Start Line, ideally at right angles to the axis of the coming advance, to ensure that the first wave was lined up facing in the right direction, and well clear of the opening line of the artillery barrage. On 26 June, the only appropriate feature that 6th RSF could find to use was a sunken road diagonal to the axis of advance and in places precariously close to the barrage: barely 125 yards.

Stepping off as the barrage opened, at 07.30 hours sharp, A Company on the right fared relatively well, but B Company on the left soon began to experience casualties to 'friendly' artillery rounds falling short. For the first time, and far from the last, comrades set the helmets of the fallen atop their rifles, markers sprouting 'like strange fungi' in the fields, warning following tanks to avoid the space where a man lay helpless.

The German front line, facing the 6 RSF approach, (from viewpoint shown opposite).

The sky above was overcast. The bursting shells ahead left a lingering pall of smoke in the damp, still air. German observers to the east around Carpiquet airfield likewise had no clear view of the advance, but nor did they need any. It was sufficient for them to drop shells and mortar bombs directly behind the long line of the barrage. All along the British line of advance the defensive fire took its effect, but nowhere worse than on the extreme left of the line, closest to Carpiquet, adding to the losses of the Fusiliers' B Company. Still their sections plodded on, walking upright over open fields bereft of cover, over a slight rise then down a shallow slope into the valley. And at last, as the foremost sections reached the narrow trickle of the Mue rivulet, the defending infantry were encountered.

The narrow trickle of the Mue rivulet.

St-Manvieu was well sited for defence. Not only did it lie in a valley, largely out of sight of the British Start Line, but it was a straggling place with clusters of fortifiable stone buildings

Church

HQ I Bataillon
26.SS-Pzgr Rgt

The depleted Fusiliers infiltrated the western side of the village, while surviving groups of *Panzergrenadiere* clung to the south and east.

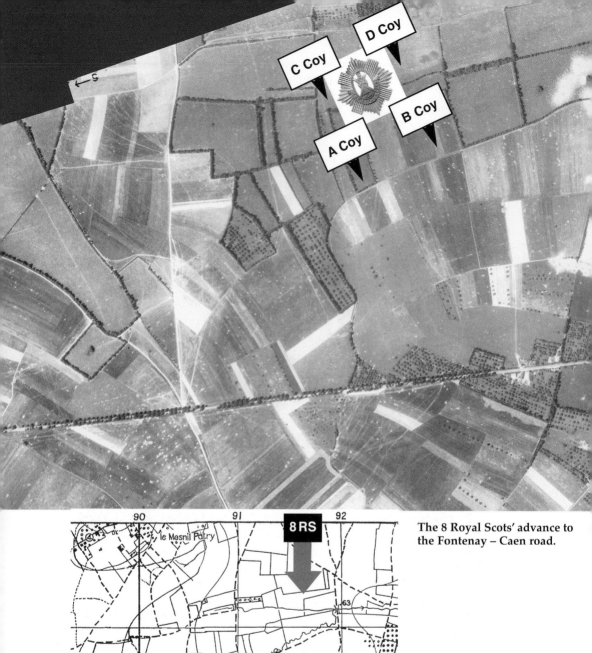

C Coy

D Coy

A Coy

B Coy

The 8 Royal Scots' advance to the Fontenay – Caen road.

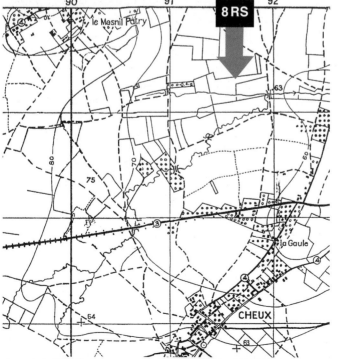

8 RS

le Mesnil Patry

la Gaule

CHEUX

interspersed with open spaces offering fields of fire. The Fusiliers' first battle quickly descended into platoon and section firefights. The defenders were outnumbered, but sure of their ground. By sheer weight of numbers the British were able to progress into the village, but actually clearing it proved 'a slow and costly procedure' as the combination of well-sited machine gun positions and individual riflemen opening fire from unexpected directions wore down the Scots infantry. Only by 17.00 hours, almost ten hours into their battle, could 6th RSF claim even the northern parts of the village cleared, *'by which time the Bn was very thin on the ground as the result of cas'*.

Like the Fusiliers, the 8th Royal Scots stepped off at 07.30 hours with A Company on the right and B on the left. Churchill tanks of B Squadron, 9th RTR, followed in close support. Covering the mile and a half to the main road in less than two hours, the companies exchanged places in accordance with the plan: A and B dug in while C and D respectively were 'passed through' on their way to the objectives. These were taken by 10.30 hours, though the process of 'clearing' took substantially longer[9]

While spared the worst of the ordeal of the Fusiliers on their left, the Royals nevertheless had a stressful afternoon waiting for the concerted counter-attack that never came. As the day wore on and the rain grew in intensity, losses to enemy shelling and mortaring grew. By evening, casualties had topped the hundred mark. D Company in its little wood had to be supplemented by B Company, replaced in its rear right-flank position astride the road by elements of the reserve 6th KOSB (first to arrive at the wood was the Borderers' mobile Carrier Platoon, later relieved by their entire D Company). A sergeant summed up *'a nightmare of a day. We reckoned up our casualties, saw to the promotion of NCOs to fill gaps, checked equipment, and every now and then we had to dive into a slit trench.'*

By afternoon, back in St-Manvieu, the depleted Fusiliers were in trouble. But so too were the defenders. The command post of the first battalion of *26. SS-Panzergrenadier-Regiment* was located in the farm complex of le Perron, on the east side of the town, alongside the Cheux-Rots road (the modern D 170). There, *Sturmbannführer* Krause and his staff sheltered in the cellars from the artillery drumfire, with only a handful of lookouts above. Telephone lines had been destroyed and all radio contact with the forward companies lost. The general situation was unclear until a wounded runner from *2. Kompanie* appeared with the news that both company commander and deputy were killed, and the company effectively overrun. Krause sent messengers forward to organize pockets of resistance, and rearward to plead for armour support. This was not forthcoming. The local *Panzerkompanie* commander refused – probably with good reason – to commit his few mobile tanks to the static defence of a fortified village. Further appeals went out from St-Manvieu to Krause's two right-flank companies, lying to the east of the main assault. Meanwhile, as isolated groups of *2. Kompanie* grenadiers continued to defy the Fusiliers' attempts to clear the place, a new threat appeared. Flamethrowing tanks of 141st RAC ground their way slowly and menacingly forward towards the remaining outposts.

141st Royal Armoured Corps (The Buffs) was a battalion equipped with Churchill 'Crocodiles': tanks with a bow-mounted flame projector fuelled from an armoured trailer. Having only arrived in Normandy three days previously, the battalion's A Squadron was placed under command of 31st Tank Brigade for EPSOM: Troops 1 to 3 under command of 7th RTR and Troops 4 and 5 under 9th RTR, supporting 6th RSF against St-Manvieu. Many costly lessons were to be learned about the use of flame throwing tanks in the first weeks of combat. In particular, that they should be employed *en masse* (in full troops of three tanks if not half-squadron strength of six or more), and always with infantry in close support. In all likelihood, when Lieutenant Harvey's lone Crocodile approached the walled estate of le Perron, it was in the mistaken belief that the place was already taken. In fact, it was the heart of the continuing defence, Krause's battalion headquarters.

No heavy antitank guns had survived the British bombardment. Krause had up to now ignored the growing numbers of British tanks milling around on the open slopes to the north. Now, with the Crocodile sitting in the entrance to the walled estate, he turned briefly from organizing his remaining outposts to give the order, 'That tank has to go!' Antitank gunner *Unterscharführer* Emil Dürr rose to the challenge. Dürr grabbed a *Panzerfaust*, dodged through the orchard to close range, and fired. He missed – not unusual for such an inaccurate weapon. Hit or miss, the usual fate of a *Panzerfaust* user was to be mown down by avenging return fire. And Dürr was indeed caught by a burst from the tank's turret-mounted BESA, taking a bullet wound to his chest. Nevertheless, as recounted by a German war correspondent, he returned having collected a second *Panzerfaust*, this time

Crocodile tank enters walled garden

le Perron

Fighting extended from the village of St-Manvieu to the sodden slopes above.

aiming lower and breaking the tank's track. Again he limped back. For his third attempt, Dürr reportedly tried a magnetic antitank mine (had they run out of *Panzerfäuste*?), which first fell off the tank, then detonated moments after he had re-attached it, mortally wounding the resolute gunner. According to German sources, the tank blazed; according to the Buffs, the tank was recovered the following day with only its track damaged, though Harvey's crew were nowhere to be seen, presumed captured.[10]

Into the evening, the fight for St-Manvieu continued amid smoke and confusion. In the village, flames raged as the rain poured down. On the slopes above, even the self-propelled artillery of 11th Armoured Division became embroiled in the battle. A gunner officer recalled, *'This was a bloody battle where infantry, tanks and self-propelled guns, ours and the Germans' were at times inextricably mixed. At one point, in a rift in the ground midway between Norrey*-en-*Bessin and Ste Manvieu, I brought my four* [Sexton] *guns into action in the midst*

The church, still today in ruins, where pockets of Fusiliers grimly hung on awaiting relief. A new church was later built nearby as the village grew.

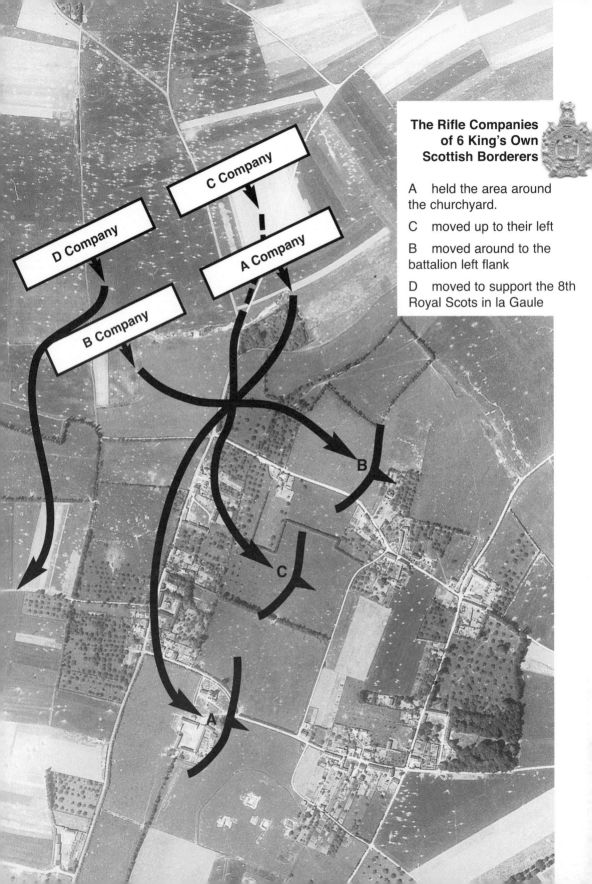

The Rifle Companies of 6 King's Own Scottish Borderers

A   held the area around the churchyard.

C   moved up to their left

B   moved around to the battalion left flank

D   moved to support the 8th Royal Scots in la Gaule

D Company

C Company

A Company

B Company

B

C

A

of hand-to-hand bayonet fighting between a Scottish company and some panzer grenadiers, which I watched (and almost had to take part) as a horrified spectator.'[11]

Krause assembled scratch forces of *Panzergrenadiere* to maintain his hold on the north-eastern corner of St-Manvieu. At last, around 18.00 hours, assistance promised by *21. Panzerdivision* arrived, and a depleted company of *Panzer IV* lent support to the Hitler Youth grenadiers' counter-attack.[12] The depleted and tired 6th RSF risked being overwhelmed, but at their colonel's side was the Forward Observation Officer of the 181st Field Regiment, Royal Artillery, whose 24 twenty-five pounder guns were to earn the Fusiliers' gratitude and trust all the way from Normandy to the Elbe. Unlike the German and American armies, the British FOO was a senior gunner officer, authorized to command not merely request fire. Back at the gun lines there was momentary surprise at the order: 'Scale 40 Fire!' Each of the 24 guns was to fire forty rounds on the same map reference as fast as they could reload. As the Scots' history relates, 'the very ugly counter-attack died almost at birth.'[13]

Still the pressure was maintained on the Fusiliers. Two hours further into the evening, with yet another German counter-attack forming up and his own casualties passing the hundred mark, including two company commanders, the colonel had to call for the help of a fresh rifle company. The brigadier recognised that this was not a time for half measures. He ordered forward his entire reserve, 6th King's Own Scottish Borderers, less the company already loaned out to cover the 8th RS flank.

6th KOSB had not been idle. As others would find on this day and the days to come, SS infantrymen over whom the tide of battle had rolled were not behaving as expected. Instead of resigning themselves to their fate and meekly surrendering, they would pop up unexpectedly in ones and twos to continue the fight behind the front lines. (Of course, many of them expected that as SS they would be shot rather than taken prisoner, a rumour fostered by German propaganda and frequently borne out by their erstwhile Canadian

The direction of the belated German counter-attack.

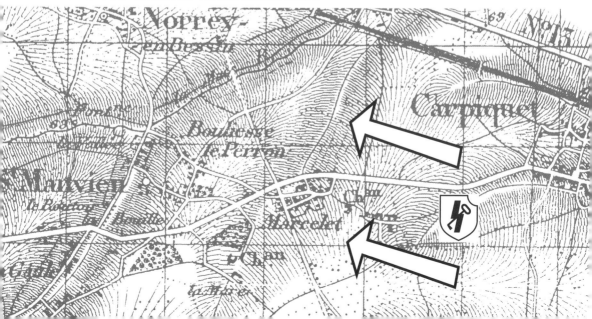

The line held at the end of the day (with many pockets of Germans still resisting).

adversaries.) Larger groups would stay in hiding, awaiting a chance to rejoin their unit, or to assist a counter-attack. The Borderers had been busily seeking out such 'snipers' (a term generally if mistakenly applied to all the SS infantry, whose unique camouflage smocks resembled those of the specialist British snipers).

Now, the men of A Company, 6th KOSB in their tin hats and waterproof gas capes sloshed through the dripping cornfields towards the smoking ruins of St-Manvieu, C Company following some way behind. The scene was one of devastation, scarred and scorched ruins inhabited by depleted sections and platoons. One such group was found sheltering in the German bunker they had taken: *'Scots Fusiliers, twenty-eight of them, and all that were left of a company that had crossed the start line that morning. The company commander was dead and a tired captain… reduced to a state of fatalism.'*[14] The relief of the scattered pockets of Fusiliers would take some time, as successive companies of Borderers came on the scene and as further counter-attacks, threatened and actual, disrupted the handover. In the confusion, the Fusiliers' D Company came under command of 6th KOSB, enabling the Fusiliers to claim that they remained in St-Manvieu till 23.00 hours.[15] The Borderers too lost a company commander, Major Going, in their first day of combat. But St-Manvieu was held, at least along the line of the Rots road. And during the night, the long battle gone quiet, the position was handed over to 43rd Division.

THE RIGHT: 46 BRIGADE
46th (Highland) Brigade was tasked with advancing on a narrow front, barely one thousand yards, setting off from le Mesnil-Patry to cross the 'Cassino' objective (the Fontenay road), secure the small town of Cheux and the hamlet of le Haut-du-Bosq, then pass-through its reserve battalion with supporting tanks onto the '100 metre ring contour' feature south east of Cheux. In classic style, the brigade formed with two battalions 'up'. On the left, 2nd Glasgow Highlanders would advance on a two-company front, supported by Churchill tanks of B Squadron, 7th Royal Tank Regiment. On the right, the 9th Cameronians and C Squadron, 7th RTR formed in the same manner.

Plans for the brigade's first battle were prepared in painstaking detail. Since each leading battalion had a frontage of barely five hundred yards, and would enjoy the benefit of a strong creeping barrage, two rifle companies per battalion appeared more than sufficient to prosecute the advance. Consequently, not only the two reserve rifle companies, but also the reserve platoon of each of the two leading companies were tasked with 'mopping up' any German survivors of the barrage and the first wave. Each of the two battalions would hold back its Support Company (carrier, mortar, and antitank platoons), plus the Medium Machine Gun company and Royal Artillery antitank troop attached to each, to be brought forward when the final objectives were secured. Each leading rifle company would be supported by two troops of Churchill tanks – three tanks per troop – one troop level with the company and one giving cover from the rear. The tanks' 38 Sets would be in communication with the infantry company headquarters, also with attached Sherman 'Flail' tanks should mine clearance be required. As a final detail, each battalion posted a right-flank guard comprising seven Bren carriers, two three-inch mortar detachments (mounted in their carriers), and two troops of 7th RTR 'Honey' reconnaissance tanks (six in all).

Such was the plan. But even before the start of the battle, problems were evident. The ground had proved impossible to reconnoitre properly. The Canadian 3rd Division holding le Mesnil-Patry only grudgingly allowed recce parties forward: 'Don't bunch, and go quiet'. But there was little of value to be seen. Beyond the plateau to the south, covered in three-foot high corn, the first objectives lay in dead ground. Far-off Cheux was invisible. The long-suffering Canadians had formed little impression of the enemy's positions or strength and had no knowledge at all of enemy minefields. The Glasgow Highlanders found that 'The maps of the area were bad.' (In fact, they were quite accurate but lacking in detail since the ground was mostly open country.) Fortunately, aerial photographs taken as recently as April permitted detailed planning of the route.

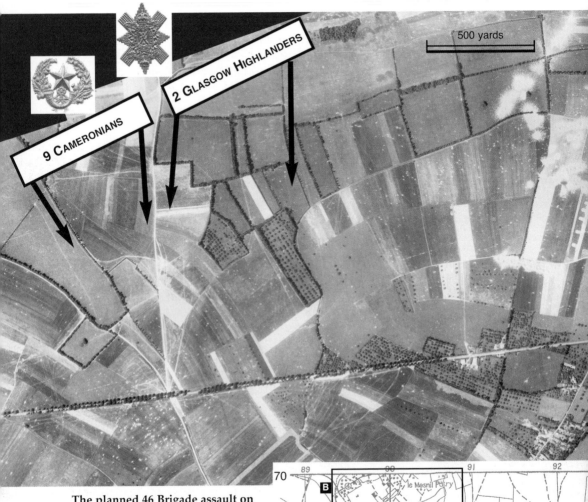

9 CAMERONIANS

2 GLASGOW HIGHLANDERS

500 yards

The planned 46 Brigade assault on a front of barely 1,000 yards.

Planning aside, practical preparations were rushed. The Glasgow Highlanders had only disembarked on Friday, 23 June. The battalion completed its assembly only at 22.00 hours on 24 June, a mere half hour prior to moving off to the Forward Assembly Area for the pending attack. Vehicles were not even completely de-waterproofed before the battle. 7th Royal Tanks had landed a day earlier, on 22 June, losing six tanks whose LCT

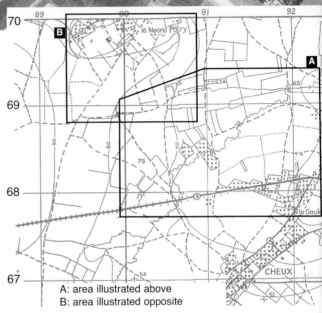

A: area illustrated above
B: area illustrated opposite

struck a mine. Time was lacking for familiarization between tank troops and the infantry companies they would be supporting. Due to the close terrain of le Mesnil-Patry, narrow sunken lanes with steep banks, the tanks were not even able to accompany the Jocks in their initial advance, but instead would rendezvous en route. And there was no time for 'netting' the tanks' 38 Sets

The battalions set off from le Mesnil-Patry: 2 Glasgow left (with B Squadron 7th RTR) and 9 Cameronians right of the boundary road (with C Squadron).

with those of the infantry.

The Glasgow Highlanders set off at 07.30 hours towards the ground being pounded by the barrage. Their Start Line was 1,200 yards north of le Mesnil-Patry, giving them a total of 4,000 yards to cover to their objectives in Cheux.

2 Glasgow Highlanders' advance to the 'Cassino' objective.

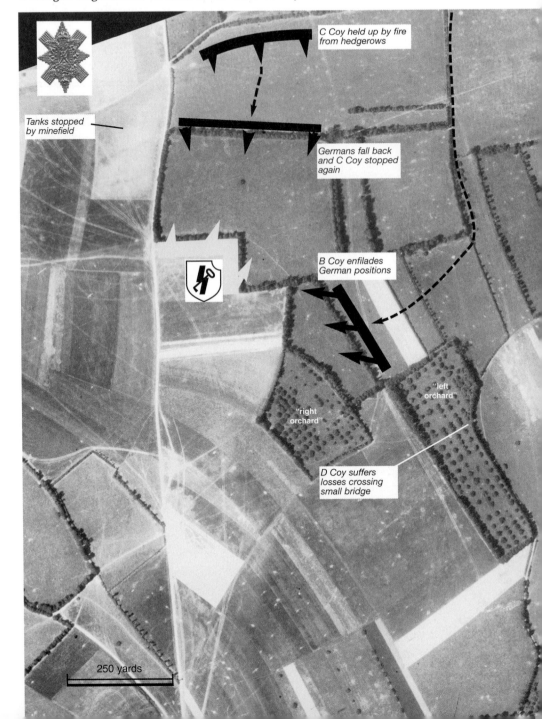

C Coy held up by fire from hedgerows

Tanks stopped by minefield

Germans fall back and C Coy stopped again

B Coy enfilades German positions

"left orchard"

"right orchard"

D Coy suffers losses crossing small bridge

250 yards

They closed well up against the barrage before its first lift, but thereafter found it difficult to keep up with the wall of fire. South of the village, the tank squadrons attempted to join the marching companies. Only now was it realised that radio communication between tanks and infantry was impossible. Not a single infantry 38 wireless set worked. And the terrain ahead was not conducive to joint operations: while the infantry plunged into hedgerows and woods, the tanks tried to get around these obstacles through open fields. So the leading foot soldiers pressed on, keeping to the left of the dirt track running south from le Mesnil which marked their regimental boundary. Ahead lay by an east-west wall of tall hedgerows, beyond which the air photographs showed two large, polygonal fields of trees, dubbed 'left orchard' and 'right orchard'. As the forward companies closed the hedgerows, the commanding officer received the first indication of trouble in a signal from C Company's 18 Set.

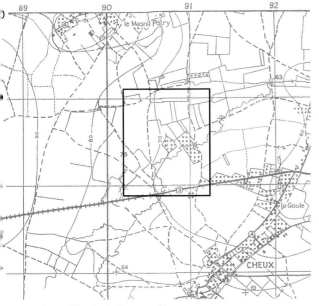

Area illustrated opposite.

The treeline in front of C Company had erupted in machine gun fire: the company was pinned down while nearby a mine field was taking a toll of carriers and supporting Churchill tanks. The colonel did not dare call in artillery, since D Company's continuing advance had taken it on ahead, abreast of the German positions. All he could do was order C Company to do the best it could with its own weapons, and urge A Company forward to assist. Eventually, C Company got moving again. But at the very next hedgerow it was again stopped dead, this time with even heavier casualties. The situation was helped when B Company, following D, came alongside the German-held hedgerow and enfiladed the defenders.

Meanwhile, it was D Company's turn to encounter trouble. Approaching the 'left orchard', D suffered casualties, which became heavy as the company was caught by mortar fire pre-registered on the tempting target of a small bridge, where the men were predictably bunching. A pause was necessary for re-organization, and the company's 'mopping up' platoon was called forward to assist. By the time D Company reached its first objective, the Fontenay road, it had long lost the barrage (which had paused on the objective only fifteen minutes and long since moved on). The company was short of NCOs and effectively reduced to two platoons. Due to mines, the colonel's mobile command post was unable to reach the planned rendezvous, and the tanks too were stuck in the rear. The remnants of D Company had to resume the

German
bunkers

Former German
bunker used as
2 Glasgow
Highlanders HQ

2 Glasgow Highlanders' advance south of the 'Cassino' objective and into Cheux. Note in the top left hand corner field hospital air markers. Nearby is a squadron of Sherman tanks.

advance unsupported.

The opposition on this section of the front was the Hitler Youth engineer battalion. Although specialists in their field, it was understood that *12. SS-Pionierbataillon* would also fight as foot soldiers, and so it was that its companies took their place in the thinly stretched defensive line north of Cheux: alongside the first and second companies of *26. SS-Panzergrenadier-Regiment* and squarely across the path of the Glasgow Highlanders. Though shocked by the artillery drumfire, *'unimaginable for anyone who has not lived through such barrages'*, the surviving pioneers gave a good account of themselves. And although landmines were not in plentiful supply for the German defensive line, those antitank mines available had been artfully sited on the pioneers' front, taking a heavy toll of the British armour and further disrupting cooperation between tanks and infantry. (Such was the British determination to regain the impetus of the advance that neither the infantry pioneer platoons nor the supporting Sherman Flail tanks conducted any serious attempt at mine clearance.) But the defensive line was thin, and the underpinning German armour was absent, sent west to the defence of Rauray. By the time the depleted Glasgow Highlanders moved south of the Fontenay road, they were already in the German rear areas, overrunning (though not recognising or capturing) the *Pionierbataillon* command bunker. The road ahead to Cheux was relatively clear. Arriving in the western part of the little town, the infantry encountered little opposition. Battalion headquarters came up and established in a German emplacement; the Regimental Aid Post set up in a large barn opposite.

On the Glasgow Highlanders' right, the 9th Cameronians' experience had differed in being an advance over open ground. They too had lost the barrage, and lost tank support to a belt of mines. Just as the company on the left of 44th Brigade's advance suffered from flanking fire, so did the right-most company of the 46th find its flank open to enemies to the west, around Fontenay. The right-flank A Company suffered such heavy losses on the approach to the 'Cassino' road that the colonel had to direct C Company to take over that side of the advance. The battalion kept going, losing its direction somewhat and running into the 2nd GH in Cheux, but nevertheless by 13.00 hours in possession of the main objective, the cluster of buildings at le Haut-du-Bosq. The Cameronians' first half-dozen hours of combat had come at a high cost, with over a hundred losses, including several officers and the second-in-command.

Meanwhile, the brigade's

The 9 Cameronians' planned advance (with area illustrated opposite.)

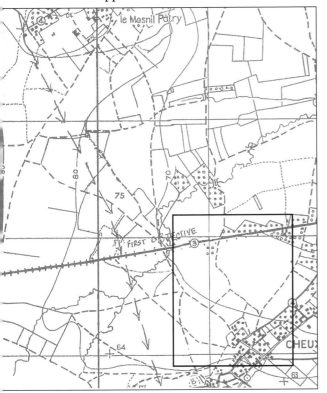

reserve battalion, the 7th Seaforth Highlanders, having spent the morning successfully mopping up pockets of German survivors, came forward in the afternoon. The Seaforth's B Company and some Churchills got as far as a reverse slope just south of Cheux before being held up by enemy fire sweeping the open ground. Losses had been slight; the Seaforth's trial by fire was yet to come.

THROUGH THE CENTRE: 227 BRIGADE

The plan had seemed so straightforward. Two brigades to advance behind a wall of artillery fire and bludgeon through the German lines; a third brigade to take up the baton, two of its battalions securing the northern slopes of the Odon valley and a third battalion dividing to open two river crossings; then the tanks of 11th Armoured Division could pour through on their way to the River Orne. 44th and 46th Brigades had indeed accomplished their assigned tasks, albeit at heavy loss and much later in the day than the plan allowed. Only in the late afternoon, after a day of frustrating inaction, did the 2nd Gordon Highlanders on the left and the 10th Highland Light Infantry on the

right struggle forward to their respective Start Lines around Cheux and Haut-du-Bosq. Sergeant Green of the 10th HLI recalled, *'The Padre, Ian Dunlop, and I played a game of pocket chess during halts in the straggling approach march... we were pretty keyed up. We did not finish the game... The jeep began to come past with the stretcher cases and the sight of the bloodstained field dressings and the urgency of the driving brought home to us that this battle was real and likely to get worse before it got better.'*

All along the line of march, shots from unexpected directions revealed that pockets of German resistance remained uncleared. Cheux itself was a nightmare: its narrow lanes between

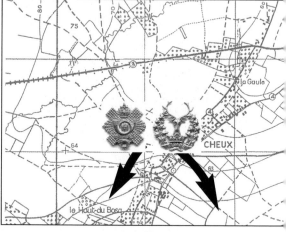

Advancing to the 227 Brigade Start Line: HLI right to Haut-du-Bosq; Gordons left towards Colleville.

rubbled stone buildings already congested by vehicles, streaming with rainwater and deep in churned-up mud. Moving off the congested road along tracks made through minefields by the preceding 46 Brigade, Sergeant Green observed one of several Churchill tanks immobilized by a mine. *'We thought the tank crew were a merry lot in the circumstances but we were to realise later that their high spirits were caused by their relief at being alive and free of the battle for a while.'* By 18.30 hours, the two battalions still had not reached their Start Lines, but were clearly already embattled. Both stepped-off to push south. As was becoming normal, communications with the supporting 31st Brigade infantry tanks had completely broken down; in the murk the Churchills sprayed BESA in all directions, *'a source of fear to all and sundry, Scottish and*

The Gordons' B Company advanced ahead of the battalion to the Colleville level crossing.

German'.

The 10th HLI had barely begun their advance when a young *Panzergrenadier* in a camouflaged smock sprang up out of the crop. His fate is not recorded, but his sudden appearance provoked *'an immediate scare that snipers were all around. Firing at tree tops began until no one knew which way to look and this nervous start to our attack boded ill for our chances.'* To make matters worse, a heavy storm broke just as the advance was getting under way and, *'in the driving rain and smoke the Battalion lost direction and attacked towards Rauray* [i.e., west instead of south] *which was heavily defended. The enemy opened up with bursts of machine gun fire... Lieutenant Bell was killed when a shell burst at the base of a tree and toppled it as the carrier in which he was riding passed underneath. The C.O., realising what was happening, came tearing up and halted the advance... By the time the Battalion were re-formed facing in the proper direction it was dark, raining heavily and the momentum had been lost.'* The HLI dug in for a wet and miserable night.[16]

If the Gordons achieved somewhat more than the HLI, the achievement came at a high cost and was of dubious value. The battalion moved off around the eastern side of Cheux, two companies 'up': A Company on the right, B to the left. A Company very quickly began to take casualties from the same defenders who had stopped 10th HLI. Pausing to regroup in an open field, they were further mauled by a well timed mortar strike. By the time the colonel could come up with the two reserve companies, these too had suffered heavy losses. Colonel Colville *'then decided on re-organising what could be collected of the Bn and a small defensive position was made beside the CHEUX-COLLVILLE road.'*[17] The position was all the smaller since all contact with B Company had been lost. To their credit, they had continued the advance as far as the railway crossing at Colleville, where they represented the extreme tip of 15th Scottish Division's penetration of the German line.

THE ARMOURED DIVISION

Even by midday, four and a half hours into the battle, it was becoming clear to VIII Corps headquarters that progress was falling well behind schedule. Corps commander General Sir Richard O'Connor had made a name for himself in the desert war as an imaginative and dynamic leader of mobile forces. Now returned from a career-disrupting spell as a prisoner of war in Italy, he was determined to show that he was the equal of commanders who had been promoted during his enforced absence. But a Montgomery-style 'set piece' such as Operation EPSOM left little scope for a corps commander. Hardly surprising therefore that O'Connor was tempted to prove himself by intervening at the tactical level.

Though O'Connor's meddling was to become a cause of annoyance to his divisional commanders, his first tactical intervention during EPSOM appears with hindsight to have been sound. It was clearly laid down in the EPSOM plan that *'If sqn 2 N Yeo are able to rush the crossings over R. Odon they will do so and 29 Armd Bde will follow as quickly as possible.'* The 2nd Northamptonshire Yeomanry's squadrons of Cromwell tanks (of which only two, A and C, had so far arrived in Normandy) were officially classed as 11th Armoured Division's 'reconnaissance regiment', a role into which they never really developed though on this occasion they perhaps came closest. When in early afternoon of 26 June the order came down from VIII Corps to loose the Northants Yeomanry on a dash to the Odon bridges, their divisional commander was sceptical. *'I never had much hope of this succeeding unless the enemy were highly disorganised and virtually in flight.'*[18] His scepticism was based on the assumption that the German forces opposing the advance were considerable, and far from disorganised. His own 11th Armoured Division intelligence summary prepared on the night of 26 June drew the conclusion that, *'as yet only the fwd defences had been driven in and that his main defences had still to be tackled.'* This was a sound appraisal of normal German defensive tactics: multi-layered, based on a main line of defence screened by forward outposts, with reserves ready to throw in to regain lost positions. On 26 June, this appraisal was simply wrong.

In truth, 15th Scottish Division had penetrated the main German line. In front of the division by the afternoon of 26 June were only outposts and pockets of retreating engineers and *Panzergrenadiere*. *'The sniper fire all over the area, greatly intensified by wildly-aimed retaliation in all directions, was not recognised for what it was: not snipers at all, not a thin screen out in front of the main German battle line; those scattered shots, with the occasional burst of machine-gun fire was the main German position – all that was left of 12th SS Panzer Division on that front, a handful of determined teenagers, toughly arrogant at the havoc they were causing.'*[19] Only in the early evening were reinforcements hastily thrown in by a profoundly alarmed *I. SS-Panzerkorps* to fill the gap: a handful of *Tiger* tanks from the east, companies of *Panzer IV* from *12. SS-Panzerregiment* to the west, and armoured cars and infantry of the Hitler Youth reconnaissance battalion to try to plug the gap forced around Colleville. They stiffened the resolve of the infantry in the area, and in the confusion and the rain these *ad hoc* forces prepared to confront the Scots.

Forward into this confusion struggled the nineteen Cromwells of A Squadron, 2nd NH Yeo, accompanied by a single Crusader antiaircraft tank and an artillery Forward Observation Officer's Sherman. The approach to their first battle was not quite what the young Yeomen had expected. Instead of the glorified fox-chases they had practised across the rolling fields of Northamptonshire, they had first to bypass stationary 15th Scottish traffic lining the road south of Norrey, then to struggle through the narrow, congested, rubble-strewn lanes of Cheux. Nor did their first contact with the enemy match expectations. Even before the squadron had cleared Cheux, tank commanders' exposed heads were being targeted by enemy fire. The squadron 2 i.c. Captain Raynsford became the regiment's first casualty, killed by a shot in the head. 2 Troop tank commander Corporal 'Reg' Spittles recalled, *'The town was totally destroyed and the Germans were there, as many Germans as 15th Scottish! They just couldn't find each other.'* Spittles crouched in his open turret hatch, hurling white phosphorous grenades at young *Panzergrenadiere* who in turn were trying to slap magnetic mines on his Cromwell.

By the time the tanks were clear of the place, the artillery fire plan laid-on to cover them had already moved ahead. The squadron rolled south regardless. Lieutenant Alex Stock's 4 Troop got far enough forward to shoot up a light anti-aircraft battery near Grainville, and rumour had it that he reported intact bridges over the Odon (a remarkable feat, if true: presumably at Gavrus, south of Grainville). But most of the squadron found themselves trapped in a large field surrounded by uncrossable ditches, under fire and unable to make progress. At first, 29 Brigade ordered them to hold position. But by 14.50 hours the futility of the exercise became evident. The squadron was recalled and returned north to harbour.

Still came the pressure from VIII Corps to regain the timetable. At 18.00 hours, 11th Armoured Division forwarded the instruction to their armour: *'29 Armd Bde ordered to act boldly with intention of reaching line R. ODON tonight.'* The idea was that the Sherman tank regiments of 11th Armoured Division would do what the Churchill tanks of 31st Tank Brigade had failed to do: namely to support the Scots infantry in their southward push. In hindsight,

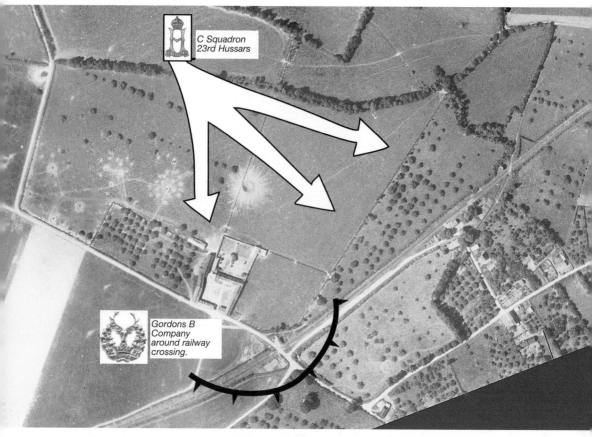

C Squadron
23rd Hussars

Gordons B
Company
around railway
crossing.

A few of C Squadron's Sherman tanks reached the Gordons at Colleville.

the attempt was futile. With the exception of the company of Gordons around the railway crossing at Colleville, the advance of 15th Scottish had halted around Cheux and was not going to resume this day. Nor were the supporting Churchills going to carry on the fight. C Squadron of 9th RTR had lost five tanks supporting the Gordons' attack over the ridge south of Cheux and with fuel and ammunition running low the rest retired to laager at dusk. 7th RTR's A Squadron had lost five tanks knocked out and three on mines; *'We became a Sqn. of ten tanks and wiser and more sober men. We had lost some of our best officers, NCOs, and men in a few hours after years of intensive training.'* In blinding rain, *'tank commanders were not sorry to pull back to Forward Rally.'*[20]

In the failing light, two of 11th Armoured's tank regiments pressed forward. On the left, 23rd Hussars had worked their way around the eastern side of St-Manvieu and past the farm of la Bijude. On the way, they could see burning Churchills south of Cheux, and in their turn the Hussars experienced their first losses. *'Those who witnessed it will always remember the shock of seeing for the first time one of the Regiment's tanks go up in flames. One moment an impregnable monster... the next, a crack of terrific impact, a sheet of flame, and then… nothing but a helpless roaring inferno.'*[21] A few C Squadron tanks got as far forward as Colleville, where the presence of tanks doubtless gave heart to the otherwise isolated company of Gordons before leaving the infantry and returning to harbour under cover of the night.

On the right, the 2nd Fife and Forfarshire Yeomanry took their turn to struggle through Cheux. Earlier in the day, B Squadron and the Recce Troop (of Stuart light tanks) had led; now C Squadron under the experienced Major Nicholls went ahead. Even beyond the ruins of Cheux, manoeuvre was impossible as the squadron advanced in single file between high embankments. And as soon as the protection of the embankments was lost, the leading tank was knocked out. A second tank edged around the wreck and suffered the same fate. *'Hemmed in between steep banks we could see nothing. There was no room to turn round, and we couldn't reverse because of the tanks lined up nose to tail behind us… We heard the commanding officer, Lieutenant-Colonel Scott, frequently coming on the air urging the squadron leader to advance. But Major Nicholls had had considerable experience and retorted that he would advance only when the gain justified the losses. That was a great morale booster to us!'*[22]

The Fifes' A Squadron attempted to edge around the western side of Cheux, only to find itself similarly encumbered on the narrow road leading to le Haut-du-Bosq. Here, in close country and unaccompanied by supporting infantry, the tanks were easy prey to resolute *Panzerfaust*-equipped Germans.

A and C Squadrons of the Fife and Forfar Yeomanry ran into *Panzer IV* (two companies) of *Hitlerjugend*.

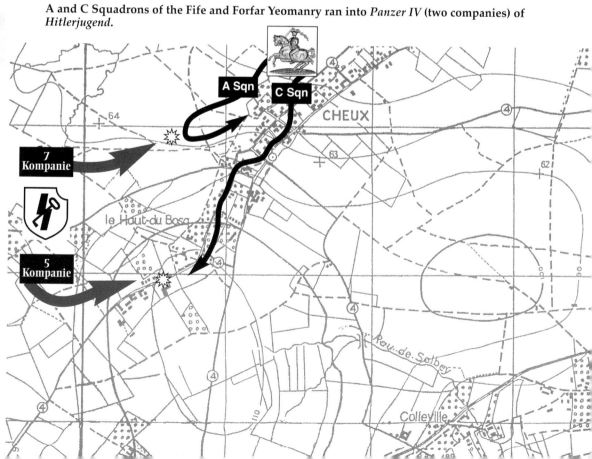

Come nightfall, both A and C Squadrons were pleased to be recalled, the tanks inching cautiously backwards through the gloom to harbour for reequipping, maintenance and the chance of a precious few moments of sleep. A Squadron had lost two tanks; C, for all Nicholls' caution, had lost seven. The regiment consoled itself that, on average, three men had managed to escape from each knocked-out tank.

THE END OF THE FIRST DAY

On 26 June, eight of the infantry battalions of 15th Scottish Division (and three tank regiments of 11th Armoured) experienced for the first time the shock of battle. Most of the infantry battalions suffered losses of men running into three figures, a substantial percentage of their rifle strength. On the positive side of the equation, replacements were still available at this early stage of the campaign. All three battalions of 44th Brigade were actually relieved by fresh units before the dawn of 27 June (a respite unimaginable for a newly-committed German unit in Normandy!), and a further two (2nd Glasgow Highlanders and 7th Seaforth) would be relieved in the course of the following day. Time was granted for these units to reflect on the many harsh lessons which only combat could teach.

The first day of EPSOM revealed alarming shortcomings in cooperation between infantry and tanks. (Though this was balanced by the outstanding degree of cooperation between the infantry and their supporting artillery – bonds of trust and confidence strengthened in this battle would last throughout the campaign for North West Europe.) Some of these

All three battalions of 44 Brigade relieved at the end of their first day of combat.

shortcomings were to do with equipment, in particular radios. But most resulted from flawed doctrine and training, in particular the assumption that armoured and infantry units unfamiliar with each other could fight in seamless symbiosis. It was not to be.[23]

At the highest level, Montgomery radiated confidence. His end-of-day wire to Supreme Commander Eisenhower referred to *'weather very bad with heavy rain and low cloud but very good progress made and leading troops of 8 Corps now available on railway line at Colleville.'* The fact that only a depleted and isolated company had reached that feature and was now seeking a way back was glossed over. He continued, *'Fighting will go on all day and all night.'* This was an outrageous fabrication: no one expected British tanks to fight in darkness, nor that the infantry would do any more than organize small-scale night patrols. However, *'I am prepared to have a showdown with enemy on my eastern flank for as long as he likes'* offers a particularly interesting insight. Having begun the day in the firm belief that a breakthrough to the Orne River crossings was feasible, Montgomery was already preparing a fall-back position to save embarrassment in the event that objective was not achieved. Later he would claim that his intent all along had been defensive: a strategy of drawing the enemy armour onto his own front. For now, however, the original plan for a strategic breakthrough was maintained. The order telegraphed to 15th Scottish, to be repeated to all brigades, read, *'TOP SECRET: enemy now reduced to last reserves on our front. Essential to secure crossings over R ODON as early as possible tomorrow 27 June.'* The stage was set for the second day of EPSOM.

Montgomery closed his report to Eisenhower with reference to the fall to the Americans on 26 June of the port of Cherbourg. Its surrender by *General* von Schlieben was a milestone for the Allies and a symbolic shock for German Seventh Army. No less than the Scots' forcing a four-mile corridor through the *Hitlerjugend*, the capitulation of a port designated by Hitler as a fortress to be defended to the death sent ripples of consternation through the defenders of Normandy. The consequences would be significant for EPSOM.

References

(1) Sergeant Hugh Green memoirs
(2) Woolcombe, p 48-49
(3) Martin, p 34
(4) *Six Armies in Normandy*, John Keegan, p 171
(5) Observations by General Hubert Gough on the later stages of the Somme battle in which some battalions had 'not a single platoon organized', merely telling-off groups of men for specific duties, and allocating the small quota of Lewis machine guns in a casual manner. Quoted in Graham, *Against Odds*, p 38
(6) The base plates and sometimes other pieces of the exploding shell might fly backwards, but most of the force went outwards through the sides of the shell. Given the forward and downward trajectory of the shell, its main blast effect was projected within a forwards arc, hence the characteristic 'horns' extending forward from shellholes often visible in aerial photographs of shelled ground. (This is why higher-trajectory weapons, such as howitzers and especially

mortars, were more efficient since their projectiles descended more steeply and less of their sideways blast and splinters were dissipated into the ground or up into the air.)

(7) 2nd Argylls, War Diary

(8) For interpretation of British map references, see Appendix I

(9) The battalion War Diary appears somewhat 'optimistic' in the timings given, in contrast to more modest records of their progress noted at division and corps level.

(10) Conflicting sources for this story include Meyer, p 106 and the Buffs' June War Diary. The latter account is less dramatic but perhaps more reliable than German propaganda dramatized by a Kriegsberichter.

(11) Memoirs of E A Powdrill, acting Troop Leader of D Troop, H Battery, 13th Royal Horse Artillery

(12) *12. SS-Panzerdivision* recorded that they were promised companies of tanks and of assault guns. It is clear from *21. Panzerdivision* records that their (improvised!) assault gun *Abteilung* did not participate in the action; nor would its lightly armoured guns have been suited to such an assault.

(13) Martin, p 36

(14) Woolcombe, p 60

(15) British War Diaries need to be interpreted with an eye to regimental pride. 6th RSF recorded *'The operation of clearing the village was well carried out by the Bn.'* whilst 6th KOSB reported proceeding *'to the assistance of 6RSF at ST MAUVIEU, where final objectives had not yet been taken.'*

(16) This and previous passages from Sergeant Hugh Green memoirs

(17) 2nd Gordons June War Diary

(18) *From the Desert to the Baltic*, Roberts, p 159

(19) McKee, p 180

(20) *"A" Squadron Diary*, Major Richard Joscelyne

(21) *The Story of the 23rd Hussars*, Bishop, p 46

(22) Trooper Ron Cox, C Squadron

(23) See Appendix VII for a review of tank-infantry cooperation during EPSOM.

An armoured brigade headquarters at rest alongside the Fontenay-Caen road.

Chapter 4

TUESDAY 27 JUNE:
TO THE ODON

27 June dawned on a wet and miserable scene. All through the night, British Medical Officers and their stretcher bearers struggled valiantly to cope with a tide of casualties. Those so far unscathed settled into their slit trenches. *'We dug in for the night under intermittent mortar fire. To add to our wretchedness, the rain still persisted, although we were already so wet that we scarcely heeded the downpour; the mortaring and the rain made sleep almost impossible… When it came, breakfast was cold tinned sausage and the tea a muddy concoction.'* The 10th HLI battalion cooks with their three ton lorry back at le Mesnil-Patry had been bothered by an aircraft droning in the pre-dawn darkness, extinguishing the cooking stoves at every pass: 'Put that bloody light out!' After the long drive to the front, the half-brewed tea and partly cooked soya link were *'a pitiful*

With drains blocked by rubble, the rain flooded the streets of Cheux.

breakfast to offer the condemned men.'[1] Nor was life any easier in the tank lines. *'That night, after our first day in action, I don't think that anyone slept. The petrol and ammo took three hours to reach us, the enemy were only a few hundred yards away, and everybody was shattered by the day's events. Long afterwards you thought about Cheux as just about the worst.'*[2] German survivors overtaken by the British advance emerged from hiding, profiting from the rain and general confusion to make their way back through the lines. Small groups of *Panzergrenadiere* formed into *ad hoc* platoons. With daylight, the battle resumed.

SIEGEL ON THE SALBEY

Of the nine infantry battalions of 15th Scottish, three began 27 June in the front line. First into action were the 10th Highland Light Infantry. Their objective was unchanged: to press on south, seizing Grainville-sur-Odon to

The German line had been penetrated and Siegel's *8. Kompanie* arrived to plug the gap.

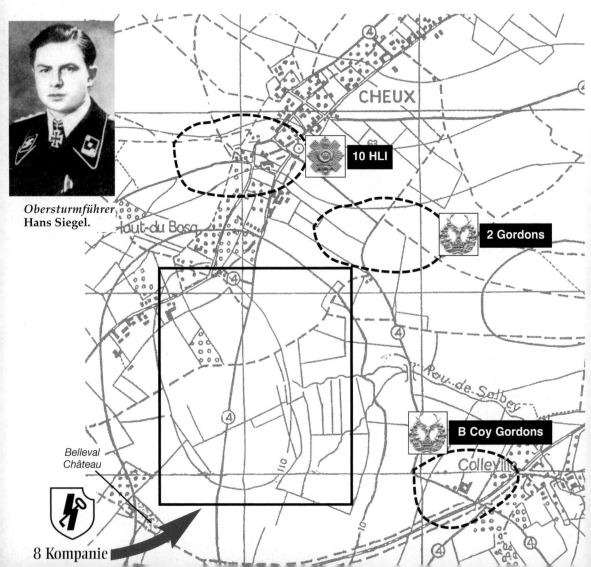

Obersturmführer **Hans Siegel.**

CHEUX

10 HLI

2 Gordons

B Coy Gordons

Belleval Château

8 Kompanie

Salbey Stream

open the way to the western crossings over the Odon River. At first light, the battalion prepared to advance to their Start Line, south of Cheux. Waiting for them was *Obersturmführer* Hans Siegel.

Late on 26 June, Siegel's *Panzer IV* of *8. Kompanie, 12. SS-Panzerregiment*, had disengaged from the fight around Fontenay and pulled back to the northeast of Rauray to replenish fuel and ammunition. The regimental headquarters was still in Rauray, and its commander, *Obersturmbannführer* Max Wünsche met Siegel with new orders. Alarmed at the risk of a British breakthrough to the east, he was despatching the fifth and seventh companies of his *12. SS-Panzerregiment* to return to their original positions behind the divisional engineer battalion (arriving too late to regain those positions, they would instead fight a mobile action against advancing British tanks through the afternoon and evening). Siegel's orders were to move to cap the southernmost enemy penetration: no infantry was available; he would have to deal with the situation as he found it. With four tanks, Siegel roared away south-east.

Between the estate of the Belleval château and the railway north of Grainville, the evening of 26 June found Siegel's troop on the high ground north of the railway line, with a clear view north towards Cheux. Siegel quickly realised that the enemy was present on the high ground opposite. After some long-range shots at distant vehicles, his four tanks edged forward down the dirt road into the shallow valley of the Salbey rivulet. Leaving the

tanks under cover of a hedgerow, a reconnaissance on foot confirmed that this was indeed the German front line, lightly held by a handful of exhausted grenadiers and engineers and a nearby battery of *Hitlerjugend* artillerymen, whose guns lacked any gun tractors to extract them from their precarious forward position. Bringing up his tanks, Siegel sited them to maximize fields of fire. Siegel's own remained on the road north of the bridge over the stream, its width filling the narrow lane, whose earth banks shielded

1: Siegel's clear view towards Cheux.

2: Edging forward across the Salbey

3: The covering hedgerow.

Advancing to the hedgerow, Siegel sited his four Panzer IV to maximize fields of fire.

the sides of the vehicle. From here, Siegel could cover an arc from the north towards Cheux to north-eastwards along the stream. The other three took up north-facing positions behind a hedgerow in a large field just west of the road. A stout earth bank protected their hulls; from their turrets, disguised by the thick foliage, the gunners enjoyed a clear view across open fields to the crestline barely a hundred metres distant. Here the tanks sat out an uneasy night. The tank crews were unaccustomed to spending the night so far forward, having to defend their own vehicles against occasional marauding enemy patrols. Siegel made contact with the nearby headquarters bunker of *II. Bataillon / 26. Panzergrenadier-Regiment*. Later, he reported back to his own commander's headquarters, now relocated eastwards from Rauray to nearby Grainville. Later still, his tanks began to tow out the artillery pieces stranded nearby to relative safety south of the railway. Come the dawn, Siegel's men settled back into their tanks and the small band awaited events.

10th HLI were due to attack at 06.30, but once again there was difficulty linking up with the tanks due to support them. Only at 07.30 did B Company

step off. They did not even reach their Start Line before being mauled by a mortar barrage. Reaching the crest above Siegel's position, the infantry were silhouetted against the sky, but the unseen defenders held their fire until the bulk of the company was in view. Then, opening fire simultaneously, four co-axial machine guns raked the advancing ranks. *'Struggling forward through chest-high corn, the Jocks were cut to pieces by dug-in Panther tanks firing at close range. Frantically they went to ground, but mercilessly the enemy mortars plastered the cornfield. Training had*

The 10 HLI Start Line: right flank indicated by the modern Haut-du-Bosq water tower.

The German tanks unseen behind this hedgerow.

taught them much, but could never teach the horror of seeing their friends torn to pieces before their eyes.'[3]

B Company having 'had a bad time', D passed through to resume the advance, but were likewise stopped. By 08.30 hours, A and D Companies had still barely reached the Start Line. The Churchill tanks of C Squadron, 7th RTR arrived but failed to tip the scales. As the Churchills appeared on the skyline, Siegel's tanks opened up with their main guns. At short range, a fair proportion of rounds from their high-velocity 7.5cm guns tore through the frontal plate of some of Britain's most heavily armoured tanks.[4] C Company tried a flanking move to the right, but still fell within the tanks' arc of fire. The infantry continued the fruitless struggle and, *'though some elements succeeded in reaching the start line, they could not consolidate their gain.'*[5]

Siegel's tanks' field of fire: the Churchills appeared sillouetted on the skyline.

Before midday, the 10th HLI attempt to advance was abandoned. During the afternoon, the surviving tanks of C Squadron returned north to harbour, claiming 'at least three enemy tanks' knocked out. The men of 7th RTR could be forgiven their mistaken claim; various units in the vicinity of Cheux that morning, tank and antitank regiments alike, all claimed successes from long-range shots into the woods. But still Siegel's four tanks held their ground.

Standing-by since dawn to the east of Cheux, the Fife and Forfar with their Sherman tanks were intended to pass through any opening made by the infantry and the Churchills. The Fifes' A Squadron was to lead. *'The Churchill attack got nowhere, and we took over. We were to advance up a slope, over the skyline, then down into the woods beyond, where the enemy positions were. We had two troops up, Freddie Craig on the right, and myself behind him. As he topped the ridge, three of his tanks were brewed, and his took cover in a slight hollow. I had to take his place, so kept going.'* [6]

Already, the Sherman troops were learning the 'form' for Normandy. No longer would the troop commander lead the way. Instead the four-tank troop would advance with the troop sergeant's tank in the vulnerable leading position. The single 'Firefly' with its seventeen-pounder gun, *'the only effective antitank gun in our troop'*, would lag behind the others. With its distinctive long gun and elongated hull, the Firefly was a choice target for the enemy, and so was typically manned by the troop corporal, the troop's lowest-ranking tank commander. Of Steel Brownlie's 4 Troop, the sergeant's tank was brewed, his own broke down, and when the Firefly was called forward to engage hard targets, *'the trouble was that the corporal commanding it did not*

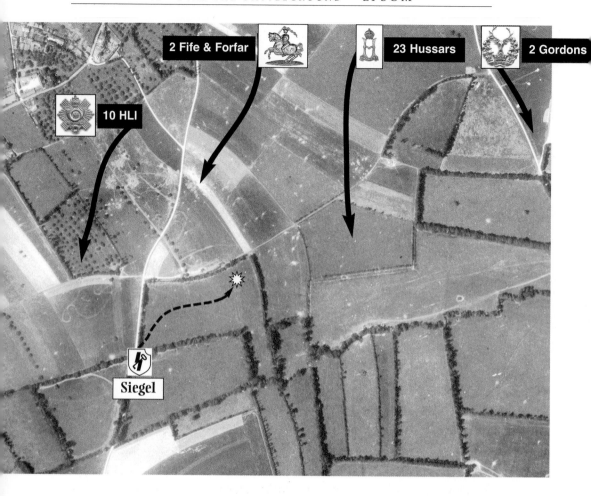

intend to be summoned, and would not even keep up, but lagged behind in spite of my orders over the air.' To Steel Brownlie, as to many others, it seemed that 'everything went wrong.' In fact, something was achieved. Conscious of his open flanks, Siegel sensed that his right risked being overlapped by the advancing Yeomanry Shermans. Moving off from his covered position to obtain a clearer field of fire eastwards, Siegel's tank presented its right flank to a hitherto unsuspected Sherman.[7] Before Siegel's gunner could traverse his turret to the three o'clock position, an armour piercing round burst through the hull, killing the driver. Siegel and three crew members got out, all scorched, the gunner mortally (he alone lacked one of the flame-resistant leather suits that *Hitlerjugend* had looted from the Italian navy). His tank lost, he and his surviving crew suffering from burns, Siegel's own fight was over. Although the approaches to Grainville remained blocked, the easterly track from Cheux to Colleville was now open.

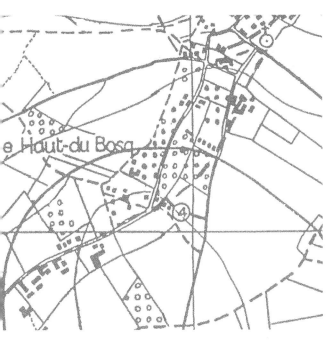

LE HAUT-DU-BOSQ

46th Highland Brigade had passed the night grouped around Cheux: the Glasgow Highlanders in Cheux itself, the Seaforth in brigade reserve to the north, and the Cameronians licking their wounds around the hamlet of le Haut-du-Bosq. The word went out to those Cameronians LOB ('left out of battle') to rejoin the unit. They would be needed. The unit had experienced heavy losses and was very much in the front line. Harassing enemy fire continuing through the night and into the morning. As in other units, the inexperienced infantry tended to ascribe any stray bullet passing nearby to aimed 'sniper' fire, and people remained jittery.

Since Guards Armoured Division had not completed its formation in time for EPSOM, the 43rd (Wessex) Division had joined VIII Corps for the operation. Elements of the 43rd Division had already relieved the 44th Brigade around St-Manvieu, and others were to relieve the Cameronians in order for them to undertake the next stage of their battle. At 18.00 hours on 26 June, an advance party of the 5th Duke of Cornwall's Light Infantry had visited the Cameronians' headquarters to recce the position. The Cameronians were in a hurry to move out. 11.00 hours on the morning of 27 June found them already relocated around a position a good eight hundred yards north of le Haut-du-Bosq. Meanwhile, the 5th DCLI had been delayed. Their history politely mentions of the Cameronians that *'by an unfortunate misunderstanding some of them withdrew before the Fifth could replace them... this complicated matters.'*[8] It certainly did. The enemy re-entered the place. The two forward companies of 5th DCLI who arrived expecting a smooth handover were greeted instead by hostile *Panzergrenadiere*. Taken by surprise, they were thrown back. Only after some time had passed was the battalion able to re-take the place. It was well into the morning before the rifle companies of 5th DCLI were able to dig themselves in around the buildings and orchards of le Haut-du-Bosq, and prepare fighting patrols to deal with aggressive 'snipers' in the cornfields.

All this time, frantic efforts were being made by the German Seventh Army to move forces into the gap that had been opened up on 26 June. From the east there had already come a handful of *Tiger* tanks, a dozen or so representing two companies of *101. schwere SS-Panzer-Abteilung*. But the bulk of 1. *SS-Panzerdivision* (the *'Leibstandarte'*, Adolph Hitler's lifeguards) was still stuck in the St-Germain area awaiting fuel supplies, and the promised *II. SS-Panzerkorps* with its two powerful armoured divisions was even further from the front. While the *Hitlerjugend* and *Panzer-Lehr* divisions worked to close the gap that had opened between them west of Fontenay, the best force that could be assembled to cap the Scottish corridor comprised the first, *Panther* tank-equipped battalion of *2. Panzerdivision* ('Wien') with an infantry task force made up of the first elements of *2. SS-Panzerdivision* ('Das Reich') arriving from the south of France. *Generaloberst* Dollmann recommended that these now form an impromptu battle-group, and Rommel gave permission.[9]

The plan was conceived in haste and cut across normal reporting channels. *12. SS-Panzerdivision* appears not to have been informed, though Hans Siegel reports being approached by a *Hauptmann* of the 'Vienna' division's *Panther* battalion on the morning of 27 June. This captain had brought up his tanks overnight, and was diligently conducting the customary ground reconnaissance before launching his attack. Rather than the full *I. Bataillon* of *3. Panzerregiment*, he commanded only a single company, though it appears to have been up to strength with its full complement of seventeen tanks. Siegel's advice was that the unit should drive into the dangerous gap he perceived to the east of his position, where the British had already probed as far as the railway crossing at Colleville. Why the *Hauptmann* did not follow the advice is not known. He may well have been keen to hold his unit further west in the hope of being joined by the promised infantry escort. But in the confusion, these never arrived. On their arrival, the SS infantry battalions had come under the command of *Panzer-Lehr-Division* and were committed further west around Fontenay, in the gap between *Lehr* and *Hitlerjugend*. Thus was the gap east of Siegel, around Colleville and Tourville, left open. Important consequences would flow from this later in the day.

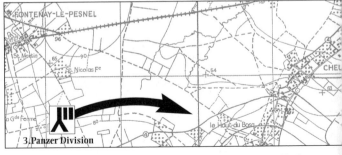

Seventeen Panther tanks of the 3. *Panzerdivision* rolled east over open fields.

So, in mid-morning, the unaccompanied *Panther* assault set off across the battlefield. From a starting position south of Fontenay, the seventeen tanks rolled eastward over open fields. Their objective was Cheux, the little town whose clogged lanes were the lifeline of the entire corridor carved by 15th Scottish. But although these were the best battle tanks of their day, they were terribly exposed by the lack of an infantry escort. As the commander of their division was shortly after to record: '*It is no longer a question of employing tanks in the classic manner, as for example is the case in Russia. In Normandy they can be used only in support of troops of infantry… It is imperative that the enemy antitank must be neutralized before they open their attack, and since the ground greatly favours short-range antitank weapons, each individual tank engaged in combat must enjoy the strong protective cover of foot soldiers.'*[10]

In le Haut-du-Bosq, the 5th DCLI were still settling-in when the first German tanks arrived. A column of six *Panther* approached along a dirt road, the high earth banks and clouds of dust thrown up briefly disguising them so that they were past B Company before they were recognised. An officer of D Company at the heart of the position recalled: *'The wireless was working to battalion headquarters and life seemed to be a little better and more like an exercise around Folkestone...I was walking back to company headquarters having flushed a German sniper from a farm building. Cpl. Ronan and I both had a fresh egg in our hand and life seemed better than ever. About ten yards up the road we were surprised and glad to see six nice big tanks trundle up the road and turn into Company Headquarters' orchard. "Always nice to have armour in support – pretty decent guns on them – funny camouflage they have. My God! German crosses on their turrets!"'*[11]

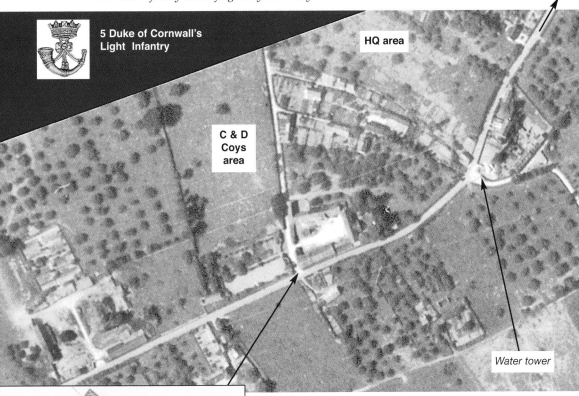

5 Duke of Cornwall's Light Infantry

HQ area

C & D Coys area

Cheux

Water tower

A troop of RA seventeen-pounders was cut down on the Cheux road.

Mayhem ensued. The leading enemy tank reached the road leading north to Cheux, where it machine-gunned to destruction an entire troop of Royal Artillery antitank guns, still limbered. The foot soldiers dived into their slit trenches while the tanks milled around the

First one and then another Panther was knocked out at close range.

company areas. Some prayed as a tank stopped, its tracks inches from the lip of their hole, its long gun swaying overhead. But, menacing though they were, the tanks were vulnerable to infantrymen with the courage to use their short-range antitank weapons. The shout went up for the three platoons of C Company to mobilise their PIAT teams. Soon, these were joined by PIATs from the nearby D Company. As the tanks wreaked havoc, brewing carriers and battalion transport, individual men carrying the cumbersome PIATS hopped from trench to trench in pursuit of the flank or rear shot that might defeat a tank's armour. A couple of the DCLI antitank platoon's six-pounders struggled to come into action, but a one-ton gun took time to manhandle and at fifty yards range presented an easy target. One gun was credited with a lucky flank shot which brewed a *Panther*. (The frontal armour of a Panther would not be defeated by a six-pounder round; conversely, *Panther* tanks whose side armour was penetrated had a propensity to blow up.) Both six-pounders were knocked out by the tanks. The commander of the battalion, Lieutenant-Colonel Atherton himself manned one of the guns, replacing a wounded crewman until he too was hit.

The tanks' lack of infantry support began to tell. With PIATs in resolute hands loosing repeated bombs at extremely short range, first one and then another *Panther* was knocked out. Two trying to escape the scene were engaged by C Company PIAT teams. Hits were scored, one of the two was knocked out and the other overturned as its driver steered blindly in his haste to get away. The successful outcome eclipsed the battalion's earlier embarrassment (though it was sadly marred by the death of the well respected Colonel Atherton). The story, heralded as an example of inexperienced British infantry defeating SS tanks, was a propaganda triumph and a boost to the whole of 43rd Division in its first battle. (Mistaking the army tanks for SS was a pardonable error, likely encouraged by the black uniforms routinely worn by the Panzer crews.)

Less pleased were the long-suffering 10th HLI who, recoiling from yet another costly failure to reach their Start Line, found their own headquarters area threatened by German tanks approaching from the 'rear'. Six-pounder guns of their antitank platoon positioned to cover the southern approaches to Cheux had to be hurriedly manhandled through 180 degrees to meet the new threat. *'The Battalion antitank gunners stuck to their guns and a duel developed, with the Regimental Aid Post and Battalion HQ in the middle, between two fires. The* Panthers' *shells were chipping lumps from the top of the wall sheltering the wounded, as all and sundry grabbed stretchers and hurriedly got the casualties away, crouching low behind the wall.'*[12] Again, the unescorted tanks, constrained amid buildings and rubble, lost the duel as a number of wrecks (variously reported as four or five) gave testimony. But the grievance felt by the highlanders went deep when they saw Sherman tanks in the lanes nearby, hatches firmly shut against the sniper scare and indiscriminate shooting that seemed to be everywhere, awaiting orders over their radios. *'What little space there was left in the lanes of Cheux seemed to be filled by our own tanks, closed down and deaf to all appeals.'*[13]

THE ADVANCE RESUMED

The previous day, the 2nd Battalion ('Reconstituted', after its predecessor was lost at Singapore), The Argyll & Sutherland Highlanders had expected to play a starring role in the battle. As the climax of the division's evolutions, as soon as the 10th Highland Light Infantry had taken Grainville-sur-Odon and the 2nd Gordons Tourville, the Argylls were to have passed a half-battalion through each place on the way to the Odon crossings at Gavrus and Tourmauville. It was not to be.

Instead, the Argylls passed a 'rather maddening' 26 June on the muddy track leading south from le Mesnil-Patry, moving forward in fits and starts as they awaited the call to action that never came. High hopes turned to annoyance and discomfort as drenching showers alternated with brief sunny spells and the men's waterproof gas capes were continually unpacked and then rolled up again. At last, when word came that they would not be in action that day, the battalion spent a miserable night in the mud and pouring rain, thoroughly exhausted just like their fellow battalions of 15th Scottish, but unlike them with nothing at all to show for it.

Argyll & Sutherland Highlanders position

The 2nd Argylls followed the muddy track to pass an uncomfortable night north of the Fontenay highway.

The morning of 27 June promised little improvement. The battalion arose from its sea of mud. At least there was breakfast to look forward to, as Lieutenant-Colonel Tweedie went off to a 227th Brigade 'O' Group. Suddenly, the colonel was back and issuing urgent orders for the unit to get ready to move immediately. Breakfast was abandoned in the rush. Company commanders passed orders to platoon leaders as they were in the act of moving out. Some wondered whether this would turn out to be another example of the British Army's characteristic alternation of urgency followed by interminable delay: 'hurry up and wait'. The regimental history records that, *'It was something of a tribute to the Battalion's training in Battle Procedure that it was managed at all... everybody felt at the time that it was all far too hectic and confused.'*[14]

Tweedie's orders were to lead the battalion to the far side of Cheux, passing through the Gordons' positions on the Colleville track, and on south to cut the Caen to Villers-Bocage road at Tourville. Unlike the previous day's plan, there would be no two-pronged advance by half-battalions of Argylls. 227th Brigade now recognised that the only feasible route south was down the single country lane opened and precariously maintained by the 2nd Gordons. So the Argylls moved in a single column: A and B Companies leading the way, C and D following, and the regimental vehicles somewhere behind. The foot soldiers' move through Cheux was mostly unopposed but still not easy. Reaching the place, the leading sections *'groped their way, having been instructed to "leave the church on their left" and searching for any fragment of Gothic architecture which would identify the building.'* And if their progress was

Trees line the Caen to Fontenay highway

The highway: Objective Cassino.

Cheux church reconstructed.

difficult, for the following vehicles the advance became a nightmare. Tweedie later recorded that Cheux, *'was still infested with snipers and blocked with tanks and tpt. [transport] Bn. HQ and the Tpt., and especially the ATk guns were jammed in the chaos… We literally fought our vehs through.'* In Cheux, the unit suffered its first casualty when Corporal O'Hara of the Carrier Platoon received a bullet through the neck, from which he died later in the day. Inevitably, the stray bullet was attributed to a 'sniper'.

Earlier, as Hans Siegel's tanks were fighting their battle with the 10th HLI, the young *Obersturmführer* had caught glimpses of the Argylls' leading companies advancing down the parallel track a thousand metres to his right.

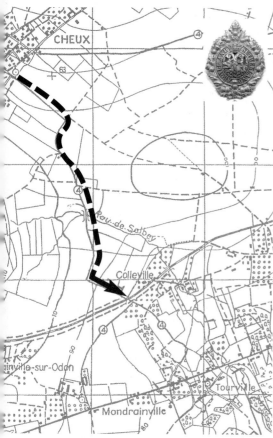

The Argylls' march south from Cheux.

The modern road bridge viewed from the site of the former lever crossing.

As he feared, the flank was open. In the early hours of the morning, the main body of the Gordons had reunited with their stray B Company, yet stayed in contact with the railway crossing at Colleville. The Gordons watched with undisguised relief as the Argylls passed through. The Argylls noted the Gordons' dead along the road: the blackened body of a despatch rider lying beside his cycle on the sharp bend before the railway; dead Gordons caught on the railway crossing. Captain Mackenzie, 2 i.c. B Company, *'advanced quite easily until we reached the railway line at Colleville. Jerry had left a Spandau to fire along this line and when the leading section of 12 Ptn started to cross this gun opened fire killing one man and wounding several others.'* The gun was silenced by High Explosive bombs lobbed by the 12 Platoon two-inch mortar. Then with 12 Platoon holding the line, 10 and 11 Platoons passed through. After the open fields around Cheux, this was very close country indeed. From Colleville to the main highway at Tourville was barely a thousand yards. Yet it was ideal defensive terrain. If the patchwork of tiny fields

The winding road into Tourville.

Tourville

and dense hedgerows had been contested, progress would have been awkward. Instead, the advancing riflemen reached the main Caen to Villers-Bocage road (the N175) almost unopposed.

Cutting this important artery was in itself an important achievement, and the leading rifle companies began to clear the buildings. At first, they met only French villagers, 'who greeted them with kisses and wine', until someone cried 'Bosche!' and they all disappeared. A German armoured car was the first of several vehicles motoring down the highway, at first passing by unsuspecting, but increasingly a problem to the unsupported infantry. One section of 11 Platoon attempting to move west along the road to Mondrainville became pinned down by an armoured car, taking cover in a field with only the corn to hide them. B Company Private Peter Bocock recalls the 'Spandau' with its high rate of fire scything the crop, clipping the heads off the corn, before the order was given to cut through the hedgerow behind and escape. Machetes were drawn and chopping commencing when a further burst encouraged the party to plunge through the still uncut obstacle. Bocock was hit in the legs and shortly after travelled back over the Colleville railway crossing on a jeep ambulance. From his stretcher he noted the dead Gordons still lying there, now crushed by Sherman tanks which had backed into the cover of the railway cutting.

Back in Cheux the guns of the

antitank platoon received an urgent call to get forward to meet these threats. Jimmy Campbell of number two gun in Sergeant Brand's section recalled moving through the devastation of a sister regiment's antitank guns, heavily mortared outside the town. Pressing on over the Colleville level crossing they were met by their officer, Captain Muirhead, who directed them westward, where B Company was encountering opposition as they continued to press towards Mondrainville. The gun unlimbered by a five-bar gate covering the main road. Joining the gun crew some time later, Muirhead was unhappy with its position *'which it must be admitted looked a little precarious'*, though it did at least command a field of fire over the road. Time went by. In the warm sun, the gun crew dozed until someone whispered loudly, 'German tank!' There on the road, framed in the gateway, stood a German tank. The crew manned their gun, loaded one of the new APDS 'sabot' rounds, then scrabbled in the grass for the gun layer's dropped pipe. (They were new to combat!) In the interval, a number of cows moved between gun and target. The gunners' dilemma: to wait, or to attempt to fire through the animals? *'The decision was soon made for us. The tank fired straight down the road and then turned toward us, at about forty-five degrees on, and fired again. The muzzle blast hit the heifers who scattered in a panic. I yelled, "Fire!" and Davy fired… There was no tracer. I could only assume we were too close… the loader who must have been hit by the recoil was laying over the trail… I grabbed another round and loaded. This time there was a large tongue of flame. In went another round. Someone shouted, "We've got him!" The tank commander shot out of the turret. When the third round went in the driver too came out. Both were well alight. Then the whole tank blew. Off came the turret.'*[15]

In this and other accounts, the German tank destroyed in Tourville is consistently referred to as a *'Tiger'*. This should not be taken literally, as the tank was a *Panzer IV*. Nor should any deception be suspected. The British infantry were not good at tank recognition. Besides, for many of them the term *'Tiger'* became generic, applicable to almost any German armour, just as they referred to the German light machine gun as a *'Spandau'* (after the manufacturer's stamp on some MG34 and MG42), all rifle bullets signified the presence of 'snipers', and virtually all German artillery

shells were reported fired by *'eighty-eights'*.

TO THE BRIDGE

With the Argylls' B Company astride the main road to the west, A Company covered the headquarters in Tourville, somewhat enigmatically described in the battalion history as 'a rather precarious firm base'. Major Hugh Fyfe's C Company then began the descent into the Odon valley, towards the final objective.

The road from Tourville down to the Odon has today changed little, apart from the impressive Lion Rampant monument to 15th Scottish Division encountered half-way down, in recent years most unfortunately surrounded by a tall hedge obstructing the view across gently sloping open fields. As the sections of C Company advanced in alternating bounds, buildings and copses on the fringes of Tourville were routinely cleared. Machine gun nests opening up were summarily dealt with. One such emplaced in a stone building was silenced by an Antitank Platoon gun putting six-pounder solid shot through the upstairs and downstairs windows. (The six-pounder High Explosive round was relatively ineffective and rarely used.) The whole advance went smoothly, hailed by the Argylls' history as *'probably the most classic manoeuvre carried out by the Battalion at any time in the campaign... The final assault, down over open cornfields... was brilliant.'* For that final dash, Major Graham

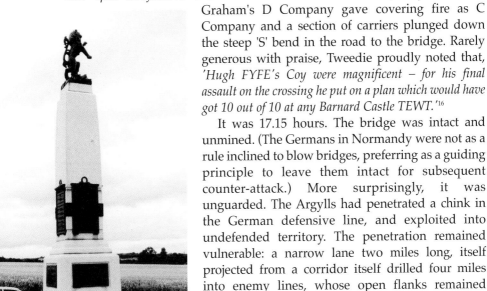

Graham's D Company gave covering fire as C Company and a section of carriers plunged down the steep 'S' bend in the road to the bridge. Rarely generous with praise, Tweedie proudly noted that, *'Hugh FYFE's Coy were magnificent – for his final assault on the crossing he put on a plan which would have got 10 out of 10 at any Barnard Castle TEWT.'*[16]

It was 17.15 hours. The bridge was intact and unmined. (The Germans in Normandy were not as a rule inclined to blow bridges, preferring as a guiding principle to leave them intact for subsequent counter-attack.) More surprisingly, it was unguarded. The Argylls had penetrated a chink in the German defensive line, and exploited into undefended territory. The penetration remained vulnerable: a narrow lane two miles long, itself projected from a corridor itself drilled four miles into enemy lines, whose open flanks remained barely two miles apart and whose whole length was criss-crossed by enemy fire. Tweedie recognised both the weakness of his *'firm (?) base at TOURVILLE [held] we felt rather "by kind permission!"'* and that at the bridge, *'A determined counter attack with armour just at that moment might have made things very sticky.'* As C Company was joined by D and parts of B, the

The Lion Rampant commemorating the 15th Scottish Division.

The Tourmauville bridge over the Odon

Sixty years on, Argylls and friends return to the bridge.

Argylls pushed a two hundred yard defensive perimeter up the southern wooded slopes of the valley. Members of the Antitank Platoon arrived and, though suitable locations for their own six-pounders were hard to find, advised the rifle companies on siting their PIAT teams to cover the approaches.

To the rear, the spreading news of the bridge's capture was celebrated throughout VIII Corps. Pip Roberts, the dynamic commander of 11th Armoured Division was quick to respond. The leading elements of the division had not interacted at all closely with the infantry advance. In the words of the VIII Corps history, up to now they *'had no very clear picture of the infantry situation, being virtually out of touch with the Scots.'*[17] Nevertheless, the 23rd Hussars were not far behind. Looping east of the Fifes to cross the railway at Colleville, the Hussars were held up at Tourville. There the Germans, now alerted and thoroughly alarmed, knocked out two Shermans and three carriers in quick succession with long range fire as they emerged from the Colleville side-road onto the highway. (Inevitably, the German was said to be an 'eighty-eight'.) An M10 self-propelled antitank gun of H Troop, 91st Antitank Regiment was directed to engage all the firing positions to the west where an enemy tank or 'SP' could lurk. A half-dozen rounds were fired and the offending gun disappeared. Still, Tourville remained an unpleasant spot. Some time later, a *Panther* tank positioned itself a thousand yards away to the east, in Mouen, with a clear line of fire down the dead-straight road. Tanks ran the gauntlet of its fire, dashing in ones and twos across the road, until the arrival of Brigadier 'Bosun' Hilton, 15th Scottish Division's much respected CRA (Commander, Royal Artillery). The brigadier commandeered a seventeen-pounder to take on the German, but sadly for him and the division, *'the tank had been the quicker on the draw.'*[18]

Meanwhile, relieved at Tourville by the Gordons, Colonel Tweedie himself had arrived at the bridge with his A Company and headquarters. Impatiently awaiting relief by 11th Armoured, the irascible colonel was annoyed when *'A somewhat timorous liaison officer havered for some time because he was uncertain whether the bridge was sufficiently robust, but Col. Tweedie, commanding the 2 Argylls, made up his mind for him by saying that if 29 Armoured Brigade did not want the bridge he would withdraw and blow it up.'*[19] 29 Brigade certainly did want the bridge. So did their parent 11th Armoured Division, noting happily at 18.07 hours, 'RE recce party report br 13' wide and able to carry all vehs.' The 23rd Hussars had already been alerted to 'push on and gain contact'. Now C Squadron raced to the scene, preceded only by a

Panther tank on the highway overlooking Tourville.

platoon of their attached motor infantry (H Company, of 8th Rifle Brigade).[20] Accounts differ widely as to when the first tanks arrived. The Argylls maintained that not until 'after dark' did the tanks turn up (in other words not before 22.00 hours). 11th Armoured recorded C Squadron at the bridge by 18.45, and a second squadron (B, with half the battalion Tac HQ) crossing by 19.25. No less optimistically, 11th Armoured headquarters also recorded 159 Brigade beginning to cross the Odon at 21.45 hours, which as will be shown they most certainly were not! 11th Armoured Division signals log also records at 23.20 hours, '23 H two sqns over R ODON', this signal a full half-hour after the first indication that '23 H in action against enemy tks at pt 112.' Confusion was rife. At any rate, by the time of the tanks' arrival, the Argylls had pushed their defensive perimeter out beyond the wooded slopes as far as the southern fringe of Tourmauville, covering the road to Baron. And, crucially, 11th Armoured Division was already demonstrating a determination to throw its whole armoured brigade across the Odon, even if the whole advance was to be dependent on one small, thirteen-foot wide stone bridge.

So, at last, the Argylls cheered the Hussars' tanks across the Odon. They

A Loyd carrier of 53rd (Welsh) Division crosses the second, culvert bridge over the Odon.

were further encouraged by the arrival of Quartermaster Captain Kenny, *'defying every law and traffic jam with his thin-skinned vehicles, determined to get a hot meal up, however far forward the Battalion had got. He reported that the name of the Argylls was one to conjure with the whole way up the line on the strength of the captured bridge.'*[21] Even as the tanks and half-tracks poured across the bridge, the Argylls remained alert through the night, which proved quiet except for the Argylls' first experience of screaming rockets launched by the German *Nebelwerfer*. Tweedie recalled: *'We had a taste of the "sobbing sisters", a typically NAZI anti-morale weapon – twelve rockets coming at you in the gloaming is a bit upsetting.'*

As to the strength of the little bridge, in a short space of time it was to withstand the passage of over two hundred tanks and a host of other vehicles, its parapet progressively battered by glancing blows from the passing armour, but its arch still standing. The greater problem was not the bridge itself, but the steep curving approach down the northern side of the valley. When Colonel Harding of the 23rd Hussars arrived on the scene, his command Sherman ignominiously slithered off the bend and ditched itself below. The next day, the Royal Engineers were called in to repair damage to the road surface, and construct a second crossing. They bulldozed a track straight down through the wooded slopes, and improvised a fascine bridge over the Odon, just east of the original bridge (two weeks later, on July 11, this would be improved to Class 40 standard by 2 Platoon, 282 (Welsh) Field Company, RE, by laying bulldozed earth over an Armco culvert and further improving the approaches).[22] Thereafter the stone bridge itself was mainly used by wheeled vehicles (and officers in their carriers unwilling to suffer the long queue – under fire - for the 'tracks' crossing!) Lessons perhaps had been learned from the earlier failure to bulldoze a satisfactory passage for vehicles through the choke-point of Cheux.

WIDENING THE CORRIDOR: WEST TO GRAINVILLE

Evident to all the British was the vulnerability of the Scottish Corridor (as the ground gained since the previous morning was now being called). With an armoured division beginning to cross the River Odon, for several miles back along the narrow corridor literally thousands of vehicles were competing to progress along deteriorating country dirt roads, most of which were under intermittent enemy fire.

To the east of the corridor, tanks and guns positioned around the '100 metre ring contour' enjoyed fairly good arcs of defensive fire over open cornfields. But south of the railway line, from Colleville to Mouen, the dense orchards and hedgerow-lined fields were enemy territory. Late in the afternoon, the 23rd Hussars had sent an A Squadron troop out towards Mouen 'to deal with an enemy tank reported there.' The troop ran into heavy fire from an unknown number of guns; only one of the four Shermans returned. To the west, the railway itself posed a problem. The single-track line westwards from Colleville, past Mondrainville, and on to beyond Grainville ran in a steep-sided cutting, impassable to vehicles. First to move on Grainville were

Jeep ambulances struggled with the tide of casualties.

A 1st Middlesex (Machine gun) Battalion carrier shelters with other 15th Scottish vehicles by the Colleville level crossing.

the Fife and Forfar.

By day's end, the 10th HLI south of Cheux had exhausted themselves in fruitless efforts to reach the morning's assigned Start Line. Not only their stretcher bearers but also jeep drivers and all the carriers of the antitank and mortar platoons were keeping up a continuous evacuation of casualties. So, the Fife and Forfar pressed forward alone: *'The daring decision was taken to send the armour forward without infantry support.'*[23] By remarkable fortune, the Fifes found the road to Grainville-sur-Odon now clear. The surviving three *Panzer IV* of Siegel's *8. Kompanie* had withdrawn to replenish fuel and ammunition. Advancing cautiously but unopposed, the British tanks reached the railway line, and once over the crossing found themselves looking down on the rooftops of Grainville. From Steel Brownlie's Sherman, *'This was a commanding position, and I did an HE shoot on some camouflaged vehicles 3500 yards ahead. Don Hall and I sat in the shelter of smoke from a burning house, and watched Kenneth Matheson's Recce Troop go into the village to see if it was clear, which it wasn't.'*[24]

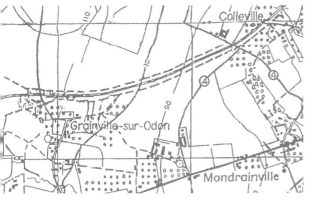

The cutting of the single-track railway proved an obstacle between the crossings at Grainville and Colleville

A *Panther* tank lay in waiting, tucked into a lane by the church. Its high-velocity 7.5cm gun put a shell clean through the leading Stuart tank, whose crew were fortunate to scramble to safety. Matheson and the rest of his troop pulled back hurriedly. *'As he was belting past us, having done his job, Colonel Scott came on the air and asked him for his exact position. He replied: "Position be buggered! Wait. Out."'* [25]

Now it was the turn of the infantry and Churchill tanks. The Cameronians had reorganized north of Cheux. Moving south, following in the tracks of the Argylls and the Gordons, they joined forces with the Churchills of B Squadron 9th RTR, some of the Cameronians actually hitching rides on the tanks. Crossing the railway at Colleville, the joint force prepared for an attack westward, between the railway line and Mondrainville. About 19.30 hours, on the northern edge of the village of Grainville-sur-Odon, contact was made with an outpost on the Fifes' left flank. 'They reported believed village clear, but possibility of tanks.'[26] The report was overly optimistic.

The Cameronians' D Company advanced into Grainville with six Churchill tanks of 9th RTR. Three were promptly knocked out, but the infantry struggled on. Around 21.00 hours, Lieutenant-Colonel Villiers persuaded his brigadier that it would be better to postpone the operation to the morning. But how to get the recall order to D Company commander Captain Leggat-Smith? With no radio contact, Villiers himself took on the job, going forward into the maelstrom of fire around the Grainville church to find Leggat-Smith and order him back into the regimental defensive position for the night. The Churchills and the Fifes' Shermans pulled back to their respective harbours. The Cameronians expended their last reserves of energy to scrape foxholes, into which they collapsed. The colonel did the same, after both his 2 i.c. Major Law and his batman represented to Villiers that he was completely worn out and in no fit state to continue. Only at midnight was it realised that some of D Company were unaccounted for, and their weary company commander gathered the Padre, the MO, and four stretcher bearers to return into Grainville in search. They found their two missing comrades, wounded and alone. The Germans had left. Grainville could have been taken by any force still on its feet. Leggat-Smith reported the news to Major Law, but the two were unable to wake the colonel from his exhausted sleep to order an advance. The Cameronians slept on; the chance was lost.

As Grainville was reduced to rubble the 19. Panzergrenadier Regiment used the church sacristy as an ammunition store.

WIDENING THE CORRIDOR: EAST TO BARON AND MOUEN

Pip Roberts' 11th Armoured Division continued through the day to stream south. By evening it was the turn of 159th Brigade, the division's three lorried infantry battalions, to move down the narrow way to Colleville. The brigade had experienced all the frustrations of stop-start movement towards battle without quite entering it. Now, as the lorry-borne infantry 'de-bussed' in front of Colleville, a brigade O Group was called to explain the brigadier's intentions. The three battalions would form up, using the Caen to Villers-Bocage highway as a Start Line conveniently parallel to the Odon River: 4th King's Shropshire Light Infantry left, 1st Battalion The Herefordshire Regiment right, and 3rd Battalion The Monmouthshire Regiment in brigade reserve. Zero hour was set for 21.30.

There were mutterings. Starting the brigade's first battle unprepared, in haste, as night fell seemed imprudent. The Shropshires' colonel noted that the maps showed no bridge where his (left flank) advance was to cross the Odon. He later recorded: *'The plan was somewhat vague, and no arty sp was laid on, infm about the enemy was very scarce, infm about our own tps almost scarcer… it was not known whether the river line was held or not.'*[27] The Herefords' colonel did not think his unit could get to the line in the time allowed, and said as much. *'I shall start when I am ready and not before – it may be as late as 23.00 hours.'* Roused

now to anger, the brigadier shouted at him to *'start at 21.30 and that is an order; get on with it or suffer the consequences.'*[28] In the end, the KSLI got going about 22.00 hours, at which time the Herefords were still shaking-out at Colleville preparatory to their advance.

The leading company of 4th KSLI took the instruction to advance at right angles to the highway literally, heading off south-east to the Odon. Dense woods gave way to wooded parkland. The company commander led the way, the rest of D Company marching in single file behind. *'We knew every type of attack in the book blindfold... I little thought that D Company would deliver its first live battle attack in single file, led by its company commander reading his map!'*[29] Crossing the Odon over an ornamental foot bridge, they arrived at Baron. Company by company, the KSLI assembled around the château of Baron, linking later with the Herefords who had taken the more direct route over the Tourmauville bridge, passing through the Argylls' defensive perimeter and on eastwards. The KSLI Headquarters, and all their vehicles, had also to use the Tourmauville bridge, where the colonel's patience was further taxed by traffic congestion, reports of *'Tiger'* tanks at various points along the way, and finally a broken down Sherman tank stuck on the bridge itself. Gradually, the two battalions assembled. To the rear, the brigadier complained that *'Up till midnight little reporting of posn, but it was gathered that 4 KSLI and 1 HEREFORD had gained their objectives.'* By 02.00 hours, the Shropshires and the Herefords were in defensive positions, tired but encouraged by their first exposure to concentrated mortar fire to dig deeply before sleeping.

Of the Monmouths, there was still no sign. Their attempts to push vehicles forwards down the Tourmauville road had got nowhere. An officer was run over by a self-propelled antitank gun. Shortly after 22.00 hours, the battalion had suspended movement. Only after midnight did the brigadier arrive with his Tac HQ, to get the battalion on its feet again. Through the dark and the rain, *'We stumbled over the battle-scarred ground. There were frequent stops. It was difficult to keep the men awake.'*[30] Indeed, after one stop, a dozing file-leader lost contact with the troops ahead and fifty men found themselves separated from the unit for the rest of the night. At last, the order was given to stop, *'All round defence – enemy territory – no noise – no digging in.'* The Mons had wandered off to the east, ending up in the vicinity of Mouen and passing what remained of the night on ground slated for attack by *I. SS-Panzerkorps*.

References

(1) Sergeant Hugh Green memoirs

(2) W Steel Brownlie memoirs (2nd F&F Yeo), 'And Came Safe Home'

(3) Sergeant Hugh Green, 10th HLI, quoted in McKee, p 173. Even the British tank men were not yet very adept at identifying enemy tanks; it was not to be expected that an infantryman would do any better against well camouflaged Panzer IV.

(4) Purists might quibble that 31st Brigade was equipped with a mixture of Mk III, IV, and VI Churchills, and did not at this time possess any of the Mk VII Churchills which enjoyed up to fifty percent thicker frontal armour; relatively few of these were present in Normandy in June, though all the flame-throwing Crocodiles present were based on Mk VIIs.

(5) *'Campaign in Europe: the Story of the 10th Battalion, The Highland Light Infantry'*, published by the regiment, p 12. Note: the 10th HLI War Diary for June was lost along with much of the

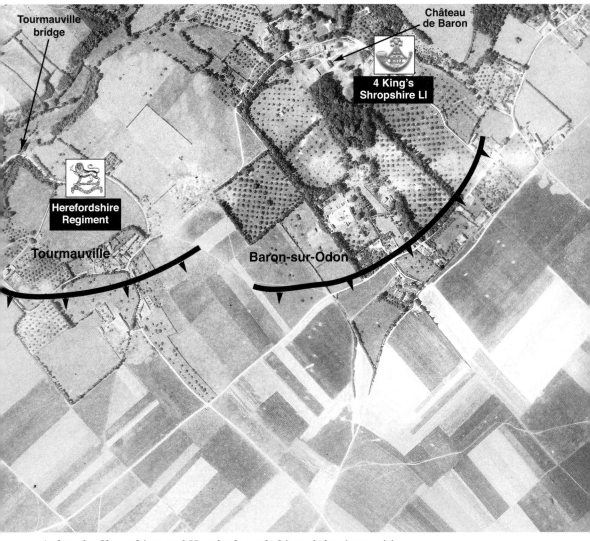

At last the Shropshires and Herefords settled into defensive positions.

headquarters transport and equipment in the opening days of the battle.

(6) W Steel Brownlie memoirs

(7) In some accounts, Siegel is quoted as saying that his entire force of four tanks changed position during this action, moving out into the open; in others he states that only his own tank relocated. It is sadly not at all uncommon for soldiers who have been telling their tales for many years to change details of their stories as time goes by. In this case, after detailed study of the terrain, the author concludes that it would have been pointless if not suicidal for the three Panzer IV under Siegel's command to have moved out from their excellent defensive positions west of the track.

(8) *The History of the Duke of Cornwall's Light Infantry*, E G Godfrey & R F K Goldsmith, p 222

(9) To clarify a confusing mixture of names within this planned *Kampfgruppe*: the Panther tanks were to come from *I. Abteilung, 3. Panzerregiment*, the tank regiment of the (Army) *2. Panzerdivision*. The infantry component comprised two battalions of *2. SS-Panzerdivision* ('*Das Reich*'): these being the first battalions of each of the *3. SS-Panzergrenadierregiment* ('*Deutschland*')

and the *4. SS-Panzergrenadierregiment ('Der Führer')*.

(10) *General der Panzertruppen*, Heinrich Freiherr von Lüttwitz, extract from 'Top Secret' report of 14 July, 1944, copy captured by American forces on 26 July.

(11) Godfrey & Goldsmith, p 223

(12) Sergeant Hugh Green memoirs

(13) Martin, p 39

(14) McElwee, p 22

(15) Corporal James Campbell, interviews with the author. Campbell's memoirs are also preserved on Imperial War Museum Sound Archive no 20983.

(16) 'Tactical Exercise Without Troops'; Barnard Castle was home to one of the founding Battle Schools.

(17) Jackson, p 39

(18) Martin, p 42. The author has been unable to identify this later seventeen-pounder. An M10 of 146 Battery of 91st Antitank Regiment (the VIII Corps antitank regiment) seems a likely candidate, though the battery admits to no losses on that day. Alternatively, it is just possible that Hilton commandeered a towed seventeen-pounder from J Troop, 346 Battery, 97th Antitank Regiment (under command 15th Scottish), though they too recorded no guns lost. For once, the identification of a Panther was correct!

(19) *The History of the 5th Argylls (91st Anti-Tank Regiment)*, D Flower, p 114. The officer who was acting Adjutant of the 2nd Argylls at the time has queried the accuracy of this story. This author nevertheless presents the anecdote, reported in the history of a regiment which Tweedie himself later commanded. Tweedie doubtless had sight of the account prior to publication, and might well have been its source; his reported comments certainly seem in character.

(20) '8th Battalion, The Rifle Brigade' was the motor battalion of 11th Armoured Division: one of its armoured infantry companies was normally attached to each of the division's tank regiments to give close support. In 1994, plans for a plaque indicating that an infantry battalion of 11th Armoured Division was first to the bridge were abandoned after protests from the Argylls; the mistake was apparently an honest misunderstanding.

(21) McElwee, p 27

(22) 'Welsh Bridges to the Elbe', John H Roberts, p 101-103; also 'One Chap's War', memoirs of Tom Geddes, 91st Antitank Regiment, p 236

(23) 'The Fife and Forfar Yeomanry', R J B Sellar, p 162

(24) W Steel Brownlie memoirs.

(25) W Steel Brownlie memoirs. How the crew of the disabled Stuart escaped injury is not recorded. It is quite possible that at such short range, the high-velocity Armour Piercing round could have passed straight through the lightly-armoured tank, especially if - as often occurred - a faulty fuse failed to detonate its High Explosive charge after the initial penetration and the round continued on its way. Note that a few days after this action the order was given by 29th Armoured Brigade to remove the turrets from these light Stuart tanks, making them less conspicuous targets, more appropriate to their reconnaissance role.

(26) 9th Cameronians, June War Diary. Note that the Cameronians War Diary consistently attributes their Churchill tank support on the day to 7th RTR whereas in fact it was provided by 9th RTR throughout the fighting for Grainville on 27 and 28 June. A conspicuous example of failure of communication between units!

(27) 4th KSLI June War Diary

(28) The Herefords' Lieutenant-Colonel Jack Churcher (soon after promoted to command the brigade) later maintained disparagingly that his predecessor had *'held no formal "O" group, but stood on the roadside waving his arms and shouting "Into battle!" – a most extraordinary performance.'*

(29) *The 4th KSLI in Normandy*, Ned Thornburn, p28

(30) *Hill 112: Cornerstone of the Normandy Campaign*, J J How, p 88

Chapter 5

WEDNESDAY 28 JUNE THE SCOTTISH CORRIDOR

Once again, the fighting had died down during the short summer's night. 28 June dawned on an inherently unstable battle. The British advance was behind schedule, and had already revealed some unhappy failures of coordination between infantry and armour. VIII Corps was still striving for the Orne River crossings, with its principal striking force at the very tip of a perilously long and potentially vulnerable wedge driven into enemy territory. As to the defenders, consternation caused by the weight and ferocity of the assault was accentuated by deepening crises among the leadership. And yet there appeared the possibility of turning the battle into a British disaster if only the newly formed salient, barely four thousand metres across, could be 'pinched out' by converging counter-attacks. All was to play for.

THE GERMAN GENERALS
The Normandy campaign presented many a German general with deep dilemmas. At the strategic level lay questions about the futility of the continuing war, now becoming recognised as unwinnable. On 28 June, as the fighting raged around the Scottish Corridor, Rommel experienced what was to be his last meeting with Hitler. The field-marshal had long since expended whatever influence he enjoyed with the *Führer*. Hitler's intent now was simply to enthuse his old warhorses (von Rundstedt

Left: Rommel and Hitler in happier times.
Below: Hitler's mountain retreat above Berchtesgaden.

Above: Gerd von Rundstedt.

had been summoned as well) with new optimism and drive for the planned counter-strike in Normandy. Rommel for his part hoped, with a courage born of desperate frustration, to discuss the reality of his armies' suffering and the hopelessness of the position in Normandy. In the battle of wills there could be only one outcome. Both grew angry. The field-marshal was moved to speak out: *'My Führer, I must speak bluntly. I cannot leave without speaking of the subject of Germany.'* Hitler dismissed him. *'Field-Marshal, be so good as to leave the room. I think it would be better like that.'* His generals no longer dictated strategy, far less state policy.

At the tactical level too, German commanders had to face unenviable stresses. Their whole society had for a decade been steeped in the imagery and belief systems of National Socialism. Open criticism of Nazi doctrines was not conducive to advancement, or even survival. While the German Army had long traditions and a 'culture' of its own, the German military was now riven with conflicting rivalries and even competing ground forces: Himmler's *Waffen SS*, Goering's *Luftwaffe* divisions... And ultimately, the two functions of Army commander-in-chief and of political leader of the state the Army served both resided in a single individual. An individual who by mid-1944 was issuing tactical directives which appeared to defy military logic. Like many a modern business manager, the generals found themselves being asked to achieve more with less. Lack of resources was rarely an acceptable excuse for failure; blame for failures could only be deflected by promises of future success, raising the stakes ever higher. Unlike modern management, the cost of failure was not merely career-threatening, but sometimes mortal. No surprise therefore that many a German general remained in constant stress: torn between conflicting demands of professionalism, oaths of loyalty, and abject fear (even setting aside any moral considerations).

In the early hours of 28 June, Rommel and von Rundstedt had answered Hitler's summons to the Berghof above Berchtesgaden. This left Seventh Army commander *Generaloberst* Friedrich Dollmann as the most senior German officer in Normandy. His situation was lofty, lonely, and exposed. The previous day, Dollmann had assured Rommel that the defensive actions fought on 26 June had been successful. His confidence had extended even to advising that Hausser's slowly-arriving *II. SS-Panzerkorps* might even be held back as a force in reserve. As the day wore on, Dollmann found optimism harder to maintain. And now that he alone was in charge, responsibility weighed heavily. Shaken by the news of the British breaching the Odon line, Dollmann appealed to *II. SS-Panzerkorps* to intervene to throw them back. The orders went out early on the 28th. But Hausser's response was negative. He made it clear to Dollmann that his two

General der Waffen SS
Paul Hausser.

Generaloberst **Friedrich Dollmann.**

divisions could not be made ready for action before 29 June at the earliest. Dollmann became desperate. In his mind was growing the ghastly spectre of Hitler's revenge for the loss of Cherbourg. Though surrendered by von Schlieben, the fortress was nominally the Seventh Army chief's responsibility. At 10.00 hours on the morning of 28 June, in his bathroom at le Mans, Dollmann made an end of his terrors by taking poison. (Though in conformity with the report submitted by Dollmann's loyal adjutant, the army commander was officially credited with having suffered a heart-attack induced by the stress of defending the Reich.)

Gruppenführer
Wilhelm Bittrich

The consequences for the German opposition to EPSOM could hardly have been greater. The immediate replacement of Dollmann by Paul 'Papa' Hausser was confirmed in mid-afternoon of 28 June. For the first time, a general of the *Waffen SS* would take command of a German field army including both SS and a substantial proportion of *Wehrmacht* divisions. Indeed, the order stated that Hausser would assume overall command in Normandy until the return of Rommel. What is more, the departure of *SS-Obergruppenführer* and *General der Waffen SS* Hausser from command of *II. SS-Panzerkorps* occurred just after Dollmann's (despairing) order for that corps to plunge prematurely into the battle. The order would stand, and now its execution would depend on a command structure in which key individuals would be new to their jobs. *SS-Gruppenführer* Wilhelm Bittrich stepped up from *9. SS-Panzerdivision* to command the *Panzerkorps*, and behind him a flurry of hasty promotions rippled through the organisation.[1]

MOUEN
The 3rd Monmouths had spent a tense few hours of darkness on the western fringes of Mouen: east of Colleville and south of the railway line.[2] Officers recognised that they were out on a limb, in 'no man's land'. Come the dawn, they were keen to abandon this isolated position and rejoin the brigade. Marching west in the direction of Colleville, the main body of the battalion passed their own C Company, left behind as rearguard the night before; then onward south to form a brigade reserve on the slopes just north of the Tourmauville bridge, where they were joined by the brigadier and his headquarters. Later, the fifty strays of the previous night also passed through C Company to rejoin the bulk of the battalion.

The precise details of C Company's movements later that morning remain unclear.[3] At some point the company was relieved of its job of screening the Colleville level crossing. It is possible that the company then proceeded further eastwards, amid the narrow lanes and small fields in the vicinity of Mouen. Wherever the precise position of C Company may have been, it lay squarely in the path of an overwhelming German counter-attack.

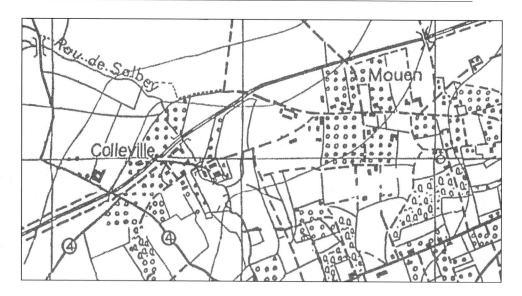

For the German defenders of Normandy, a trend was now beginning which would be one of the decisive factors in the EPSOM battle. On 27 June, early-arriving infantry battalions of *2. SS-Panzerdivision, 'Das Reich'* had been hurled piecemeal into the fight. Next, on the night of 27-28 June, the 'gathering of the clans' continued with the arrival in Normandy of the first elements of *1. SS-Panzerdivision,* Hitler's *Leibstandarte.* Tactically, the arrival of a fresh regiment of elite *Panzergrenadiere* was a godsend for Kurt Meyer, whose own *Hitlerjugend* division was dangerously depleted and over-extended. But from a wider perspective, the release of these *Leibstandarte* battalions to Meyer's command was an act of desperation which carried longer term implications.

Through the years of conquest, from 1939 to 1942, and on through the years of dogged defence of the *Reich,* the triumphs of the German armoured divisions had been achieved by concentration of force and integration of their different arms. The German army could not win the battle of logistics in Normandy: Allied air and naval power saw to that. The German's only (slim) hope for maintaining any sort of strategic initiative lay in assembling the two *Panzerkorps* that faced the British and loosing them in a concerted counterblow. Instead, *Hitlerjugend* and *Panzer-Lehr* had already spent weeks being worn down in the front line, and the new arrivals risked a similar fate.

For now, the major concern of the senior *Leibstandarte* officer present, *SS-Obersturmbannführer* Albert Frey, was the tactical meshing of his infantry regiment with supporting arms of another division. The German *Panzerdivision* was designed as a balanced offensive force. It was at its most effective when its constituent arms were integrated. Yet Frey had no sooner arrived with two of his regiment's three battalions, than he was subordinated to *12. SS-Panzerdivision.* Frey voiced his concerns, requesting that his unit

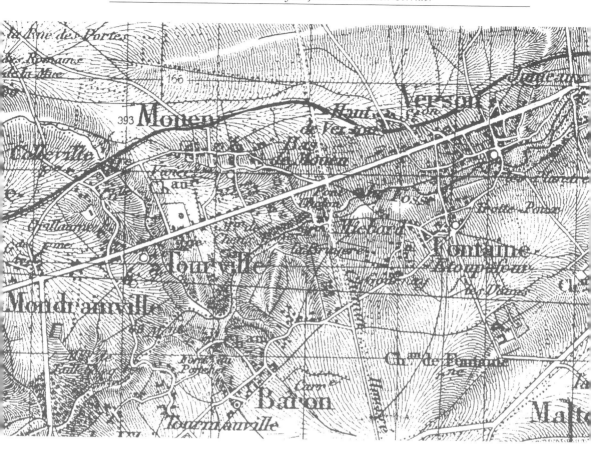

await the arrival of its own *Leibstandarte* artillery support. The request was denied. Meyer was conscious only of the urgency of penetrating the British salient, and of the depletion and fatigue of his own division. In order to meet the requirement for a west-bound pincer to match the planned push by *Kampfgruppe Weidinger* on the far side of the British corridor, he had to make use of whatever forces came to hand.

So it was, 'with a heavy heart', that Frey gave the order to his first and second battalions to prepare for attack, trusting in the promise of *Hitlerjugend* artillery (though, tellingly, no artillery liaison officers were received to direct the promised fire). Also in support were tanks of *21. Panzerdivision* (a formation in action continuously since 6 June and now sadly depleted) and a handful of heavy *Tiger* tanks of *101. schwere SS-Panzer-Abteilung* (it appears that no more than three were available at any one time during the day's operations). The order was to advance astride the Caen to Villers-Bocage highway: *SS-Hauptsturmführer* Lotter's *I. Bataillon* to the right, *SS-Sturmbannführer* Hansen's *II. Bataillon* to the left of the highway. From their forming up area around Venoix, the battalions were to force a way through Bretteville-sur-Odon and Verson, to penetrate the British salient at Mouen,

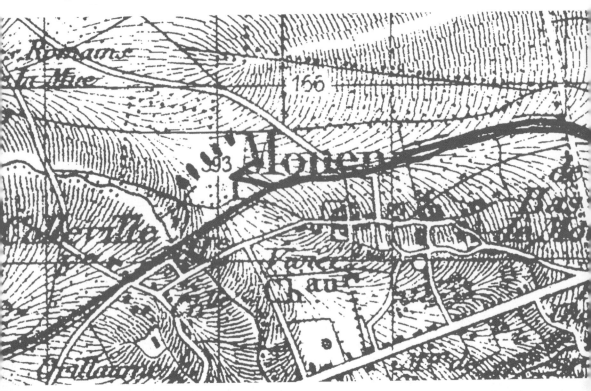

The route of the five remaining tanks of *4. Kompanie* along the railway, drawn by Werner Kortenhaus, then a 19 year old radio operator.

and join forces with an east-bound battle-group around Tourville. 11th Armoured Division along with all the other British units in the Odon valley would then be trapped in a pocket, isolated, confused, to be smashed by the fresh *II. SS-Panzerkorps*.

As with previous formations experienced in war but new to Normandy, before coming to grips with the enemy, before even leaving their forming-up area, the *Leibstandarte* had to undergo the novel experience of Allied artillery bombardment. This was unlike anything they had known on the Russian front. The volume of fire the Royal Artillery could sustain was awesome, and all the more disconcerting for being supplemented by naval guns of up to fifteen inch calibre, capable of reducing a battle tank to shards of metal. Worse still, as Frey had feared, there was little with which to respond. Such fire support as he was going to receive on 28 June would come largely from his own heavy weapons companies, including that of his *III. Bataillon*, under *SS-Obersturmbannführer* Weidenhaupt, still assembling south of Caen around May-sur-Orne and Louvigny.

II. Bataillon had only reached Verson when its commander Max Hansen was wounded (for the ninth time!) and had to be replaced in command of his battalion. The battalion advance continued, angling left to the south-west, through Fontaine-Etoupefour towards the little hamlet of Gournay. To their right, between the highway and the railway, the *I. Bataillon* advanced due west, casting uneasy glances to their own, exposed right flank. There, to the north, lay the wide open, rolling ground between Cheux and the Carpiquet airfield. For flank cover there was only what *21. Panzerdivision* could grudgingly spare from their defence of the north side of Caen: the fourth company of *22. Panzerregiment* with its remaining Mark IV tanks. Not daring to venture onto the exposed open fields, yet unable to penetrate the dense orchard and hedgerow between Verson and Mouen, the leading *Zug* of five tanks followed the path of the single-track railway, advancing in single file with railside earth banks and hedges for cover.

The *Panzergrenadiere* passed the wrecks of the 23rd Hussars tanks which had ventured east of Colleville the day before. Now, with the Hussars moving south over the Odon, it was tanks of 4th (independent) Armoured Brigade, temporarily under command of 11th Armoured Division, which were assigned to screen the vital Colleville rail crossing. As the German force neared Mouen, three British tanks burst out of a forest lane, across the face of the grenadiers. These appear to have been Stuart light tanks of 3rd County of London Yeomanry, returning to their unit after reconnoitring a way forward.

The battleground around Mouen railway station.

Station

Reaching the railway, all three were knocked out in quick succession at very short range by the leading *Panzer IV*, number 412. Emboldened by this success, tanks and grenadiers plunged forward onto ground still held by the 3rd Monmouths' C Company. These were overrun.

There followed a period of confusion in Mouen as *Panzergrenadiere* mopped up the captured position amid burning vehicles and British infantry resisting, surrendering, or attempting to escape. One of the *Panzer* men recalled, '*a wilderness of abandoned equipment and dead British soldiers'*.[4] With tank wrecks blocking the railway ahead, the column of *Panzer IV* abandoned the narrow railbed for the cover of a small, hedgerow-lined field, bringing down railside telegraph wires which snarled the tanks' running gear. At last, by late afternoon, the captured position on the western fringes of Mouen was secured. The Monmouths' losses were considerable: by the end of the day the regiment acknowledged the loss of three subalterns and sixty-one Other Ranks. But for the Germans the day was yet far from over. While the infantry occupied and improved the British positions, the leading five tanks established flank cover in their small, triangular field north of the railway, alongside the road to Cheux. The storm broke over them some time after, presaged as ever by an intensification of the British artillery 'drumfire'.

The Monmouths' continued presence in Mouen had been fortuitous but accidental. The defence of the area was by now the responsibility of the 15th (Scottish) Division, whose 2nd Glasgow Highlanders had already been caught up in the fight around Colleville itself, supposedly 'behind the lines', and along with some passing troops of Churchill tanks had joined in with resisting the continued *Leibstandarte* advance. Additionally, in the belief that the Colleville position was secure, steps were afoot in the late afternoon of 28 June to extend the corridor eastwards from here. From licking their wounds around Cheux, the 10th HLI were relieved by the 6th KOSB and ordered forward to Mouen. Their mission was to clear the area around Mouen. Orders were brief and lacking detail, but little resistance was expected. In support came the tanks of 3rd County of London Yeomanry, from 13.55 hours temporarily placed under command of 227th (Highland) Brigade to help deal with the situation in Mouen.

About 19.45 hours, two rifle companies of 10th HLI led the advance, each with a tank squadron loosely in support. (And it must be said that their support was very loose indeed, with little worthwhile contact between the two units.) The left-hand A Company, '*were only faintly apprehensive, in view of the fact that we had been told that the area was clear of Germans. We were well into the field when the enemy, who had let us get very close, opened up with machine guns… the leading section of A Company tumbled like wheat before a scythe.'* D Company, advancing south of the railway was likewise cut down. Sergeant Green of the Intelligence Section found the battalion commander '*riding up and down in his Bren carrier… frantic in his desire to urge on the attack'*, but frustrated by his inability to penetrate the confusion. 3rd CLY noted dryly that, '*the CO of the infantry lost contact with all his Coy commanders which made it impossible to keep a coherent account of events.'* The CLY plunged forward with

B Squadron left, C right, and A in reserve. A single *Panzer IV* held its fire before opening at point blank range. Its combination of excellent fire discipline and smokeless rounds succeeded in its knocking out three Shermans in succession. But gradually, by sheer weight of numbers, the defending *Panzer IV* were worn down. 422 took a turret hit which deformed its outer *Schürzen*, preventing traverse; 413 had a track broken; the commander of 421 standing in his turret for a better view had his head blown off; 425 dodged enemy tanks, discharging its smoke dispensers in all directions until at last, disabled and burning, it was abandoned by its crew.

The German advance was held, and not solely by the HLI and the Yeomanry. Unbeknown to those units, also engaged nearby in the defence of Colleville were the 2nd Glasgow Highlanders and supporting Churchill tanks of 7th RTR, on their way to take up positions around Mondrainville.[5] By the end of the day, the five *Panzer IV* remaining to 4/22. *Panzerregiment* and the *I. Bataillon* grenadiers had failed to penetrate beyond Mouen. But even so, the Germans now held a line from the rail crossing north of Mouen, south to the quarries on the banks of the Odon, and eastwards to the crossroads at Gournay. The disconsolate Jocks of 10th HLI *'could advance no further and dug in for the night in a position a few hundred yards from their start line'.*[6]

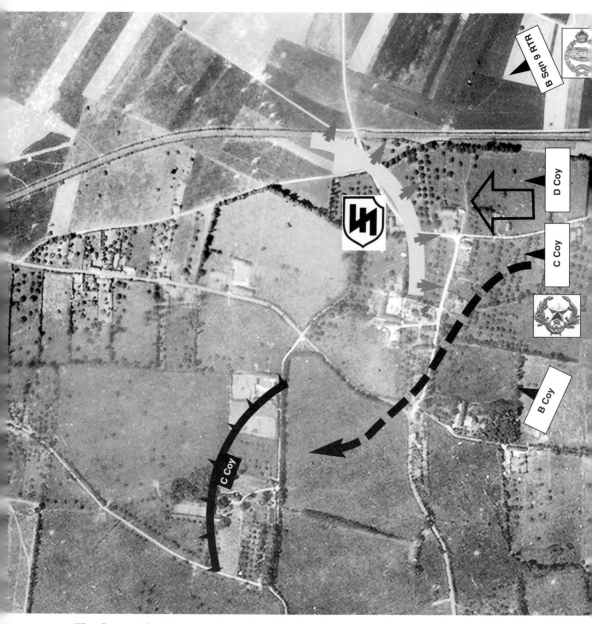

The Cameronians' renewed assault on Grainville.

GRAINVILLE AND LE VALTRU

The EPSOM plan was conceived with scant regard to the local road network. Most worthwhile communications ran east-west across the Scottish corridor; only a few dirt tracks ran parallel to the British advance. The rubble of Cheux and the surrounding muddy fields were obstacle enough to the advance and provisioning of an army corps, regardless of enemy shelling and periodic armoured assault. That a reinforced armoured division might rely solely on the awkward Tourmauville crossing over the Odon valley for its advance, supply, and ultimate withdrawal seems with hindsight somewhat optimistic (if not foolhardy). And mid-way between these two choke points, the steep-sided cuttings of the single-line Caen to Villers-Bocage railway presented an obstacle to all wheeled and most tracked vehicles.[7] On the morning of 28 June, the only practicable way over the line available to the British was the level crossing at Colleville. All the more reason, therefore, to widen the corridor at this vital point.

The 9th Cameronians' exhaustion the night before had lost them the prize of Grainville-sur-Odon, but morning found the battalion arrayed on the eastern side of the village and ready to renew the assault. The men stood-to soon after dawn. The officers attended an O Group to hear Colonel Villiers' detailed plan for seizing the village. With B Company providing a fire base, C and D would execute a right-flank attack, covered by Churchill tanks. It was not to be. Observers had the Cameronians' Forming Up Place and Start Line in their sights, and the attack was broken up by enemy artillery before it got under way. A new O Group was held at 11.00 hours. This time, elaborate flanking manoeuvre was rejected. C and D Companies would make a frontal assault, preceded by a ten-minute artillery concentration by an entire field regiment. The attack went in at 12.15 hours.

The Cameronians were none too soon. After the previous day's failure to coordinate with their assigned tank company, the *Das Reich* infantry battalions of *Kampfgruppe Weidinger* had been re-oriented to an eastbound advance, today with armour of 2. *Panzerdivision* ('*Wien*', the Vienna division) in close support. Their axis of attack paralleled the Villers-Bocage to Caen road. They arrived at Grainville as the Cameronians were securing the place. Heavy fighting ensued: infantry struggled in the buildings around the church, while Churchill and *Panther* tanks traded rounds at close range near the railway line. The regimental history records that '*several hours of confused street fighting followed,*'[8] whereas the battalion War Diary relates by 13.00 'mopping up proceeding' and by 14.00 'Bn. consolidates ground gained.' In any case, by 14.00 hours it was possible for C Company to exploit westward of the village, to form a 'breakwater' outpost in a nearby farm.[9] The B Squadron Churchills had taken a toll of enemy tanks in the close combat, and had not themselves suffered as badly as the day before. German observers still had the place under observation, and in the days to come the Cameronians would suffer a steady drain of casualties. But as of 15.00 on 28 June, the objective was reported securely held.

As well as launching the Cameronians into Grainville, 46th (Highland) Brigade's Brigadier Barber had plans to extend still further the bounds of the corridor. 2nd Glasgow Highlanders had been summoned from Cheux to hold a brigade reserve position around Mondrainville (only to become caught up, as has been seen, by the fighting between Colleville and Mouen). Next, the brigade's reserve battalion was brought forward. The 7th Seaforth Highlanders were to pass through Colleville, intent on a move to seize the

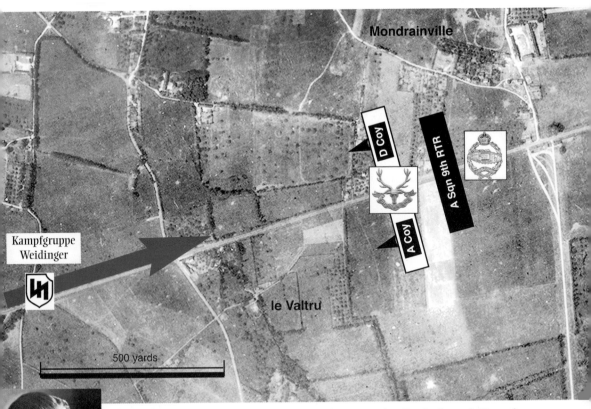

The scene of the headlong encounter between the Seaforth and *Kampfgruppe Weidinger*.

Sturmbannführer **Otto Weidinger** commander of *Kampfgruppe Weidinger*.

crossroads at le Valtru. Possession of this location would not only shield the western approaches to Tourville, but also link the road leading south from Cheux, through Grainville, in the direction of a second crossing over the River Odon: the twin bridges of Gavrus.

After struggling past the railway crossing, over which 11th Armoured Division was still flowing southbound, the Seaforth shook out into battle formation. Conscious that the battalion was advancing into enemy territory (Grainville was as yet unsecured), Lieutenant-Colonel Grant planned a 'wide diamond' formation, ready to face in any direction the enemy appeared. One rifle company would lead the advance along the Villers-Bocage highway, with rifle companies thrown out on left and right flanks, a fourth in reserve to the rear, and battalion headquarters, vehicles, and Churchills of A Squadron, 9th RTR occupying the centre.[10] For all the precautions, the enemy lay straight ahead. The formation ran straight into the main thrust of *KG Weidinger*.

Whatever had been the plan, the Seaforth tore into stiff opposition as they advanced along the main road leading west from Mondrainville towards their objective: the crossroads at le Valtru.[11] Two rifle companies led the way: A Company to the left and D Company right, fighting what the unit War

Diary described as 'a stiff advanced guard action'. The fighting was confused, flowing past enclosed orchards, around roadside stone buildings, and over a small rivulet. Churchill tanks appeared, offering what support they could. But since the wireless of the 9th RTR liaison officer accompanying the infantry battalion headquarters had broken down, Lieutenant-Colonel Grant had no more chance of talking with the tanks' squadron commander than had the Jocks on the ground of communicating with individual tanks, whose crews were 'buttoned up' against enemy small arms fire and reduced to peering through dusted-over periscopes. The Seaforth regimental history was later dismissive of the support received: *'The advance to le Valtru on 28 June was complicated by an Armoured battle.'* It does appear that the infantry and the tanks fought largely independently of one another. The ingratitude of the infantry is understandable since 'Our tanks twice went trigger-happy.'[12] The supporting tanks occasionally sprayed Besa (machine gun) fire across their own infantry, hitting a number of Jocks in the forward companies.

The objective was taken at 11.00 hours, at heavy cost. The fight cost the Seaforth two majors and a lieutenant, plus seventy-three Other Ranks. There were few defensive features in the immediate vicinity of the crossroads. A stone building by the road to the rear of the position served as a regimental aid post. The cluster of buildings of le Valtru itself, to the south, offered some cover but no fields of fire due to surrounding hedges and orchards. Consequently, much of the battalion dug their slit trenches in the open ground in front of the position. Contact was made with the Cameronians in Grainville, a few hundred yards to the north. And, like the Cameronians, the Seaforth pushed a 'breakwater' rifle company forward. C Company advanced five hundred yards westward with some carriers and antitank guns to dig in on a 'dominating ridge'. (This phrase in the regimental history is potentially misleading: assuming that the company did not venture all the way to le Bas des Forges, over a mile from the crossroads, the comment refers not to any great height advantage over the battalion position, but rather to the excellent view southwards across the Odon valley towards Hill 113.)

THE CROSSING SWEEPERS

Early on 28 June, at the Taillebosq mill alongside the Tourmauville bridge, the morning sun shone through the overhanging trees, with the promise of a fine day ahead. Barely a day before, the wife of miller Joseph Devaux had been pleading with a German corporal to take some food and lead his men away lest they risk becoming prisoners (and cause a battle to be fought for the mill!). And now, liberation. Having narrowly missed being shot by an anxious Argyll, Madame Devaux had ushered the liberators into her home. Inevitably, tea was brewed. As it was served, the rest of the family emerged from their cellar shelter. To the Jocks' amazement, the grandmother of the household exclaimed in broad Aberdeenshire, 'That's the best cup of tea I've had in five years.' The lady was from Forres, and after serving as a nurse in the previous war had returned to marry one of her French patients.

Neither the Devaux family nor the Argylls had enjoyed much sleep, as

① **The Taillebosq mill in 2004.**

Ron Lomas by the gate where Madam Devaux narrowly escaped being shot.

vehicles roared over the bridge and intermittent waves of 'moaning minnies' screamed down on the bridgehead. Now, the place was full of activity: soldiers stripped to the waist washed and even shaved, propping up fragments of broken glass as mirrors. For Lieutenant-Colonel Tweedie, the completion of the 159th Brigade perimeter around the bridgehead was something of a relief, though the night had been one of '100% vigilance, i.e., no sleep!' Now came orders from his own 227th Brigade. The Argylls' original task of seizing two intact bridges over the Odon had not been forgotten. He was to send fighting patrols up the river to scout the crossings between Tourmauville and Gavrus.

Two patrols were quickly assembled. Lieutenants Desmond Morris of A Company and Bill Edwards of B (both Canadians)[13] were to lead fighting patrols, each equipped with both 18 and 36 wireless sets for communication and recce parties from the sapper platoon. Conscious that they were moving into enemy territory in broad daylight, they blacked up and adjusted their camouflage netting before moving off, up both river banks. They departed at 14.00 hours, and within two hours both radioed back the news that all bridges were intact and undefended. Immediate preparations were made to send Major Hugh Fyfe's C Company to Gavrus. But before these could set out, someone at Brigade realised that the Argylls were no longer required to hold Tourmauville; the entire battalion was ordered up the river. C Company therefore became the advanced guard for the move of the whole unit.

The trek was a nightmare. Narrow, muddy paths twisted and turned along the steep and thickly wooded river valley. The rifle companies were strung out virtually in single file, and easy prey for any enemy. B Company commander Major McElwee recalled that *'Any well-planned ambush might have proved fatal.'* As it happened, there were indeed Germans nearby hurrying to the defence of this gap in their lines around Tourmauville. As the Argylls

The route of the anti-tank guns from the Château de Tourmauville to the Gavrus bridges.

❷ The only forest track wide enough for a Loyd carrier.

❸ The guns were manhandled through the boggy ground.

4 The omamental bridge and footpath north to Mondrainville.

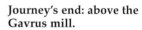

Deep gullies made the riverside path impassable by guns.

Left: Arrows indicate the two 6-pounder guns covering the northern bridge.

Journey's end: above the Gavrus mill.

marched, strung out along the river valley, F and G Companies of 8th Rifle Brigade were in action a short distance away in the woods and fields to the south west of the Tourmauville château and the cluster of buildings known as les Vilains. G Company in particular suffered casualties, two officers and twenty Other Ranks, fighting foot soldiers hastily raised from *Hitlerjugend* artillery and *Luftwaffe Flak* regiments.

A 6-pounder ready to fire. (See Appendix III)

Quite remarkably, the Argylls' antitank platoon succeeded in completing the journey with a number of its six-pounder guns. On one patch of particularly boggy ground, the Loyd carriers lost traction and the dead weight of the guns, each over a ton, had to be manhandled through the mire. At least four of the platoon's six guns appear to have been hauled in this way. By the 1990s, the gunners' memories of their route had become uncertain. So, in late June 2006, the author spent a hot day exploring the Odon valley, ultimately identifying the only track along which Loyd carriers and guns could possibly have made the journey from Tourmauville (actually, from the Tourmauville château) to Gavrus. Most if not all of the foot soldiers clearly advanced along the southern river bank (i.e., the enemy side). The guns could not have moved along riverside paths due to deep gullies on both sides of the river, crossed only by flimsy footbridges. Nor was the pasture between the mill stream and the main branch of the Odon accessible from Tourmauville: it can only be approached dry-shod from the west. Most of the guns' route was high up on the southern side of the valley, commencing from the north west corner of the Tourmauville château grounds. The difficult patch of marsh still exists, at the top of a steep-sided gully, its standing water lapping over the muddy path. Since 1944 the marsh had been drained but by 2006 was again flooded due to the culvert drains laid under the path becoming blocked up.

Mill   Bridge

le Valtru

Gavrus

Once past an ornamental stone bridge (linking the Gavrus château with the RN 175 at Mondrainville), the way became easier, the path widening as it made its descent through the woods to emerge just south of the southernmost bridge at Gavrus. There, all was quiet. As the companies arrived, some moved north across the two bridges spanning the twin branches of the Odon. By the quarry east of the crossing they encountered a reception committee, in the form of Number 6 Platoon, the Middlesex Regiment. These had been sent forward via le Valtru to support the Argylls; arriving to find no one present, their Lieutenant Atkin had set up his four Vickers medium machine guns on the high ground north of the river. At last, the Argylls' antitank guns arrived and were deployed, while the rifle companies re-formed. The men dug their slit trenches in the eerie stillness of the last hour of twilight.

References

(1) The Seventh Army Chief of Staff thoughtfully urged Hausser to complete preparations for the attack before moving on. To whatever extent Hausser heeded this advice, there is evidence of breakdowns of staff work at various levels of the organization in the hours and days following.

(2) Mouen is today a fair-sized village, clustered around the D675 (formerly RN 175) Villers-Bocage to Caen road. In 1944, its focal point was closer to the old railway line, the place nowadays known as le Haut de Mouen. It was then little more than a handful of buildings on a low hill surrounded by small orchards and dense hedgerows.

(3) Accounts of the 3rd Monmouths' locations and movements on the morning of 28 June tend to be vague and contradictory. This is understandable, as some of the Mons' officers themselves had only vague ideas of their whereabouts. Some later, oft-quoted versions of their story appear to confuse numbers of men reported 'lost' (i.e., temporarily uncertain of position) with casualties. This history gives precedence to the scanty entries in the battalion War Diary, and the account of Major Joe How, then the battalion's most junior subaltern.

(4) Kortenhaus memoirs

(5) In yet another example of poor infantry-armour communications, the Glasgow Highlanders' War Diary attributes their support to the 7th Armoured Division!

(6) 227th Brigade June War Diary

(7) The only known photograph of the railway at this time appears to be taken just west of the Colleville level crossing, showing vehicles using the railway cutting as a shelter rather than a thoroughfare. (Vehicles are parked back-to-back, see page 94.) The author feels it unlikely that any vehicles (even Churchill tanks) crossed the railway cutting between Grainville and Colleville during the battle.

(8) *The History of the Cameronians (Scottish Rifles)*, vol III, C N Barclay, p 166

(9) The British infantry appear to have been unimpressed by French architecture, frequently citing noble châteaux as 'farms'. There can be little doubt that this 'farm', forming a company strength position, was in fact the Château de Grainville with its imposing buildings surrounded by stone walls and orchards commanding the western approaches to Grainville village.

(10) The 'wide diamond' plan is described in Martin, p 43. It is unclear from documentary evidence how far this plan survived the passage of the Colleville rail crossing. The 7th Seaforth War Diary notes the squadron of Churchill tanks in support and clearly states that *'The Sqn of tanks remained about a mile south of CHEUX [i.e., near Colleville] having been warned against the possibility of German Mark VI Tanks between GRAINVILLE-SUR-ODON and COLLEVILLE... The advance was continued with two companies on independent axis.'* The likely conclusion is that, once past Colleville, the tanks continued in loose support of the infantry, but that very little coordination was involved.

(11) This objective is variously referred to in different orders as point 910635 and 911636. In fact, 912636 would have been nearer the mark.

(12) *The Seaforth Highlanders*, J Sym, p 288-289

(13) See Appendix IX.

Chapter 6

WEDNESDAY 28 JUNE: OVER THE ODON

With the 23rd Hussars across the Tourmauville bridge, and further tank regiments poised to follow, 11th Armoured Division scented a breakthrough.

OBJECTIVE THE RIVER ORNE
Up to now, the division's first experience of combat had proved intensely frustrating. A corps commander keen to demonstrate his prowess had descended to micro-managing the battle. To the great surprise of the division's tank and infantry brigades, who had trained so long in cooperation, they were separated at an early stage. 29th Armoured Brigade was thrown into its first battle in support of an infantry division with which it had no training and little means of communication. The armour general, Pip Roberts risked understating the truth when he famously commented that, *'The co-operation between the Scotsmen and 11th Armoured Division was not very close; they rather went their separate ways.'*[1] That was exactly what had happened. An officer of 159th Brigade later wondered, *'to what purpose we had spent the last three years training in close armoured/infantry co-operation if we were immediately to be separated from each other in our first battle. Little did we realise in our naivety that... Senior Generals... had only a limited conception of how closely tanks and infantry could combine together, or how effective such close co-operation could be... The fact that 159 Brigade had been left in their Concentration Area was proof in itself that the need for close co-operation between infantry and tanks had not yet been realised at the higher levels.'*[2]

Now was time for optimism. On the morning of 28 June, the division appeared at last to be functioning as intended. Its infantry brigade was across the obstacle of the Odon valley, and covering the flanks of the breakthrough. According to doctrine, this was the time for the tanks to pour through the breach. The VIII Corps objective remained the River Orne, the nearest crossings now a mere five miles away, over mostly open ground, 'undulating country... reminiscent of the Yorkshire Wolds'.[3] 'Good tank country', if one assumed that a tank advance had the same requirements as a fox hunt. (This attitude was a carry-over from the mud of Flanders and the desert of North Africa. Only slowly and painfully would the lesson be learned that almost any terrain could be 'good tank country' so long as it was not covered by antitank fire!)

The German defences had already proved deeper than anticipated. The strength of resistance as far back as the line Grainville-Colleville-Mouen was acknowledged to have surprised 11th Armoured. But now there was

29th Armoured Brigade, morning of 28 June.

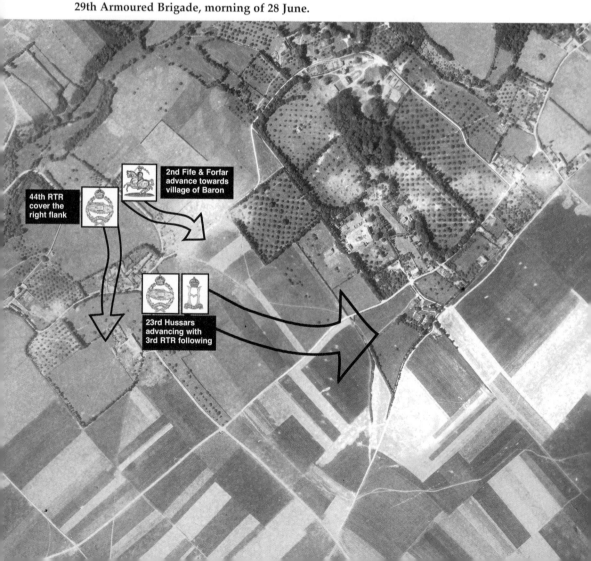

44th RTR cover the right flank

2nd Fife & Forfar advance towards village of Baron

23rd Hussars advancing with 3rd RTR following

confidence that this must have been the main German defence line, the *Hauptkampflinie* ('HKL'). Though the flanks of the corridor were still being contested, Pip Roberts' divisional intelligence section confidently predicted the way ahead to be clear. *'The enemy casualties both in inf and armour during the last two days have been hy, and the force available to him would not appear to be strong enough to org a defence posn between the R ODON and the R ORNE.'* Amid such optimism, the previous night's report (logged at 22.30 hours) of '23 H in action against enemy tks at pt 112' did not cause overmuch concern.[4]

CLIMBING 112

23rd Hussars.

The two squadrons of 23rd Hussars south of the Odon had remained overnight in fighting positions, with the result that few crewmen had managed much sleep. At first light they were rewarded by the sight of two German tanks, identified as *Panzer IV*, twelve hundred yards away towards Esquay. Both were promptly fired on: one was reported knocked out and the other disappeared. Then, at 05.30 hours, B Squadron received the order to advance towards point 112. With C Squadron giving covering fire, and A arriving across the Tourmauville bridge, B Squadron set off. First, they skirted the ruins of Baron village, following a contour as long as possible to stay in dead ground. Then, a right turn to climb the long, open northern slopes, roughly following the line of the old Roman road. One tank was immobilized by a broken track, another hit and destroyed. Fire was returned, and around 06.00 hours two further hits were claimed on enemy '*Tigers*'.

The front line of 29th Armoured Brigade as reported at 11.07 hours.

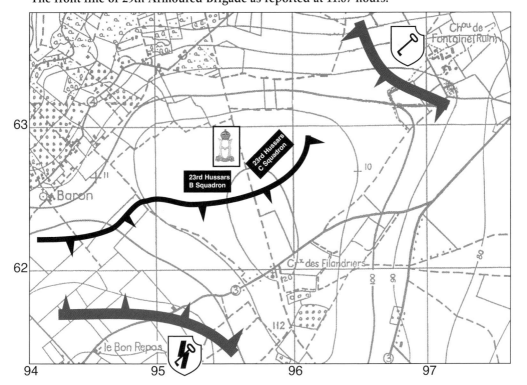

N

Viewpoint

112

At 07.05 hours, the Hussars' B Squadron reported 'nearing COUNTESS', the code name for Hill 112. But this was only the foot of the feature. On the map, Hill 112 appears as an oval, oriented roughly north-south, about two thousand metres in length. On the ground however, it is far less distinctive. From a distance, the hill barely stands out, its slopes gentle and its shape undistinguished, a simple whaleback. Driving across on the modern D 8 road, one is barely aware of having crossed a ridge; indeed, there would be nothing at all to remark about the site were it not for the post-war memorials and the Churchill tank mounted on its plinth. Only by stopping and taking time to look around does the extent of the view become apparent: a vista from the buildings of Caen in the north east to distant Mont Pinçon in the south west. And even this vista was not the cause of Hill 112's importance.

On 'the other side of the hill', the enemy was unprepared for this determined advance. So focused had the German command been on 'pinching out' the flanks of the Scottish Corridor that the possibility of the British salient being still further extended had not been fully allowed for. The forces defending Hill 112 at dawn on 28 June were artillery observers with a few antitank guns. It is all too easy for armchair generals blessed with the wisdom of hindsight to speculate on 'what might have been'. Nevertheless, it is hard to resist the conjecture that, had the 23rd Hussars taken the feature at a dash, it is conceivable that they might have swept over before significant resistance was mounted. As it was, the leading tanks took over three hours[5] to complete their cautious advance over the two miles or so from Tourmauville to the Croix des Filandriers, the sturdy calvary on the main Caen-Evrecy road, from which a line of sight extended over the shallow convexity of the hilltop past a small orchard to the small wood by the summit. Note that the view

Open country: the view south-west from Hill 112, over Esquay to the far distant Mont Pinçon (viewpoint marked opposite).

The view south over Hill 112. The modern memorial wood is entered near the base of the pylon, behind the tractor.

from the platform of the modern Hill 112 memorial, by the Churchill tank, is somewhat different from that of 1944. The original orchard, just south of the position, has disappeared. Looking along the rough track leading southwards, the memorial wood to the right of the track is a modern feature, though it does contain German emplacements which once stood in open ground. The original 'crown of thorns' wood was entirely to the left, east of the track, its north-western corner resting on the 112 metre spot-height.

For the defenders, the delay was just time enough. Fortuitously, the assembly of *Kampfgruppe Weidinger* the previous day had relieved hard-pressed units of *12. SS*, allowing some to be pulled out of the line to rest and

reorganize. Companies of *12. SS-Panzerregiment* had during the small hours moved south across the Odon. A company of *Panther* tanks was now in the area between Evrecy and Esquay; two *II. Abteilung* companies (with *Panzer IV*) had arrived around Esquay itself. *'There we stayed for about half-an-hour. Completely exhausted from the intensive days and nights of fighting, I fell asleep.'*[6] This rest was rudely cut short by the call to defend Hill 112. The ten remaining *Panzer IV* of *5. Kompanie* tore up the southern slopes. A *Halb-Zug* (half-troop)

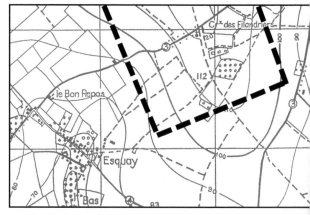

Outline of aerial photograph on page 122 indicated.

commander recalled, *'After a very short assembly we started the attack in a broad*

wedge formation ["*Breitkeil*", the standard German armoured assault formation, effectively a triangle with its base toward the enemy] *on that wooded area… We worked our way forward, each Panzer giving the other covering fire. Without firm targets, we fired antitank and explosive shells into the wood. The attack moved forward briskly… At approximately 100m we changed from wedge into staggered line… I was now driving the point Panzer. Our direction was approximately north-west.*[7] Kretzschmar's tank exchanged fire in the area of the orchard until hit and damaged. The crew returned to Esquay to collect

A wrecked *Panzer IV* in Esquay.

another tank from the repair shop before plunging back into the fray with other, newly arriving members of their battalion.

As the Hussars judged from the volume of fire, the enemy appeared to be present in some strength, and so well dug-in as to be almost impossible to hit. The attached M10s of G Troop, 75th Antitank Regiment tried to reach the enemy armour with their seventeen pounder guns. Next, medium artillery was called in. And with the improving weather, fighter-bombers were at last available. But the Typhoons could not spot any enemy tanks. When field guns tried to assist by marking suspected targets with red smoke, some of the shells fell short among B Squadron, and tank commanders quickly hurled out the yellow smoke canisters that identified friends, the red and the yellow swirling about to the mystification of the Typhoons (and the consternation of Colonel Harding's crew when he dropped a yellow smoke canister in his turret!). The exchange continued, intensifying as enemy antitank guns to the west in the area of le Bon Repos joined the fire fight. By 09.40 hours, C Squadron had moved up in support, passing behind the stalled B Squadron to loop around the relatively quiet north-east side of the 112 feature. Shortly after, the Hussars' attached motor infantry arrived: H Company, 8th Rifle Brigade. These promptly left their vehicles and advanced ahead of the tanks into the orchard, where they dug-in. They held the position at the cost of moderately heavy losses. By midday, regimental headquarters arrived with the reserve A Squadron, closely followed by 270th Forward Delivery Squadron, with eight replacement Shermans (the first the Hussars had received during the battle). Exceptionally, instead of the older, experienced FDS crews being replaced by 'unhorsed' Hussars, these were flung straight into action. Three were

promptly knocked out. *'It was a most unfortunate occasion. In the space of a few minutes, we lost some good friends and some of the best reinforcements ever sent up to us.'*[8]

THE ODON BRIDGEHEAD

Meanwhile, 29th Armoured Brigade continued to pour across the Tourmauville bridge. By 06.30 hours, 3rd RTR was across and deploying its squadrons south east of Tourmauville, closely followed by Brigadier Roscoe Harvey's Tac HQ, established around the buildings of the little settlement. 3rd RTR's accompanying motor infantry, G Company of 8th RB, ran into trouble patrolling the woods west of Tourmauville, losing twenty men and two six-pounder guns. By 10.30 hours, the 2nd Fife and Forfar were across, taking over from 3rd RTR, 'to watch 23H right flank and possible counter-attack from ESQUAY 9460.'

3rd RTR in turn moved east. Shortly after midday, an A Squadron tank ran onto mines in Baron village, blocking the main road and slowing the advance while a way was found across country. The battalion took position on the open northern slopes of Hill 112 (in map square 9562). There they covered the exposed left flank of the Hussars, and kept a watch over the wooded country to the north east, where the arrival of *II./1. SS-Panzergrenadierregiment* infantry and antitank guns posed a growing threat.

Towards the end of the morning, 44th RTR (detached from 4 Brigade, under command of Harvey's 29 Brigade) crossed the Odon with their motor infantry, B Company, 2nd King's Royal Rifle Corps. 44th Tanks moved west with a view to relieving the Fifes. The augmented 29th Armoured Brigade

was now complete in the Odon bridgehead, its four tank regiments and their supporting motor infantry companies deployed in a four-mile arc, from south of Gavrus to the north-eastern slopes of Hill 112. Nowhere was free of fire – even Harvey's Tac HQ south of Tourmauville had been engaged by antitank guns from the direction of Esquay, and Liaison Officer Lieutenant Rogers wounded in the face by a *Nebelwerfer* bomb.

But the 112 feature remained the focal point of the advance. There the Hussars tried repeatedly to force their way to the top: led first by B Squadron commander Major Seymour, later by Colonel Harding himself. The colonel was everywhere: dismounting from his tank to direct antitank M10s, encouraging H Company's efforts to hold the small orchard. At length, frustrated by the poor field of vision from the gently-sloping ground, Harding directed his tank onto the western slopes. From there, at last he could see the enemy hotbed of Esquay. And the enemy could see him. Harding's command tank was promptly knocked out – fortunately with no loss of life.

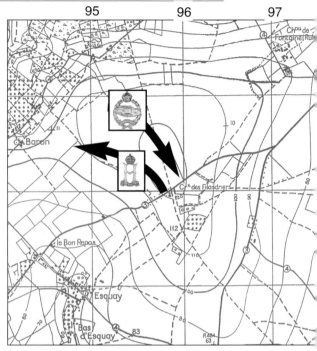

By 13.45, the Hussars were reporting ammunition running low. There was no question of running three-ton lorries into the maelstrom, so preparations were made for the Hussars' relief. At 15.00, 3rd RTR moved up the hill, followed by their motor infantry. The tanks led, the riflemen behind in a column of half-tracks, and the light carriers with their machine-guns covering the flanks. By 15.30 the relief was complete. The Fifes urgently despatched a squadron to take over 3rd Tanks' covering role on the left flank; the rest of the regiment to follow as soon as the handover to 44th RTR was achieved. The Hussars fell back to leaguer around Tourmauville. *'Calmly, and under perfect order from the Colonel, we withdrew into our original positions. About nine we got back into harbour, unshaven, tired out and hungry... I had then been in my tank constantly for more than twenty-seven hours – it seemed more like twenty-seven days.'*[9]

On the hill, the fight continued. Left behind by the Hussars, H Company still clung to the little orchard, which was already becoming stripped of branches and foliage, a 'crown of thorns' atop otherwise open hillside. 3rd

23rd Hussars pull back from Hill 112, leaving H Company, 8th Rifle Brigade. 3rd RTR move up in support.

RTR tried to edge forward where the Hussars had failed. At 17.00 hours, 11th Armoured Division recorded that '3 R Tks reach N slope of pt 112 feature.' But the predicament faced earlier by the Hussars was unchanged. '*Numerically we were overwhelmingly superior in tanks but the position was a commanding one and the enemy knowing its importance full well had taken every step possible to deny it to us. He need not actually occupy the hill.*'[10] This was the simple truth. The summit of 112 was untenable by tanks. Vehicles without cover silhouetted on the crest would inevitably be picked off by guns on the reverse slopes. '*Death stalked the rider who attempted to mount its broad saddle… neither* [combatant] *could hold the place, and each could deny it to the other.*'[11]

One A Squadron tank commander present was somewhat aggrieved: when his original Sherman had earlier broken down, he appealed to 3rd RTR's unwritten rule that officers found a new mount but NCOs stayed with their tank. He was overruled. As a surviving desert veteran in a unit with many newcomers, his squadron commander needed him in the battle. Taking over another tank, Corporal 'Geordie' Reay noted, '*The crew weren't exactly over the moon about my arrival. I heard them talking about my DCM and hoping I wouldn't do anything stupid.*' Indeed, recognising the risk of cresting the hilltop, becoming hull-up to the enemy guns, he radioed back for artillery support: '*I couldn't see any point in rushing into trouble.*' It was not forthcoming. From 3rd RTR's Colonel Silvertop, via A Squadron commander Bill Close, came the order to advance regardless. '*All Bill could say was, "Jig One Able, you'll have to get on." I knew what would happen the moment we showed ourselves and told the crew, "We're going in but we're going to be hit. It'll be every man for himself… Driver advance." And the next thing I knew I was slumped down on the turret top with the tank in flames.*'[12]

By the afternoon of 28 June, the German defences included a number of heavy, antiaircraft 8.8cm guns. Though air defence remained their primary role, and their bulk prevented effective emplacement in the hard, stony ground, nevertheless while they remained in action they proved effective long-range tank killers. Still the 3rd Tanks fought on. '*One tank… burst into flames. It seemed as if we were exposed to fire from three directions, both from Tiger tanks and 88mm Flak guns. I asked permission to pull back to slightly less exposed positions but from where we could engage the enemy.*' And this time, caution prevailed. '*We remained in these rather negative positions for the remainder of that day.*'[13] The A Squadron commander was not alone in his mistaken belief that he was engaging *Tiger* tanks. In fact, the German tanks on Hill 112 that day were *Panzer IV*, and they too found the position untenable. A tank man of 5. *Kompanie* relates, '*At around 17.00 hours, our total number, through newly arrived Panzer, was back to nine. The 6. Kompanie was also there. This time we tried to attack the hill by swinging wide to the left around the small wood in front of the square wooded area. Despite being covered from view to the right toward the square wood, we again came under heavy fire from tanks, had a few Panzer losses and had to withdraw again to our starting positions.*'[14]

On the hilltop, the Rifles' H Company grimly held their orchard as German mortar fire came down and tanks of both sides fired into their positions. At length, the position became untenable and by mid-afternoon had been abandoned, the company rejoining the Hussars in their leaguer. By 19.45 hours, firing had died down all around the 29th Brigade perimeter, with the exception of Hill 112 where '3 R Tks *heavily engaged if he attempts to move forward.*' By 22.00 hours, far from achieving a breakthrough, 11th Armoured sensed a general strengthening of the German line: '*3 TIGERS have appeared on the 112 feature... We are being engaged... The situation concerning 3 R Tks is slightly confused.*'[15] In the confusion, 3rd RTR pulled back down the northern slopes to pass the night in forward leaguer east of Baron.

References

(1) Roberts, p 164

(2) Thornburn, p 21-22

(3) *Bishop, 23rd Hussars*, p 56

(4) 11th Armoured Division Intelligence Summaries: No. 9, 23.00 hours, 26 June & No. 10, 05.00 hours, 28 June

(5) Regimental records indicate that the Hussars' movement began at 05.30 hours with B and C Squadrons 'established North half of Pt 112' only by midday. Although Brigadier Harvey's war diary records sometimes reflect a degree of optimism, here 29th Brigade confirms the Hussars' line as still a thousand yards north of point 112 at 11.07 hours. One wonders how far the experience of 28 June may have influenced Harvey's drive to hurry his tanks on at all costs on 18 July, the opening day of Operation GOODWOOD.

(6) Untersturmführer Willi Kändler, quoted in Meyer, p 121

(7) Oberscharführer Willy Kretzschmar, quoted in Meyer, p 121

(8) Bishop, 23rd Hussars, p 57

(9) *The Battle: a Tank Officer Remembers*, G S C Bishop, p 19-20 Assuming that the timings given are even remotely accurate, it seems that the regiment took almost as long to move off the hill as on to it.

(10) Bishop, 23rd Hussars, p 58

(11) *Taurus Pursuant: A History of 11th Armoured Division*, E W I Palamountain, p 17

(12) Geordie Reay, quoted in *Panzer Bait*, William Moore, p 130-131

(13) *A View From the Turret*, Bill Close, p 110

(14) Oberscharführer Willy Kretzschmar, quoted in Meyer, p 122

(15) 11th Armoured Division signals log. Note that no Tiger were on Hill 112 on 28 June; most likely Panzer IV were mis-identified though possibly the term was being used generically to indicate 'enemy tanks'. That very day, an intelligence report published by another unit noted that: '*The enemy has had considerable success in disguising Mk IV's to look like Tigers,* [this drawn from the mistaken assumption that Panzer IV turret Schürzen were camouflage, rather than defence against hollow-charge missiles!] *and from a distance they are almost impossible to distinguish. Almost half the Tigers reported by our tps turn out in fact to be Mk IV's. The type of tk should not be reported at all unless there is reasonable certainty that the identification is correct, but it is most important to obtain this identification if possible.*' (32nd Guards Armoured Brigade War Diary)

Chapter 7

THURSDAY 29 JUNE: THE COUNTERBLOW

Though he now bore the heavy responsibility of commanding Seventh Army, Paul Hausser remained stuck with his predecessor's last-minute change of plan for *II SS-Panzerkorps*. And Hausser's successor Willi Bittrich would have to implement the changed plan as best he could. The strategy of concentrating the German armour in a single northbound thrust to Bayeux and beyond had been irrevocably dropped in favour of a rapid response to the British EPSOM offensive. True, if successful the counter attack might cause a tactical rebuff, inflicting great losses on the British. But a turning point had been reached. Succeed or fail, the coming operation risked the loss of the Germans' greatest opportunity to regain the strategic initiative in Normandy.

BITTRICH'S TACTICAL PLAN

The newly-promoted corps commander hastily oversaw the changes to the corps plan demanded by the deceased Dollmann. The new, north-easterly axis of attack presented few tactical options. On the left, *9. SS-Panzerdivision 'Hohenstaufen'* would have to approach past Villers-Bocage, its assault on the western flank of the Scottish Corridor necessarily following the main RN 175 highway, its right flank logically resting on the valley of the Odon. The later-arriving *10. SS-Panzerdivision 'Frundsberg'* would initially be limited to attacking over the open ground between Bougy and Evrecy: its left flank on the Odon valley, and its right constrained by the difficult terrain around the River Guigne that ran west to east from Evrecy to the Orne. The river only a trickle, the Guigne valley nevertheless was overgrown and boggy. Until the engineers could improvise crossings, the Guigne would be a bar to progress.

9. SS Panzerdivision Hohenstaufen.

10. SS Panzerdivision Frundeberg.

SS Gruppenführer **Wilhelm Bittrich.**

Just as Paul Hausser had protested his inability to bring *II. SS-Panzerkorps* into battle on 28 June, so too his successor Willi Bittrich found the start line impossible to achieve by the early morning of the following day. The corps' journey from the eastern front had become progressively more difficult. Clearer weather resulted in the French roads being harried by Allied fighter-bombers. Though

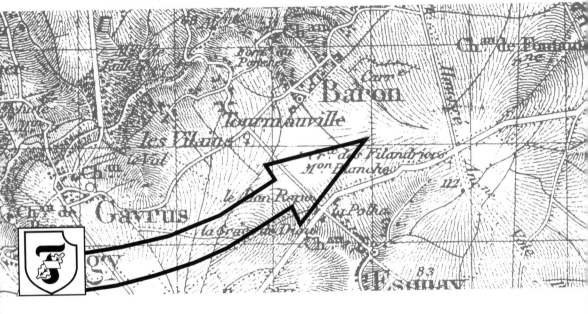

The *II. SS Panzerkorps* plan: *Hohenstaufen* to cut the Scottish corridor at Cheux (above) and *Frundsberg* to smash 11th Armoured at the tip of the corridor (below).

the German anti-aircraft guns took a heavy toll, movement towards the battle zone was greatly hampered and resupply of ammunition and fuel became a nightmare.

Given the constraints of time and territory, Bittrich's tactics had to be simple. The two divisions would be rushed into combat with minimal preparation; fully a third of the *Frundsberg* infantry (the second and third battalions of *Panzergrenadierregiment 21*) would attack directly from the line of march. And even so, the designated start time of 06.00 hours came and went with no prospect of attack getting under way before noon.

BRITISH INTELLIGENCE: EXPECTATIONS AND REVELATIONS

A painstakingly thorough intelligence summary prepared by 11th Armoured Division during the night of 28-29 June reveals key areas of knowledge and ignorance. It was recognised that the high ground ahead would continue to be contested vigorously: '*the enemy hopes to hold us up with his long range A Tk weapons in the open country on our front.*' Relief was expressed that the *2. SS 'Das Reich'* had been held on the western flank of the corridor. Relief too at the report (though it was overly optimistic) that when '*the bogy of 1 SS Pz Div raised its head again today,*' the *Leibstandarte* elements present were 'not more than a Bn in strength'. Unsuspected by the author of the report, nor indeed by his divisional commander, was the imminent arrival of the strongest armoured formation in Normandy, in the shape of *II. SS-Panzerkorps.*

To preserve the ULTRA secret, the information gained at Bletchley Park from decoding German radio communications could not be shared below the level of British Second Army. That is, below General Dempsey. True, there were ways of 'disguising' sources. On occasion, air reconnaissance would be conducted to 'reveal' enemy movements already known from ULTRA decrypts, so that friends and enemies alike would be unaware of the original source of the knowledge. In this case, O'Connor was already aware of the likelihood of new German arrivals. During the night of 28 June, without compromising the ULTRA source, Dempsey discussed with O'Connor his concerns about strengthening resistance on the VIII Corps front and his doubts about extending the Odon bridgehead in the face of the expected onslaught. He even went so far as to pass a direct Second Army order to O'Connor to withdraw from the Odon bridgehead, a mere twenty four hours after its creation.[1]

However, O'Connor's slow implementation of this order suggests that he was not yet wholly convinced of the need to 'close down' EPSOM. The corps commander still hoped to make a mark for himself in his first Normandy battle. Only at 10.00 hours on the morning of 29 June, in a meeting with division commanders held at 15th Scottish HQ, did Pip Roberts learn from O'Connor that the Orne River was no longer an immediate objective. This was welcome news to Roberts, who already felt his division 'out on a limb'.[2] Roberts had expected that by this time both of his division's flanks would be covered. Neither was. He was disconcerted to find a Canadian attack on Carpiquet airfield postponed, leaving German observers and guns with a clear line of sight to the summit of Hill 112 from the north east. And the slow advance of XXX Corps left the western flank of the corridor exposed on both sides of the Odon valley. Nevertheless, Roberts was given to understand that the delay on the western flank was only temporary.

In the 10.00 hours conference, O'Connor did not reveal the order to pull back north of the Odon. Instead, he confirmed that he was bringing up his reserve 43rd (Wessex) Infantry Division to secure and extend the eastern flank of the corridor, leaving 15th Scottish to concentrate on the west. 11th Armoured would increase its grip on the bridgehead over the Odon, still with a view to resuming progress towards the Orne when conditions permitted. By the time this directive was confirmed, 11th Armoured was already several hours into its execution.

11th ARMOURED REACHING OUT

The armoured regiments of 11th Armoured Division had spent an uncomfortable night in forward leaguer. Bill Close of 3rd RTR recalled, *'That first night was most unpleasant; we more or less stood-to in our tanks as we knew we were practically surrounded, our one consolation being that we were under the protection of the Rifle Brigade.'*[3] The night had been particularly difficult for 8th Rifle Brigade. Just as they were preparing for the brief respite of the few hours of summer darkness, there came a barrage of mortar and machine gun fire from the area of Hill 112, accompanied by reports of Tiger tanks attacking. About 21.45 hours, as the rifle companies summoned from their respective tank battalions joined H Company in its position on the northern slopes of 112, the enemy tank attack appeared over the ridge to the south. Casualties and confusion resulted as the tanks stood off and shelled the 8th RB assembly area. At length the tanks withdrew and to everyone's relief the afternoon's idea of a night attack on Hill 112 by 8th RB was called off.[4] Nevertheless, at first light the battalion was directed to return up 112 and secure the wood at 962617.

Lieutenant Stileman had already led a night recce up the hill to point 962617, at 02.00 hours reporting 'sounds of digging' from the little wood. Come daylight, H Company once again advanced up the northern slopes so recently vacated. In support was 3rd RTR, though with the experience of the previous afternoon, they were careful not to expose their tanks hull-up. Edging carefully up the slope, at 06.30 hours the left-hand squadron stopped just short of the Croix des Filandriers. 3rd RTR contented themselves with occupying a *'defensive position… of observation to SE, South, and SW all day, B Sqn on left in support of 8 R.B.'* There would be no repetition of the previous day's scrapping on the hilltop. The squadrons sat and endured 'Intermittent shelling all day'.[5]

Now, for the first time in the campaign, the companies of 8th Rifle Brigade were assembled in battalion strength (less F Company, which would rejoin later in the afternoon) under command of their own headquarters for their advance up the hill. There they found no Germans in the little wood, and took cover in the slit trenches they had dug the previous day. The plan had been to

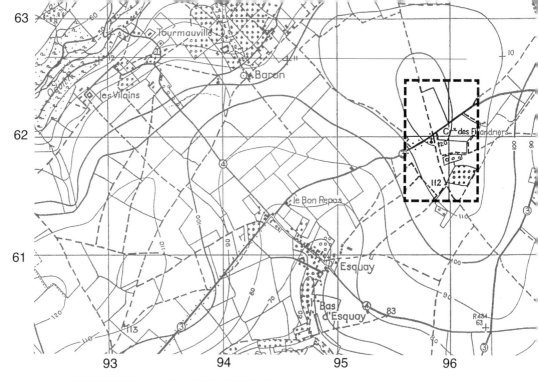

retain the battalion transport on the hill, though there was little the half-tracks and carriers could achieve there, and they would be certain to attract enemy fire. Sure enough, as wiser counsel prevailed and the vehicles moved back down, enemy artillery fire and mortaring commenced. As the day wore on, the fire continued and casualties steadily mounted, H Company's commander himself falling an early victim. Like the tanks the day before, the riflemen found that *'While the Germans could not maintain their position on the hill, they could bring very heavy fire to bear on anyone who turned them off it. Most of the Riflemen were subjected to shelling and mortaring without ever seeing a German… as vehicles burnt and shells exploded in the*

The wood at map reference 962617 (see above, also Appendix I map reference).

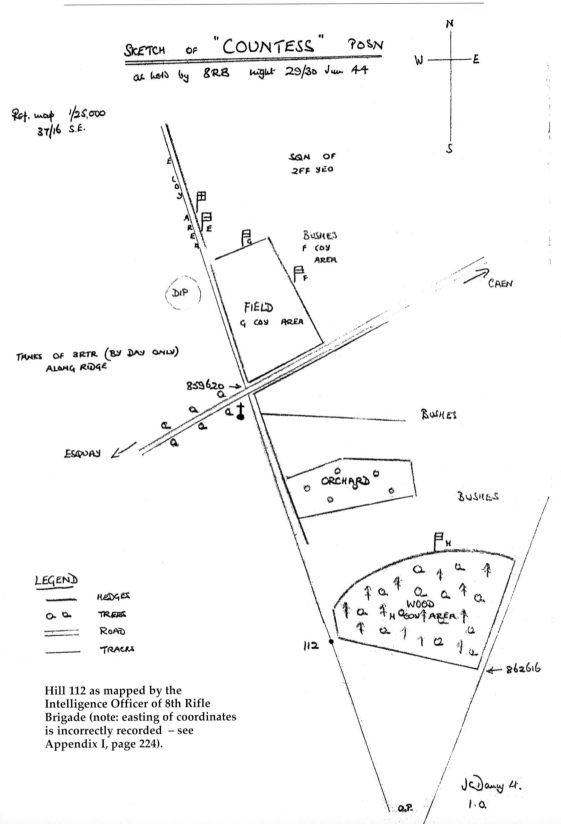

Hill 112 as mapped by the Intelligence Officer of 8th Rifle Brigade (note: easting of coordinates is incorrectly recorded – see Appendix I, page 224).

cramped area of Hill 112 the air became loaded with a fine, grey powder, covering men... so that the wounded looked even more ghastly than usual.'[6]

To their lasting credit, 8th Rifle Brigade succeeded in holding their exposed position on the summit of Hill 112. As their War Diary proudly records, from 08.00 on 29 June to the small hours of the following morning, *'This posn was held all day without change, being all the time under observed fire from 88mm's in the area CARPIQUET 9767, as well as mortars from the EAST, SOUTH and WEST.'* Doing the job that only infantry can do, they dug in and held their ground, unable to strike back at their tormentors, but able to deny the hill to the enemy.

On the other side of the bridgehead, 29 Brigade was concerned to protect the right flank of the advance over Hill 112, while also exploring the possibility of opening up a second crossing through Gavrus. The freshest armoured unit present was selected for these tasks. 44th Royal Tank Regiment had spent the night in leaguer around les Vilains, and at 06.00 hours received orders to move south west, to screen the town (or rather, the rubble) of Evrecy, while pushing out their right flank to link with elements of 15th Scottish believed to be in the village of Gavrus. The unit was well prepared. In fact, the reinforced battalion took the form of a balanced regimental combat group, with its own Recce Troop (of Stuarts), its customary motor infantry (B Company of 2nd KRRC), an attached antitank troop of four M10s (later reinforced to battery strength), and three tank-mounted artillery observers.

Positions of 44th Royal Tank Regiment, early on 29 June.

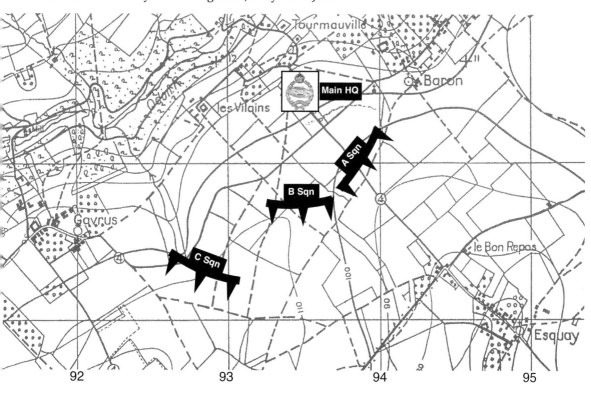

Gavrus

Bougy

Viewpoint,
pages 140
and 141

500 yards

The Hill 113 battleground.

Evrecy

Baron →

113 △

C Squadron, being already to the south west of the regimental leaguer, was allocated the lead; B Squadron was to give covering fire; while A Squadron would advance to occupy C's original position, ready to advance in support of C when called forward. The Recce Troop and motor infantry were to feel their way west towards Gavrus (where an earlier 8th RB patrol had worryingly reported no contact with any friendly troops of 15th Scottish). The squadrons shook out of their leaguers, and moved into position in a rough semi-circle. At 09.10 hours, C Squadron and B Company both began their slow and careful advance. 44th RTR was one of those units in which each squadron's seventeen-pounder 'Firefly' Shermans were trooped together:[7] C Squadron advanced with 2 Troop 'on point', 3 echeloned left, and 4 to the right, and the Fireflies together in A Troop some distance behind.

Leaving the motor infantry looking down over Gavrus, C Squadron climbed up the steady gradient towards the wide open summit of Hill 113. All going well, C Squadron proceeded beyond their objective to gain a better vantage point over Evrecy, and at 10.30 hours A Squadron was ordered

The Hill 113 battlefield in June: to the north, the Odon valley and beyond the road the village of Gavrus. (Note: there two 113 metre spot heights: one at this point and another 350 metres east.)

Bougy

forward on the left to command the Bon Repos road junction at point 946614. By midday the slow, methodical advance found C Squadron established on the northern side of the ruins of Evrecy, the tank troops arrayed around the four Fireflies, and all engaging a variety of targets with their own guns and the support of a single, distant troop of F Battery, 4th Royal Horse Artillery (four twenty-five pounder self-propelled Sextons). B Squadron was meanwhile manoeuvring around the right flank, in what was believed to be

The 44th RTR advance.

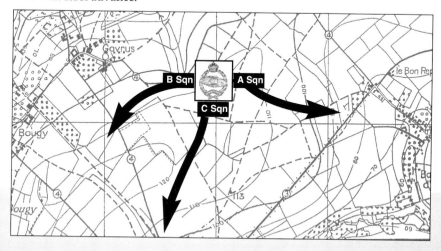

Gavrus

dead ground, to get at the western side of Evrecy. And A Squadron managed to get close to its objective, stopping on the highway just short of the crossroads to assist 3rd RTR by engaging a number of distant enemy targets. Then in an instant the tide turned. *'We were just congratulating ourselves, as they had reported knocking out two enemy tanks and a similar number of anti-tank guns, when suddenly all hell broke loose on "C" Squadron.'*[8]

In 2 Troop, two Shermans went up in flames, one of them the accompanying artillery OP. As the survivors of the troop swung right to face the threat, a third Sherman exploded. 3 Troop and the two west-facing Fireflies joined in, and they too began to lose tanks. A turret hit damaged a Firefly's gun: the crew baled out but Lieutenant Colbeck-Welch remained to reverse the tank out of action; fifty yards was gained before the tank was destroyed and the lieutenant killed. The action that had begun with so much promise was rapidly falling apart, the survivors of C Squadron falling back under cover of their own smokescreen and that of the burning tanks. Such of the enemy as could be seen were reported (accurately for once!) as 'Long 75mm on Mk III Chassis',[9] in other words *Sturmgeschütze*. B and C Squadrons fell back behind the crest of Hill 113. This dead ground offered some protection, but equally limited their view of the enemy: tank commanders were ordered to stand on their turrets for observation, whereupon the enemy

'Long 75mm on Mk III Chassis'.

dropped High Explosive rounds in their midst.

The ebullient Brigadier Harvey reported back to Division as late as 13.40 hours that the *'line EVRECY – BOUGY held in some str by inf, tks, and A Tk guns.'* In truth the position was far from secure. (Later in the afternoon, 29th Brigade was grudgingly to admit that *'making progress on that flank expensive and adv halted.'*) Some contact had now been made with the Argylls in Gavrus, but the firm bulwark 44th RTR had hoped to find on their right flank was elusive; and the seventeen-pounder antitank battery supposed to be arriving over the Gavrus bridges had not materialized at all. Worse still, the tanks' own M10 battery had chosen to withdraw, leaving the right flank exposed to growing German pressure as the enemy infiltrated the wooded valley. An aggrieved report by 44th RTR complained that, *'The 17 pdr SP guns withdrew and by their withdrawal not only uncovered B Coy, who were without their own anti-tank guns, but also exposed the flank of C Sqn, who again bore the brunt of the attack.'*[10] B Company, 2nd KRRC were even more scathing, pointing out that the battery had behaved more like tanks than antitank artillery. *'Bty S.P. 17 Pdr did not succeed in protecting flank of 44 RTR. They were in posn against just such an eventuality as that which occurred, i.e., counter-attack by armoured cars and tanks... When A.P. fire was directed against them they withdrew turret down. Instead of lining a ridge they should have been placed in trees and hedges and camouflaged.'*[11] By 16.30 hours, thoughts of advancing southwards had been abandoned. All available artillery was directed against Evrecy, where increasing enemy traffic was observed. 44th RTR was reduced to covering the western approaches to the Tourmauville crossing, and 'it was fairly obvious that we were in for a pretty sticky time.'[12]

FRUNDSBERG vs 29 BRIGADE

In venturing forward towards Evrecy, 44th Royal Tanks had run into elements of a German armoured division moving in the opposite direction. Fortunately for the British squadrons, they were first on the scene and the enemy's arrival was somewhat disorganised.

Paul Hausser had refused Dollmann's order to lead his corps into a counterattack on 28 June in the full knowledge that the deadline was impossible to achieve. Even 29 June was a challenge. *'In my opinion, the attack was prepared too quickly. I wanted to wait another two days but Hitler insisted that it be launched on 29 June.'*[13] Allied airpower, rubbled villages and cratered country roads all slowed the final stages of the *II SS-Panzerkorps* move from Galicia to the Normandy invasion front. Through the night of 28-29 June, *10. SS-Panzerdivision* struggled to prepare for battle. From crossings over the Orne, the *Frundsberg* formations looped west and north, around the obstacle of the Guigne River to the ruined town of Evrecy. There, companies of the divisional reconnaissance *Abteilung* formed an advanced guard, the battalion headquarters established in a farm just outside Evrecy itself. To the north and east of Evrecy, the ground over which the division was to attack in the early morning, small fields and dense 'bocage' hedgerow gave way to a wide expanse of rolling open country. The gentle slopes of Hill 113 blocked the

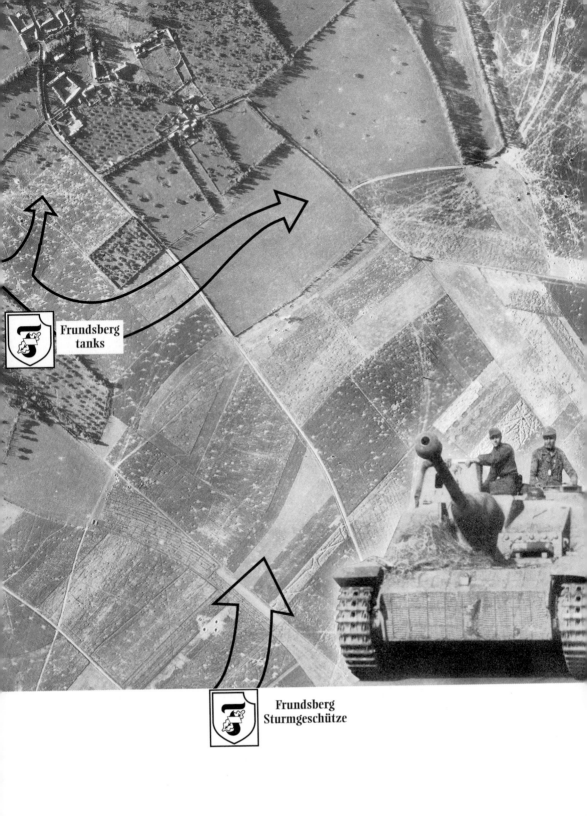

Frundsberg
tanks

Frundsberg
Sturmgeschütze

view north. To the north east, barely five kilometres distant and clearly visible come daylight, stood the dominating whaleback ridge of Hill 112. Rather further away, eight kilometres to the south of Evrecy was the divisional headquarters, in the farm of Ronde Fontaine. On all sides, troops and vehicles streamed northwards into the night, towards a distant glow and thunder of artillery. The commander put in a brief appearance, then was gone. SS-*Oberführer* Heinz Harmel was everywhere that night, receiving reports and urging units forward to their assembly areas.

By dawn, the *Frundsberg* artillery regiments were in place. The three battalions of *SS-Panzergrenadierregiment 22* were still struggling forward to their start line west of the Evrecy-Bougy road. As to *SS-Panzergrenadierregiment 21*, only one of its three battalions had yet arrived south of Evrecy. Clearly, the planned 06.00 hours target was not going to be met. The start was postponed, initially to 07.00 hours, then to 10.00, later to midday and beyond. But one unit on the start line west of Evrecy failed to receive notification of the second postponement. So, at 07.00 hours, *Obersturmführer* Franz Riedel ordered his *7. Kompanie* of *10. SS-Panzerregiment* forward. Confident that his seventeen *Sturmgeschütze*[14] were being closely followed by the *Panzer IV* tanks of the fifth and sixth companies, echeloned back to the left and right, Riedel led the way towards Hill 113. Soon after crossing their start line, the company of *Sturmgeschütze* encountered C Squadron, 44th RTR.

The *Sturmgeschütze* were not designed for offensive armoured combat. They were at their most effective in a defensive role, firing from camouflaged positions then using their mobility to avoid return fire. Their lack of turrets and co-axial machine guns presented disadvantages in close combat versus tanks. However, it appears that the advanced squadrons of 44th RTR were caught on the forward slopes of Hill 113, and that Riedel's company was able to engage at fairly long range (his own account stresses that his guns enjoyed the advantage since 'the range was calculated precisely'). But also working in favour of the *Sturmgeschütze* were their longer-ranged, high-velocity 7.5cm guns (all the more advantageous since the leading troops of Shermans lacked Fireflies); and the smaller profile of the low-slung assault guns in contrast to the larger, taller Shermans (an important factor in securing a first-shot hit). Seeing the British tanks crossing their line of advance, the *Sturmgeschütze* appear to have had time to stop and fire first. In the ensuing engagement, both sides claimed more kills than can be believed. (This was a common feature of EPSOM armoured engagements, most likely based on honest over-estimates in the heat of battle.) But there could be no doubt that Riedel's guns ended holding the field. The British tanks fell back behind an opaque white smokescreen. Becoming aware of his exposed position, Riedel quickly determined that to advance blindly would be fatal. Only then did the *Abteilung* commander, *SS-Sturmbannführer* Leo Reinhold make his appearance, somewhat comically roaring across the hill in a motorcycle combination, waving his arms frantically from the sidecar, coming to a halt to demand an explanation. 'What is all this firing? What have you been up to?'

Needless to say, the major was pleased with the explanation given, and the outcome of the accidental battle.[15]

The initial success could not immediately be followed up. Only later did supporting armour come forward, the *Panzer IV* companies of *10. SS-Panzerregiment* engaging the surviving Shermans of 44th RTR and the M10s of 75th Antitank Regiment in a swirling fight on the slopes between Hill 113 and Gavrus. Here, on the sort of open ground which the British persisted in considering 'good tank country', numerous armoured duels were fought out through the afternoon of 29 June. Individual tanks struggled on this open ground to make use of any screening hedgerow or fold in the landscape for protection. As a confused afternoon wore on, numerous wrecks of both sides' tanks littered the battlefield. Some German armour

SS-Sturmbannführer
Leo Reinhold

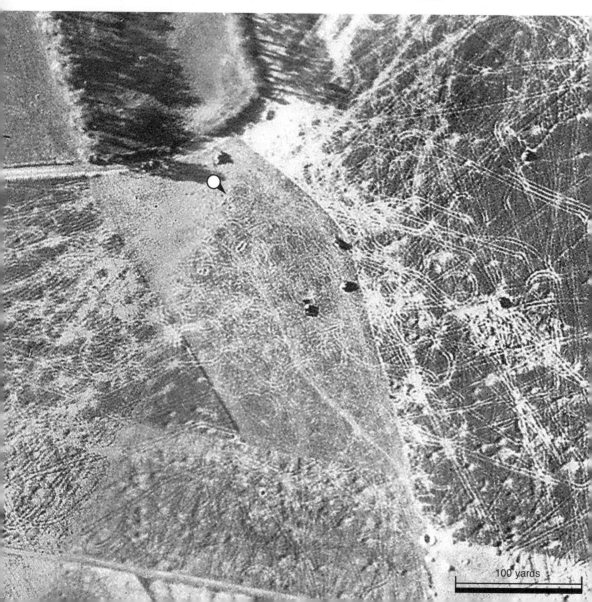

100 yards

Three Frundsberg Panzer IV knocked out. Viewed from the point shown on opposite page.

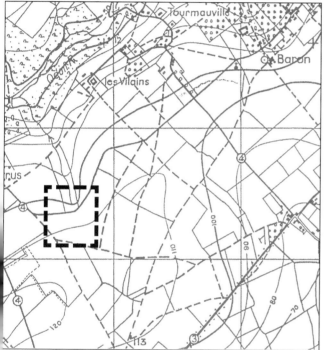

The battleground south of Gavrus. Detail of aerial view opposite indicated.

managed to find firing positions in the woods lining the Odon valley, there to support the small numbers of German infantry managing to infiltrate past Gavrus on the left flank of the division's battle.

As for the infantry attack on the *Frundsberg* right flank, it was not until afternoon that a full-scale assault by *21. Regiment* could be initiated, and even then the quantity of artillery fire coming down on Evrecy 'delayed and complicated the advance'.[16] By the end of the day, far from advancing past Esquay to threaten Hill 112, the most that the infantry had been able to achieve was to establish the regiment's *II. Abteilung*, dug-in on the northern and eastern slopes of Hill 113. Other elements of *21. Regiment* supported companies of the *Pionier Abteilung* advancing east of Evrecy into the Guigne valley, where the assault engineers blasted hedgerows and laid tracks capable of bearing armour.

FRUNDSBERG vs 2nd ARGYLLS

The more northerly assault led by *22. Panzergrenadierregiment* had also been delayed as its objectives were more distant and the troops subject to defensive artillery fire missions even before they reached their Start Line. As dawn broke to reveal a clear blue sky, the threat from the air became a reality. The regiment and its supporting arms had either to risk crossing the open ridge west of 113, or else detour still further west under orchards and along country lanes to reach their forming up places in the Odon valley. At last, by early afternoon, the advance was able to begin. Slowly the leading infantry skirmished north-eastward, the river on their left, through the little village of

Bougy, then uphill past Bougy's château grounds towards Gavrus, where the 2nd Argylls were awaiting events. (The Argylls' experience is recounted in detail in Chapter 8.) For their part, the Germans expected to find Gavrus defended, and advanced with caution.[17]

Initially unsupported by armour, when the *Panzergrenadiere* first encountered resistance, they deployed along the stone wall on the east side of the château. The wall was quickly mouse-holed to provide firing positions for squad light machine guns, and exchanges of fire continued across the western orchards of Gavrus.[18] True to their tactics, the infantry attempted to 'fix' the defenders to their front while throwing out flanking movements to either side. To the right, in the open fields south of the Gavrus-Bougy road, the only cover was the ripening grain.[19] To the left, outflanking manoeuvres were more promising. Small groups probed gaps between the Argylls' platoons, some even reaching the road between the village and the bridges. Towards evening, one platoon-strength force eventually advanced along a sunken path

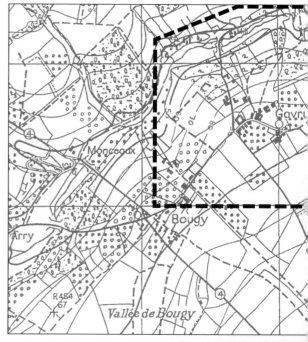

Aerial shown opposite is indicated.

The château wall (viewpoint shown by arrow opposite).

Gavrus in 1944, before the battle. The fields in the centre have recently been built over.

to drive a wedge between the Argylls on the west of the village and the larger force defending the bridges. However, this penetration was not in sufficient strength to permit further exploitation: having established an advanced fire base, the small German band was content to hold its ground.

By early evening, the *22. Regiment* left had extended still further, straying across the divisional boundary into *Hohenstaufen* territory north of the Odon valley, from whose tree-covered slopes they directed fire into the defenders around both bridges. But at no time was a concerted, overwhelming assault attempted. Soon after the battle for Gavrus, the Argylls' commander (an experienced professional soldier) recorded a degree of admiration yet also surprise at the enemy's behaviour. *'There are very few enemy but they are being very cleverly used. They fight in very small combat gp. – a tank, a team of snipers who are probably O.R.'s* [i.e., 'Other Ranks', in other words, not specialist snipers as Tweedie would understand the term], *an MG gp and so on… Only once were GERMAN Infantry seen in large numbers. They will make "battle noises" but they will not come in unless they are on a certainty.'*[20]

Most likely, the Germans' tactics were heavily influenced by the lack of armour to overcome the fire of determined defenders backed by copious artillery support. All German accounts so far discovered credit *Frundsberg Sturmgeschütze* (of 7 or 8 *Kompanie*, 10. *SS-Panzerregiment*) with penetrating the village of Gavrus. This now appears inaccurate. Assuming that some of these assault guns may have crossed northwards from Hill 113 even as far as Bougy, it is unlikely that they did any more than offer fire support from safely outside the village. Aerial photography clearly reveals traces of tracked vehicles manoeuvring to give supporting fire from the south west of the village. Such fire support, reinforced later in the evening by assault engineer detachments with flame-

Gavrus on 3 July 1944.

German armour was active in the open fields but hesitant to close the Gavrus defences.

throwers, undoubtedly ensured that the southernmost part of Gavrus village was cleared of defenders (enabling the corps commander to claim the village 'taken'). But in Gavrus itself, photographic evidence confirms that one of the 'Tigers' reported destroyed by the Argylls (and quite possibly the only tank destroyed within the village) was a *Panzer IV*, of either *5.* or *6. Kompanie*.

Meanwhile, late in the day, as the armoured battle continued to rage over the open slopes between Hill 113 and the wooded Odon valley, elements of *22. Regiment* succeeded in skirting the orchards south of Gavrus and infiltrating the southern slopes of the wooded Odon valley. But once again, this was not an assault in overwhelming force: merely enough to cause concern to the infantry of 11th Armoured Division (patrols of 8th RB and 2nd KRRC, also the westernmost company of the Herefords dug in at les Vilains). By the end of the day, the Argylls still held the Gavrus bridges and the surrounding woods of the Odon valley. The village itself was effectively 'no man's land', as British artillery pounded the area. In its first day of combat in Normandy, Harmel's *Frundsberg* had fallen far short of its objectives.

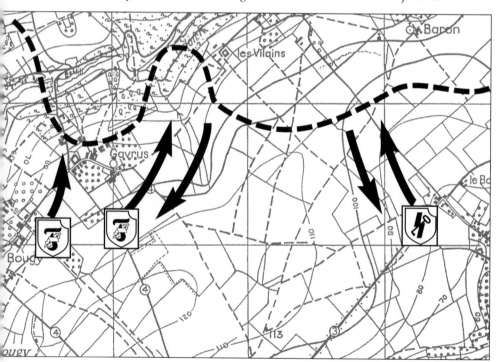

Late in the day the Odon valley remained in British hands.

HOHENSTAUFEN vs 46 BRIGADE

Like the *Frundsberg*, the *9. SS-Panzerdivision 'Hohenstaufen'* had intended to initiate its first Normandy battle at 06.00 hours. Like them, the divisional artillery worked through the night to bring up the guns, establish firing positions, and construct command and communications bunkers. By

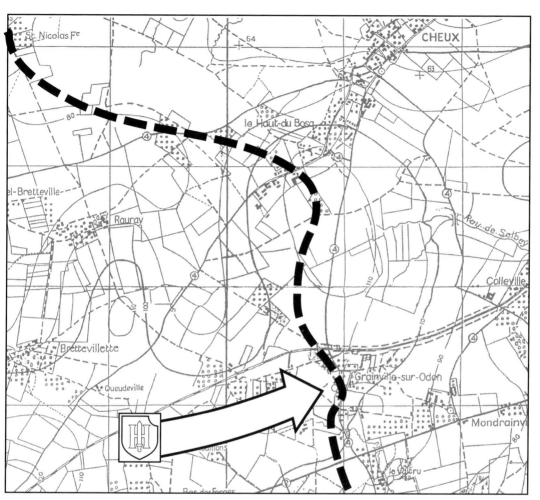

The first *Hohnstaufen* blow fell along the RN 175 highway.

morning, all was more-or-less ready, and from 08.30 hours the two forward and the single reserve battalions of 46th (Highland) Brigade astride the RN 175 Caen to Villers-Bocage road started to take losses from heavy artillery and mortar bombardment. But, as with the *Frundsberg*, the infantry intended to storm the line of the road in the wake of the artillery 'softening up' were far from ready. Held up by late arrivals, plagued by air attack, both *19.* and *20. Panzergrenadierregimenter* were forced to put back their hour of departure.

Only at about 14.00 hours did the advance get under way. Supported by a full, two-battalion tank regiment, plus surviving elements of Weidinger's *3. Panzerregiment* tanks, the objective was to break the western defences of the Scottish Corridor between the main road and the railway, burst through the Allied communications between Cheux and Mouen, and link hands with German forces heading west from the area of Carpiquet. Two battalions of *20. Panzergrenadierregiment* moved against the Cameronians in Grainville; two battalions of *19. Regiment* straight up the RN 175 towards the 7th Seaforth Highlanders holding le Valtru.

The tide broke over the forward companies. First to be hit was the Seaforth's C Company, in their 'breakwater' position astride the highway. They were overrun. A pair of *Panzer IV* suddenly appeared on the road to their front, hull-down below the crest of the road leading up from le Bas des Forges. The tanks quickly knocked out two antitank guns [21] and suppressed the two forward platoons with machine guns until German infantry swept over the entire position. Elements of C Company's third, reserve platoon survived to rejoin the main body at le Valtru, with the news that company commander Major Telfer was dead, and that their Lieutenant Woodall and Captain Hendry (of A Company) had been last seen stalking the attackers with a PIAT. (It was later claimed that Hendry had knocked one of them out before

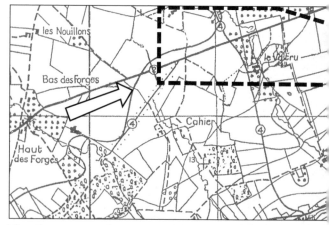

The German assault came straight up the RN 175.

The view north up the road from Gavrus: open fields to the west.

To the east, stone buildings and hedgerows of le Valtru.

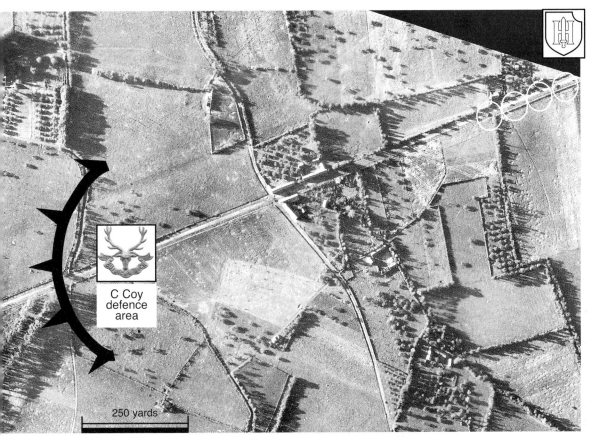

C Coy
defence
area

250 yards

After C Company, Seaforth Highlanders, was overrun four Panzer IV rampaged through the village of le Valtru before being knocked out.

dying of his wounds.) A wave of two hundred *Panzergrenadiere* then approached le Valtru itself. They were slowed by the infantry and stopped dead by the full force of the eight guns of 531 Field Battery, Royal Artillery. Now, as throughout the European campaign, the battery responded quickly and effectively to the call of 'their' infantry battalion.

Under cover of a renewed German bombardment, four *Panzer IV* rushed the Seaforth battalion position, firing in all directions as they plunged past the crossroads. The 2 i.c.'s carrier was brewed up by a 7.5cm shell, breaking Major Johnson's leg. More *Panzergrenadiere* came close behind, in company strength. Confusion followed. Some enemy infantry penetrated a short way past le Valtru to Mondrainville where they ran into the reserve battalion of 46 Brigade. After a fierce fight they were beaten off by the 2nd Glasgow Highlanders, supported by Churchill tanks. At the crossroads, the Seaforth's Lieutenant-Colonel Grant led by example, dashing from gun to gun, ensuring cohesion between companies after the loss of two company commanders, until himself hit in the leg and evacuated. Grant's D.S.O. recommendation later cited him as responsible for the defenders' elimination of the four

Lookout

intruding tanks. One individual inspired by the colonel was Corporal Cunningham of the Carrier Platoon. He loosed a PIAT bomb at a passing *Panzer IV*, but the tank moved on past intervening trees; Cunningham jumped out of his roadside slit trench to thump a second bomb into the back of the tank, oblivious to yet another following. Eventually, '*Every anti-tank weapon was let loose, and all four were destroyed. It was a great moment. These four "flamers" however, acted as an aiming mark throughout the rest of the day and night which followed.*'[22] With their front line silhouetted from behind by the blazing wrecks, the Seaforth continued to suffer enemy fire as late as 22.00 hours, when a further two officers were lost to mortar bombs, for a total of six killed and four wounded that day in defence of le Valtru. But still they held.

Barely five hundred yards to the north of the Seaforth position, the 9th Cameronians in Grainville had been severely mortared during the morning, suffering thirty casualties. The battalion noted the assault that overran the Seaforth's forward company (no doubt witnessed by the Cameronians' own forward outpost in the château). But not until 16.00 hours did the *Hohenstaufen* wave reach Grainville.

The Germans won the first round, reaching the château un-detected due to the Bren gunner on lookout over their line of approach being killed before he could sound a

Right: The straggling village of Grainville-sur-Odon ringed by orchards.

Deep railway cutting

Vital railway crossing

Church

Château

RN 175

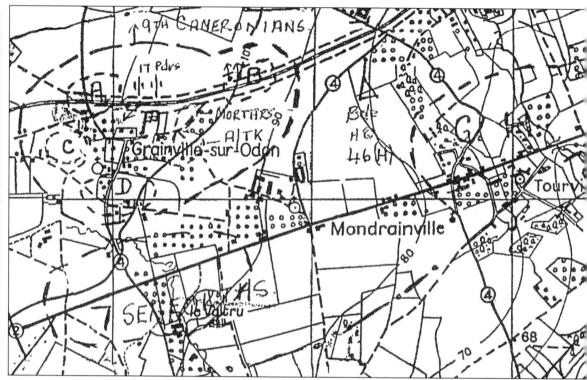

9th Cameronians' map showing rifle company and support elements' dispositions on 29 June, also neighbouring battalions and 46 Brigade HQ positions.

warning. The company headquarters was penetrated and severe hand-to-hand fighting ensued. The Cameronians' C Company was not overrun, but while the ground was held, further enemies infiltrated past. Colonel Villiers was on his way forward to investigate C Company's position when his carrier was blown up by a (British) mine. The unconscious Villiers was helped by his adjutant and driver to a defended forward position in a nearby house which soon became caught up in the general *mêlée*. The house caught fire, but its small garrison fought on. Only after a full hour was the colonel able to rejoin Battalion HQ, to the welcome news that C Company was still holding. Nevertheless, pandemonium reigned through the afternoon and into the evening.

Brigadier Barber's 46th (Highland) Brigade was drawn up in a tight triangle. With all telephone lines cut, he was reliant on liaison officers' reports. News from the front was patchy. The Seaforth and the Cameronians continued to hold, albeit precariously; the Glasgow Highlanders in close reserve were kept busy mopping up bands of Germans who were leaking through the confusion of the forward areas. But, with 43rd Infantry Division now moving up to cover the eastern flank of the Scottish Corridor, 15th Scottish was able to reinforce the vital Grainville-le Valtru sector. From 20.00 hours, Barber was given not only 7th RTR, but also 10th HLI and 2nd

Gordons, on temporary transfer from 227 Brigade.[23] Reinforced by a company of 10th HLI, the Cameronians' fight for Grainville died down. At 23.00 hours, Brigadier Barber reported all his brigade's positions intact.

HOHENSTAUFEN vs 44 BRIGADE

The German wave rolled ever further north, seeking a weak point through which to penetrate the western flank of the Scottish Corridor. North of the railway that spanned the battlefield, the corridor was worryingly narrow.

9. SS Panzerdivision Hohenstaufen.

44 BRIGADE

6th King's Own Scottish Borderers

8th Royal Scots

6th Royal Scots Fusiliers

Five miles back behind the bitter fight raging over Hill 112, there was still only one dirt road supporting the formations of VIII Corps. From Cheux to Colleville columns of soft-skin vehicles moved over open ground, braving spasmodic German fire from both east and west.

During the previous evening, Brigadier Money's 44th (Lowland) Brigade had made a concerted effort to open up a second, parallel artery to the west. With 6th King's Own Scottish Borderers firmly established around le Haut-du-Bosq, a brigade 'O' group had been held at 15.30, and by 17.00 hours 8th Royal Scots were ready to set off south from a Start Line close to the Fontenay-Caen road. Opposition was supposed to be light – no more than snipers left behind by a withdrawing enemy. The battalion accordingly moved in a shallow skirmishing line, three companies up, supported by the Churchill tanks of A and B Squadrons, 7th RTR and the seventeen-pounder M10s of Q Battery, 21st Antitank Regiment. The objective was the railway line north of Grainville. The infantry were led to expect little more than a 'partridge drive' (though the crews of 7th Tanks, still recovering from the shock of 27 June, remained 'rather sceptical about this').

The advance at first met only light resistance. The Royal Scots passed the Borderers' positions, while the tank men skirted the open ground around Cheux, looking askance at the 'Mk IV woods' by the Salbey Stream where they had come to grief two days before. But from 20.50 hours, enemy opposition stiffened. The infantry called on the tanks, but the Churchills had now moved from open ground into dense bocage country, *'poking their noses gently through the hedges before bounding to the next one,' whereupon, 'To add to the general discomfort it was discovered that several Panthers were prowling about in the woods 300 yards in front.'*[24] It appeared that further progress would require a set-piece attack. (Had the Royal Scots but known, less than a half-mile ahead, just beyond their railway objective, the Cameronians were now established in Grainville.) A formal assault would require reconnoitring the ground ahead, so in the failing light the Royal Scots dug in for the night along the line of the Belleval château's tree-lined ornamental front drive. The tanks fell back a short way to a forward leaguer, *'camouflaged and feeling only vaguely secure in the knowledge that there were infantry in the ditch in front… It is not good for morale to awake at 2 o'clock in the morning to hear a Panther prowling about.'*[25]

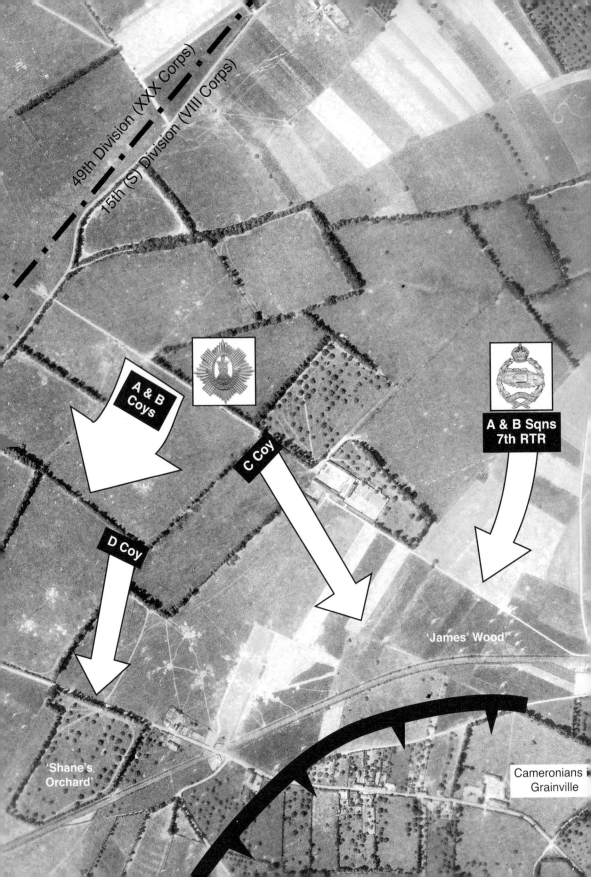

49th Division (XXX Corps)

15th (S) Division (VIII Corps)

A & B Coys

C Coy

D Coy

A & B Sqns 7th RTR

'James' Wood"

'Shane's Orchard'

Cameronians Grainville

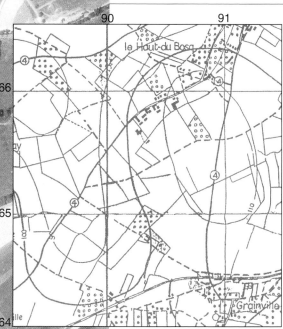

Shortly after the break of day on 29 June, the Royal Scots' Lieutenant-Colonel Delacombe held an O Group at 05.00 hours. His revised plan represented the orthodox approach to stiff opposition: a set-piece battalion attack with just two companies forward and plenty of artillery. First, while artillery prepared the way, A and B Companies would clear the hedgerow-lined fields to their immediate front. In the second phase, C and D Companies would bound through to secure a half-mile stretch of the railway line: C taking the area around 907646 'James' Wood' and D 'Shane's orchard' at 899643. B Squadron's tanks would 'run the gauntlet' over the open ground around the left flank to a position where they could cover the infantry advance.

Strong opposition was encountered from the start. To the discomfort of enemy machine gun and mortar fire were added British 25-pounder rounds falling short: the distant guns' targets were barely three hundred yards ahead of the Royals' Start Line. B Squadron's dash (insofar as Churchills moving cross-country could 'dash'!) was achieved at the cost of two tanks brewed by infantry fire. A Squadron followed. As they passed the burning wrecks, they lost squadron leader Major Coombes to a mortar shard that pierced his helmet. Then, lining up together the two squadrons and the accompanying M10s began a duel that would last most of the afternoon. *'A quick look along the vane sight and a snappy "300 yards, fire!" was answered by the gunner with "But I can't see anything." A well placed kick however and his foot went down with good results. Two more followed with the speed of a Bofors. The crew relaxed slightly... So the day wore on with almost continuous firing as a single shot from one side would be answered with a volley from the other.'*[26]

With the tanks' supporting fire, C Company succeeded in establishing themselves on the railway line around 'James' Wood'. But only with the greatest difficulty did D Company penetrate 'Shane's Orchard', and they were promptly thrown out by the customary German counter-attack[27]. They were forced back as far as B Company's hedgerow. Later in the day a further attempt by D Company, reinforced by a B Company platoon, once again achieved a toe-hold on the orchard. But losses were mounting remorselessly. The brigadier judged the time right to reinforce the fight. 6th KOSB moved up on the right and at 14.00 hours, 6th Royal Scots Fusiliers were ordered to the assistance of the hard pressed 8th Royal Scots.

Belleval château: British and German armour traded shots across these open fields.

C and D Companies of the 6th RSF were executing that particularly difficult task of relieving a friendly force under fire when both they and the disengaging 8th RS companies were hit by the full force of the Hohenstaufen assault. 8th RS had already lost most of their own antitank guns, picked off by the fire of German tanks, lying back in hull-down positions, and the supporting M10s had likewise suffered losses. Exploiting the opportunity, an armoured infantry assault swept through the orchard position. The result was confusion. Two armoured flame-throwing vehicles made their way into the company areas, *'where they milled round and killed a lot of men in a particularly*

The château at the heart of the substantial Belleval estate.

Flamethrowers 'milled around and killed a lot of men'.

unpleasant manner before they withdrew.'[28]

The line wavered and nearly broke. The Royals' D Company, anticipating and indeed busy executing its withdrawal from the battle, was overrun. *'Tanks charged the forward companies of the "Royals" at the dreadful moment when they were moving out of their trenches during a relief.'*[29] The relieving 6th RSF later admitted that 'the posns were never really firmly taken over.' The orchard was abandoned and a new defensive line established on the south face of the Belleval estate. Still the outcome was uncertain; groups of enemy infantry infiltrated the front line. Brigadier Money ordered his remaining battalion, the 6th KOSB, to assist, and their B and C Companies advanced with tank support. When 15th Scottish Division called for further reinforcements, they were willingly provided by VIII Corps – indeed, with 4th Armoured Brigade given warning orders to intervene, there were potentially more British tanks available than could effectively be deployed in the area. The 44th Brigade line held.

So was established a pattern that would be repeated over the hours and days to come. German forces were able with their superior weapons and tactics to hold ground with minimal numbers, and trained to recover ground lost with rapid counter-attacks. This had worked in Russia. But against prepared British positions the Germans were being stopped dead. The German infantry depended on mortaring and machine gun fire to suppress defenders and permit outflanking and infiltration. But they wilted under the rapid response of the Royal Artillery field regiments. The tanks enjoyed

SS-Oberführer **Heinz Harmel issuing orders from his command half-track.**

superiority in armoured duels, but proved unable to penetrate multiple layers of antitank artillery (supplemented on occasion by aerial attack). Nor should be forgotten the damage inflicted by the Royal Artillery behind the front line: on the approach to the battlefield; and by the disruption inflicted on enemy command and control. The Germans experienced devastating counter-battery fire; resupply of fuel and ammunition was problematic; identified radio locations were rapidly neutralized; maintaining field telephone lines under British artillery fire was a task often suicidal and sometimes impossible.

By the evening when the firing died down, both battalions of Royals were exhausted, drawn out of the line and replaced along the whole 44 Brigade front by the Borderers. The thirteen Churchills of A and B Squadrons still running pulled back to refit: *'As far as we were concerned it was a bloody awful day.'* Far from a second north-south road being opened, the link between 44 and 46 Brigades, across the railway line, was tenuous at best and certainly not a route for traffic. Further south, the road between le Valtru and Gavrus was now covered by enemy fire, the Argylls increasingly isolated in Gavrus. Much had been lost, and little visibly gained by the British in the day's action. But neither had the Germans' commitment of their strategic reserve yet yielded any worthwhile payback, and their finely-honed attack formations were becoming blunted.

11th ARMOURED PULLED BACK

Back to the south of the Odon, as the afternoon wore on the *Frundsberg* threat from the west became increasingly evident. Nevertheless, 8th RB were maintaining their position on top of Hill 112, and the tanks on the slopes below were holding their ground, while giving the fire support needed. Pip Roberts went forward in the afternoon to observe that side of the battlefield, then returned about 16.00 hours to Roscoe Harvey's Tac HQ above Tourmauville. There he found, 'everyone in 29th Armoured Brigade seemed rather pleased with themselves – and rightly.' Just as the general broke the news to the brigadier that further advance was to be temporarily suspended, the 44th RTR battle flared up, now only a short way to the west. Roberts' news of impending enemy pressure was underscored when, *'the "overs" meant for 44th Royal Tanks were coming very close to me and I thought I should withdraw with what dignity I could.'*[30] Even Harvey, notorious for seeking positions with direct line of sight to the enemy, saw the need to relocate. Shortly after, he moved his Tac HQ five hundred yards uphill to the south east.

It is clear that Roberts became increasingly frustrated by directives from VIII Corps as the battle wore on. During the afternoon of 29 June, Corps demanded that 3rd County of London Yeomanry be removed from Roberts' command to support 15th Scottish Division. 3rd CLY's own brigadier, well aware of the plight of 15th Scottish, nevertheless felt the order unnecessary,

The bottom of the Scottish corridor at the end of 29 June: the Argylls isolated in Gavrus.

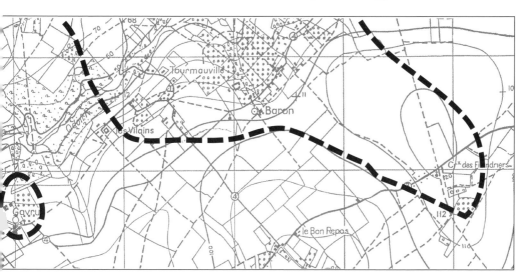

since 2nd Northants Yeomanry's two squadrons of Cromwell tanks were on hand and adequate to support the infantry; besides, he added, the battleground north of the Odon was already overcrowded. Roberts concurred with the brigadier. But VIII Corps insisted. While Roberts exuded confidence, O'Connor was desperately concerned by the *Hohenstaufen* threat to 44th Brigade. Next, at 19.15 hours, Corps ordered 44th RTR to be released north of the Odon. No doubt to their relief, the battalion moved out. The 23rd Hussars took over their section of the diminished bridgehead, while 11th Armoured suspended traffic movements on the divisional centre line to permit the 44th to exit northwards.

If these developments added to Roberts' resentment at micro-management of his division's battle by VIII Corps, worse was to come. At 22.00 hours arrived the order for his tank regiments to abandon the bridgehead altogether. Roberts was to leave his infantry brigade behind, under command of 15th Scottish, as of 23.59 hours. 29 Brigade was to pull north, clear of the battle zone, as soon as possible. The move was carried out between 23.00 and 04.00 hours: the order-of-march being the Fifes, the vehicles of 8th RB, and 3rd RTR, with the Hussars providing the rearguard above the little Tourmauville bridge.

Feelings about the withdrawal were mixed. It will continue to be debated. Brigadier Harvey was unsurprisingly resentful. General Roberts chose not to record his own feelings in print, but the attitude of 11th Armoured headquarters was clearly, if tactfully, expressed in the divisional history. *'The wisdom of these decisions is not here questioned; but the general feeling that, in spite of tank losses a further sweep southwards from Hill 112 coupled with the continued repulse of enemy attacks on the flanks, was well within its powers, was indicative of the high state of the division's morale.'* [31] The historian of 23rd Hussars reflected that, *'It seemed a pity to be giving up ground so hardly won.'* [32] On the other hand, many shared the feelings of Bill Close that, *'Perhaps there was some feeling of disappointment in the Division that we were not able to proceed, but I think there were few from 3RTR who regretted leaving Hill 112.'* [33]

General O'Connor's biographer, generally sympathetic to his subject, records that, *'The withdrawal of the armour was probably a mistake, though understandable.'* [34] This view is of course informed by hindsight. The ground so hard won and then abandoned would prove even harder to regain in the bitter and protracted fighting over Hill 112 that was to follow in July. In the course of 29 June, the impressive concentration of experienced Panzer divisions on the British front and the precarious communications with the bridgehead – a single river crossing at the end of a narrow salient – were daunting challenges. Alongside O'Connor's evident slowness in executing the withdrawal order, it should also be remembered that the responsibility for the decision lay squarely with Dempsey.

Lieutenant-General Dempsey's decision to pull back from the Odon bridgehead has been much criticized by historians as 'understandable but unfortunate',[35] his conduct of the battle 'marred by the tragedy that [he] misread the balance of advantage.'[36] Ironically, it was the very failure of II.

Panzerkorps on 29 June that led Dempsey to conclude that its main blow was still to be struck. An understandable misjudgement. Though late on 29 June documents revealing the German plan were found on a *Hohenstaufen* officer, Dempsey appears – inexplicably – not to have been informed. What he did see was an VIII Corps intelligence report which concluded that 'tomorrow's attack is likely to be stronger.'

In one vital detail Dempsey was prescient. He was personally convinced that the key to the present battle was no longer the Orne River crossings, nor Hill 112. In fact his objective was no longer territorial at all. The strategic goal was now simply to force commitment of the German armoured reserves. The tactical objective was to bring on a fight in which the Germans' offensive capability would be written-down. Dempsey recognised that now, *'the vital spot to hold was the Rauray gap… where the Germans would strike.'*[37] His priority was proved correct: this boundary between VIII and XXX Corps, between 15th Scottish and 49th West Riding Divisions, between 6th KOSB and the 1st Tyneside Scottish, was to be the focal point of the battle ahead.

Last of all of 29 Brigade to leave the Odon bridgehead came the riflemen, creeping down the hill they had held, marching back over the river and away past Cheux to rejoin their vehicles at Norrey. As the sun rose, 'Even God never knew how good it was for us to see the sun again… we wondered if all warfare was like this.'[38]

References

(1) According to the VIII Corps War Diary, the order was timed at 21.00 hours, 28 June; when it was received is not entirely clear.

(2) Roberts, p 166

(3) Close, p 110-111

(4) 8th Rifle Brigade and 11th Armoured War Diaries; *The Rifle Brigade in the Second World War,* R H W S Hastings, p 357. Once again, note that whatever Germans may have been involved, there were no *Tiger* tanks present.

(5) 3rd RTR War Diary

(6) Hastings, *Rifle Brigade,* p 358

(7) This was standard practice by 4th Armoured Brigade in June. Units equipped with Duplex Drive ('DD') amphibious Sherman tanks often adopted the system as their Fireflies could not be converted and had to be landed separately. Other formations simply decided for themselves whether to allocate one Firefly to each troop or form a troop of four Fireflies within each squadron.

(8) *A History of the 44th Royal Tank Regiment in the War of 1939-45* Part III, G C Hopkinson, p 140

(9) 44th RTR War Diary

(10) 44th RTR War Diary

(11) 2nd KRRC War Diary

(12) Hopkinson, p 141

(13) From post-war interrogation, quoted in Jackson, *Eighth Corps,* p 52

(14) As detailed in Appendix IV, the division's tank regiment lacked its first Abteilung, absent while being re-equipped. Estimates of the combat strength of the second battalion's four companies are based on reports made on 1 June, giving *Kompanien 5 & 6* between them 32 combat-ready *Panzer IV* and *Kompanien 7 & 8* a total of 34 *Sturmgeschütze III*. Whatever the actual availability on the morning of 29 June, it is unlikely that higher numbers were present.

(15) *10. SS-Panzer-Division,* Jean-Luc Leleu, p 65

(16) Tieke, p 91

(17) Sad to relate, the British divisional history, Martin's *Fifteenth Scottish* is unreliable for events south of the Odon on 29 June. Among several factual errors, the attacking enemy division is wrongly identified as *9. SS-Panzer.*

(18) Since the author's first detailed study of this ground in 1997, new housing has filled these orchards. Nevertheless, at the time of writing, the wall running north from the Gavrus-Bougy road still remains as it was left in 1944: loopholed for infantry movement and fire, and breached in places where later-arriving vehicles appear to have crashed through.

(19) These fields were built-over in 2005 by yet more houses.

(20) After-action report by Lieutenant-Colonel Tweedie, original at Stirling Castle

(21) The battalion War Diary gives one enemy tank and one gun, but appears inaccurate in various details of the actions of 29 June. The usual keeper of the diary, Intelligence Officer Lieutenant Mackintosh, had been one of three officers killed the previous day. The author follows the later, more considered account in the regimental history: J Sym, *Seaforth Highlanders*

(22) Martin, p 48

(23) Remarkably, leaving Brigadier Mackintosh-Walker in Colleville commanding only the 2nd Argylls, in far-off Gavrus! The last-minute diversion of these two units from the planned relief of their sister battalion in Gavrus is indicative of the concern being felt at VIII Corps.

(24) *7th RTR "A" Squadron Diary*, prepared by R Joscelyne, p 16. Identification of the enemy as *Panther* tanks was probably accurate, though at this time they were most likely not '1st SS' as thought but survivors of *3. Panzerregiment.*

(25) Martin, *Fifteenth Scottish* mistakenly refers to Belleval château as the 'Château of Grainville' (p 46-48). Other regimental histories have followed Martin's mistake. This is presumably caused by different regiments' references to the place, whose name they clearly did not know, as being near Grainville. The two châteaux are barely a half-mile apart, though separated by the railway (today by a four-lane highway), and neither was named on the British Army map in use in 1944.

(26) Joscelyne, p 17

(27) The customary German *Gegenstoss*, a hasty response before the attackers could settle on the position; only when this was impossible was the more lengthy and deliberate *Gegenangriff* to be adopted.

(28) Martin, p 47. Contrary to British reports of 'flame-throwing tanks', these were in fact *SdKfz 251/16* half-tracks mounting twin flame-projectors (also carrying a third, portable flamethrower for separate use), open topped and lightly armoured but potentially devastating to infantry morale if they could achieve surprise, short range attacks, as was the case here. Note that, contrary to widespread belief, most *Panzergrenadier* units were not armoured infantry: of the *Hohenstaufen's* six *Panzergrenadier* battalions only one, *III./20. PzGrRgt.* had armoured half-tracks. The few of these vehicles remaining appear to have been committed on 44 Brigade front.

(29) Woollcombe, p 67

(30) Roberts, p 166

(31) Palamountain, 1945, p 20

(32) Bishop, *23rd Hussars*, p 61

(33) Close, p 112

(34) Baynes, p 192-193

(35) D'Este, p 242

(36) *Overlord*, Max Hastings, p 169

(37) Hart, p 146

(38) *From the Beaches to the Baltic*, Noel Bell, p 17-18

Chapter 8

THURSDAY 29 – FRIDAY 30 JUNE: THE ARGYLLS BESIEGED

The Argylls found the morning of 29 June 'rather a confused period'.[1] The men were pleased with the success of their first fight. At the spearhead of their division they had led the way across the Odon, and then gone on to clear a second crossing. Yet, to the Argylls' mystification, there had been no follow-through along this second route. The road north to le Valtru was still open, though sporadically swept by fire. Some of the battalion transport had managed to work its way to the unit, struggling through traffic clogging all the country roads north of Gavrus to bring up a late breakfast. However, in spite of the waiting bridges, 11th Armoured Division was nowhere to be seen. The Argylls awaited developments.

Gavrus on 24 June. Aerial photography tends to 'flatten out' the remarkably steep cleft of the Odon valley.

29 JUNE, MORNING

After a fairly quiet night, interrupted only occasionally by random enemy machine gun fire, the battalion took stock of its isolated position. As the Argylls' history relates, 'It was an awkward place to hold.'[2] Though the defensive perimeter was not wide, barely five hundred yards across, lines of sight were obstructed by the steep and tree-clad river valley. Battalion headquarters was established north of the river. Also on the northern bank was D Company in battalion reserve; nearby were elements of Support Company: the Mortar Platoon's six three-inch mortars in the small quarry to the east of the road, and the Carrier Platoon dug in around their vehicles to the west. Positions high in the woods north of the river afforded glimpses of the rooftops of Gavrus, but little more.[3] Directly ahead,

The northern bridge. Beyond the southern bridge the road climbs steeply up to Gavrus. Rooftops just visible (in June) across the deep cleft of the valley.

Position of Argylls' 'No.6' six-pounder gun covering bridge. from the east.

between the steep slopes of the Odon valley, a narrow strip of level pasture separated the two branches of the river. Straight across that pasture ran the north-south causeway linking a pair of small stone bridges. This was the only practicable crossing for any vehicles for some distance in either direction over waterways which, though narrow and shallow, were nevertheless lined by deep and steep river banks. Two six-pounder guns of the Antitank Platoon covered the northern bridge, the limit of their effective line of sight. The three rifle companies on the far, southern side of the river likewise had little or no visual contact with each other, nor with battalion HQ. On the left of the bridgehead, A Company held the woods to the south east; on the right C Company held the wooded arc between the road and the river to the south west. Pushed forward, up the narrow lane as far as the outermost houses at the bottom of the village, B Company stood astride the road.

The battalion was tired. While officers supervised the digging of extra defensive positions, the men were glad of any rest they could get. They were glad also when civilians from the village above appeared bearing gifts of eggs and milk. Officers however remained mindful of the fact that, until relief arrived, they were still in the 'front line', with only the enemy ahead, a fact brought home when the villagers handed over a surrendered Austrian prisoner.[4] There was concern over the growing numbers of civilians milling around in the village, up the hill in 'no man's land'.

Nearest to the emerging village people was B Company. The company commander Major McElwee led a party up through the village, intent on discussing with the village authorities how to control the movement of civilians, and also with a view to reconnoitring new positions to be occupied when – presumably – the bridgehead was reinforced and expanded. Arriving at the crossroads at the top of the village, McElwee surveyed the landscape. The road leading down to the west towards the nearby village of Bougy held special interest as the French had reported German movement in that direction.

Major Fyfe, the C Company commander, was also interested in Bougy.

'No.5' six-pounder gun covering bridge from north.

Earlier, at first light, suspecting the area to be the source of harassing machine gun fire, he had personally set out with a Bren gun to investigate. Somewhere in the vicinity of the Bougy road he met the enemy and 'had rather the worst of the encounter'. Later, not to be outdone and alerted to a German armoured car said to be operating along the Bougy road, Fyfe ordered a fighting patrol in that direction, also sending Sergeant Brand's six-pounder antitank gun out to a forward position covering the road. From his crossroads vantage point, McElwee spotted Brand's gun and ordered forward a B Company section under Lieutenant Edwards (11 Platoon commander, a Canadian) to give it some support. On arrival at Brand's gun, Bill Edwards observed the C Company patrol sweeping forward and took matters into his own hands, trying his hand at a 'one man stalk' in search of Germans flushed-out of the corn by the C Company 'beaters'. Instead, the lieutenant got only fifteen yards before being wounded in the foot (and narrowly escaping worse as a bullet lodged in his breast-pocket cigarette case!).

As Edwards was carried off and Corporal 'Blondie' Bell took over the section, Sergeant Brand's gun crew now caught glimpses of the suspected armoured car. Moving on the slightly sunken road, it was hull-down from their vantage point. Bertie Brand, Davy Trail the number one, and Jimmy Campbell the number two conferred urgently. When their new 'discarding sabot' ammunition had been issued just days earlier, they had been told of the unusual trajectory of this previously 'hush hush' round, dipping after leaving the muzzle then rising again. The gunners reasoned that if they set elevation by lining up on the roadside, barely 150 yards away, and fired at the German's muzzle flash, the round might just skim

A German armoured car was operating along the Bougy road.

the earth bank low enough to do some damage. As Jimmy Campbell recalled, 'It worked. As soon as the next round was fired, he fled.'[5] No more was heard of the armoured car, presumably on a probing reconnaissance mission ahead of *10. SS-Panzerdivision*. The gunners were later to learn that their Antitank Platoon 2 i.c., the much respected Channel Islander Lieutenant Jack Cornish, had been killed that morning high on the north bank of the river by a stray bullet, quite possibly from the armoured car. The Argylls had suffered their first officer fatality of the campaign.

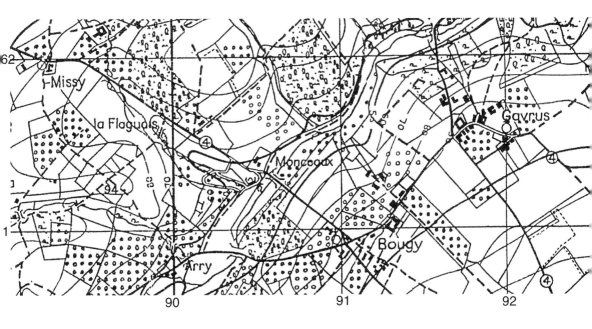

29 JUNE, AFTERNOON

As the morning wore on, Battalion HQ was in radio communication with the three companies south of the river, but had little inkling of events beyond the battalion perimeter. Only at 13.30 hours was a warning order received indicating the intentions of 227th Brigade. The Argylls were to prepare to take yet another Odon crossing: the bridge at Monceaux, a mile upstream.[6]

South of the river, Major McElwee supervised a late dinner, delayed by his prolonged recce through the village. Next, he ordered B Company to prepare for an afternoon of organized rest (a necessary precaution in case of a later move). Tossing a coin with the Company Sergeant Major, the officer won and prepared to rest first. But some time later, Bill McElwee awoke with an uneasy feeling. *'There had been intermittent and apparently very casual shelling and mortaring during the morning and there was no sudden increase of volume. I tried to analyse the difference… but I could not. I only knew that it felt purposeful and aggressive.'* The history master from Stowe School was starting to learn to 'read' the battle. Preparing to join the men in rest, he had removed his 'tin hat' and pack. Now, with just his Balmoral[7] on his head and sticking his revolver in his pocket, he brushed aside the protests of his CSM and set off to check that Corporal Bell's outlying section were wide awake.

Awake the men were, though hardly alert. The officer found them gossiping and keeping no proper look-out: years of training had still not prepared them for the reality of battle. A single glance over the hedge they were 'defending' revealed to McElwee's horror an extended line of German infantry approaching. The time was about 15.10 hours. Things then moved

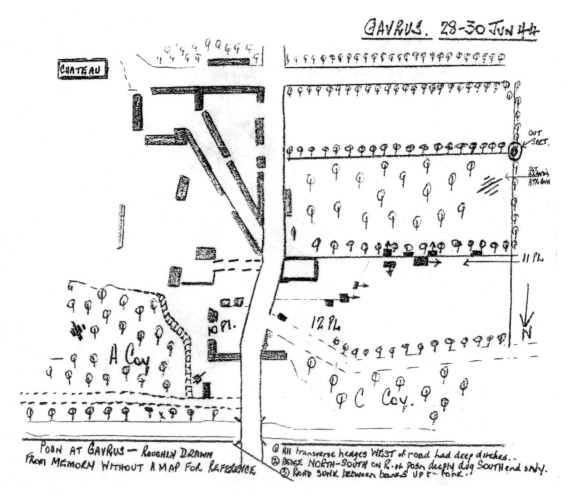

Major McElwee's sketch map 'from memory without a map for reference'.

quickly. McElwee ordered Sergeant Brand's gun out of the position. *'Major McElwee came dashing up and told us, "Get that six-pounder out of here!" Well, you never saw a six-pounder getting out of action and limbered up on the back of a carrier quicker in your life. All the stores were hauled aboard. We didn't need any prompting and as we left we came under machine gun fire.'*[8] While the gun retired across the river to the HQ area, the rifle section was pulled back two hundred yards into 11 Platoon's main position, to the west of the road. McElwee informed the CO of the situation via the company 18 Set, then dashed across the road to the 10 Platoon position. All was quiet there: the whole attack seemed to be concentrated on B Company's right, to the west of the road.

C Company offered help, which McElwee gratefully accepted. With their 14 Platoon edging up behind B Company's right flank, McElwee could afford to edge his own 12 Platoon forward to re-occupy some positions they had

The reality: Sergeant 'Bertie' Brand's six-pounder covered the Bougy road.

previously dug by the road, behind 11 Platoon's right. But 11 Platoon continued to bear the brunt of the fight, now under command of B Company's 2 i.c. Captain Mackenzie, following the loss of both Bill Edwards and the platoon sergeant. McElwee rejoined 11 Platoon, since *'In that close country of thick hedges it was quite impossible to see what was happening from Coy HQ, back*

The Germans' front line and their view east from the wall towards 11 Platoon position. This field is today built-over.

with 12 Pl and the only place from which I could contact the battle at all was up in front.' Already the infantry were learning lessons for which no amount of training had prepared them. As Colonel Tweedie was shortly after to record: *'Fighting in this country which consists of woods, high hedges and sunken roads is a job all on its own... If ever there was a Pl and Sec Comd battle this is... Man management by the Pl and Section comd cannot be overstressed.'*[9]

The fire fight continued. To McElwee's evident surprise, the Germans showed little inclination to close the range and rush the defenders, as would have been standard British 'Battle Drill', but remained content to stand off and pour in heavy automatic fire across the open fields in front of 11 Platoon. Enemy artillery also put in one heavy strike, and several times mortar fire came down, but the defenders were heartened by the apparent weight of their own artillery hitting the Germans. (In fact, unbeknown to the British infantry, merely reaching the firing line had already cost the enemy dearly, as Royal Artillery fire tasks and RAF fighter-bombers reached back over the battle zone.) The 11 Platoon two-inch mortar found its range and struck at Germans sheltering in the opposite ditch. At length (McElwee could not precisely fix the time), the incoming fire slackened. The first phase of the fight ended. McElwee *'came to the conclusion that we had won that bit of the battle at the cost of about three men wounded.'*

29 JUNE: EVENING AND NIGHT

After a brief lull, the second phase of the battle resumed with the approach of German armour. During the intermission, McElwee had received permission from Tweedie to lead a 10 Platoon patrol back up the village in search of positions from which flanking fire might be laid against any renewed assault on 11 Platoon's defended area. Thinking he could hear the sound of tanks, McElwee had his field glasses glued to the crossroads, unsure whether to expect a Sherman from Tourmauville or a German *'Tiger'* to appear. Then, as he turned to ask Corporal McLean where he thought the sound was coming from, *'the nose of the Tiger caught my eye about 12 yards away in the field.'* There quickly followed *'the precipitate and undignified withdrawal of myself and patrol down the street'*.

German tanks encountered during the battle for Gavrus were without exception described as *'Tigers'* by the Argylls. In fact, no *Tiger* tank appeared in the fight for Gavrus; the only German tanks on this battlefield were two companies of *Sturmgeschütz III*, later supported by a number of *Panzer IV*, all of *II. Bataillon, 10. SS-Panzerregiment*. Photographic as well as anecdotal evidence supports the view that only the tanks, not the turretless assault guns, actually penetrated the village of Gavrus on 29 June. This is not surprising since the *Sturmgeschütze* with their low-slung guns were at a grave disadvantage when advancing through dense terrain. One Frenchman, recognised after the war as a resistance worker, spoke with British officers during the battle and recalled his surprise that the only battlefield intelligence the Argylls were interested in was whether there were any *'Tigers'* about.

Duly warned by the major, Corporal Stewart lined up 10 Platoon's PIAT,

The main German threat came from fields to the west and lanes to the South.

and when the tank rolled into view he fired three successive rounds at it. At least two were observed to hit. The vehicle pulled back behind a wall, but when this was partially demolished by High Explosive rounds from the platoon two-inch mortar wielded by the Company Sergeant Major, the tank was seen to be burning satisfactorily. Heartened by this exchange, McElwee returned to 11 Platoon, still at the heart of the renewed action. There he found 'the same old fire fight', though now the enemy brought to bear the machine guns of two *'Tiger'* tanks.[10] Nevertheless, McElwee was by now growing in confidence. Only when one of the tanks started to approach the right of the defensive position did he become concerned. *'Having no A Tk gun I did not care to let it come too close, so I ordered MACKENZIE to engage it with the PIAT at extreme range.'* For this clumsy weapon, 'extreme range' could be anything up to one hundred yards. Three or four rounds were fired – no mean feat since recocking the spring of the firing mechanism could be awkward – and the tank sheered off. (Most if not all of the *Frundsberg Panzer IV* were equipped with *'Schürzen'*, metal 'aprons' hung about the suspension and turret, designed specifically to detonate prematurely such hollow charge rounds as fired by the PIAT; it seems more than likely that this tank crew may have been deterred by the loud explosions of the bombs even though none penetrated.)

Now begins one of the least well known episodes of the battle for Gavrus. It should be noted that it is by no means unusual for unit histories, especially those of British regiments, to omit mention of support received from other arms of service. At this stage of the fight, having earlier sent Sergeant Brand's antitank gun to the rear, McElwee realised the need to bolster the antitank defences on his right flank. *'We got up more PIAT amn to 11 Pl and the C.O. sent fwd two A Tk guns. I intercepted one of these and we manhandled it up the lanes and into the corner of the field in 12 Pl area, just in front of my carrier and Coy HQ. With that in posn I felt safe again and went fwd to 11 Pl to put in a fairly self-satisfied report into the C.O.'*

Six-pounder guns emplaced in the front line were not easily withdrawn.

What is not clear from this, nor indeed from any other surviving record of the 2nd Argylls, is that the six-pounder guns in question belonged not to the battalion's own Antitank Platoon, but to the Royal Artillery.[11] For EPSOM, the 97th Antitank Regiment's 346 Battery had been placed under command of 227th Infantry Brigade, and that battery's K Troop with its four six-pounder antitank guns under Lieutenant Morley accompanied 2nd A&SH. According to both the 346 Battery commander's personal account (handwritten on 3 July) and the Battery War Diary, K Troop fought on 29 June to the south (i.e., in front) of the Argylls' own antitank guns. The personal account records that, after K Troop had suffered mortar and MG fire, *'It is understood that Lt Morley was ordered to move a gun to a flank to counter a Tiger tank which the A.& S.H. claim to have hit with PIAT fire. Lt Morley took off a gun to do this job.'* The Battery diary subsequently added the detail that *'Lt Morley personally accompanied a gun to a point believed to be at 913617.* [This would place it at the heart of the C Company position, north-west of McElwee.] *Comd. C. Coy 2 A & S H saw Lt Morley directing the gun into action. Before the gun was properly in place the detachment incl. Lt. Morley were machine gunned.'*

It should be noted that, in addition to elements of the 97th Antitank Regiment, Colonel Tweedie also had under his nominal command a troop of the 91st (the VIII Corps antitank regiment). E Troop comprised four seventeen-pounder antitank guns, towed by Crusader tanks (turretless, converted to fully-tracked artillery tractors). Having only landed in Normandy on 27 June, E Troop was totally inexperienced. Somewhere along the road from le Valtru to the Gavrus bridges, they came under enemy fire. According to the (unusually candid) 145 Battery War Diary, *'E troop area became the centre of attraction, the results of which were not creditable, as some men thinking themselves cut off made their way back, through some bad error. I think their first experience of coming under fire was too much.'* E Troop returned to the fray the following day, only to suffer further casualties, losing all four guns and two tractors. Of the survivors, *'very few of them brought their kit and small arms.'* Whatever the combination of mismanagement and inexperience, the

E Troop's seventeen-pounders were towed by specialist Crusader tractors.

contribution of E Troop to the Gavrus action appears to have been minimal, although their plight emphasises the weight of fire brought down on the northern half of the battlefield. The presence of the tractors may account for some Argylls' observations of British 'tanks' on the northern slopes during the battle.

Although the River Odon was supposed to be the boundary between the two divisions of *II. SS-Panzerkorps*, the *Frundsberg* left flank gradually extended across to the northern slopes of the valley as the German infantry followed their standard practice of seeking to infiltrate forward and outflank the defenders. This, combined with a renewed German onslaught to their front, forced C Company to recoil. As the forward rifle sections fell back, the antitank gunners were left unprotected. Some fell and the rest were forced to abandon their gun. With nowhere else to go, the survivors later picked up rifles and fought on as infantry alongside the Argylls. The German troops followed the withdrawal, some of them now finding a sunken path between B and C Company positions, closing to McElwee's Company HQ behind 11 Platoon's right flank. Sections of C Company were driven back almost as far as the road.

McElwee was initially unaware of the C Company withdrawal. *'I shall never know exactly how the enemy penetrated the right rear of our posn. At one moment I was happily directing 11 Pl's battle. At the next I suddenly noticed that the crew of the A Tk gun were all flat on their faces, and the next after that an enemy LMG opened up on us from straight behind.'* McElwee does not elaborate on the fate of the artillerymen, but it appears likely that they numbered among the eighteen lost to K Troop that day. Thinking that 11 Platoon's fight was still the focal point of the battle, McElwee had not noticed

Parties of Germans infiltrated along hedgerow lined lanes. Note the abandoned carrier in McElwee's B Company area.

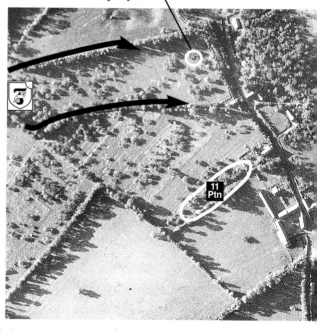

that most of 14 Platoon had been overrun, with only their right (i.e., northernmost, towards the river) section under Corporal Taylor still firing. Still, McElwee was not dispirited. *'This made the situation in 11 Pl's posn very unpleasant but not untenable. They were pinned down but could fight back on both sides.'* Confident of the platoon's ability to conduct an all-round defence, McElwee left the 18 Set with Mackenzie and set about trying to restore the situation.

From this point in the late afternoon, the Argylls' situation became very confused, with little or no central coordination. A Company, so far unengaged in the east of the village and now joined by some stragglers from C Company, sent a platoon to recover the sunken lane. But this attempt was short-lived: the platoon became pinned down by heavy fire and the platoon leader wounded. The acting company commander Lieutenant Macfarlane was himself wounded while leading attempts to extract the survivors, a process which consumed some time. As for McElwee, after encountering his Company Sergeant Major the two found themselves in the firing line, engaging an enemy machine gun with the CSM's Bren. The tension was beginning to tell on both. *'I can remember saying crossly "Take aim, Sgt Major" and the CSM retorting equally crossly "I am taking aim, Sir".'* In the end, McElwee 'left him to it' and returned to his Company HQ area, which he found abandoned, with no one to drive the vehicles away. There, amid the confusion, he was accosted by German infiltrators. One of these he dropped with a lucky pistol shot; the other flung an egg grenade *'which did me no harm, but knocked me down the bank into the road'.* The extent to which McElwee was affected by this event can only be conjectured. What is clear is that the situation was extremely fluid and – for a while at least – he could not be fully appraised of events. Nevertheless, recovering from the blow, he remained optimistic and undaunted.

McElwee's next act was to pull out of the line two sections of 10 Platoon, leaving just Corporal Stewart's PIAT team to guard the southern entrances to the village. This task they went on to perform admirably. The Corporal soon after stalked and hit a further *Panzer IV* before being himself dazed by a High Explosive round fired in reply, leaving Private Mantz to finish off the tank with his own A Company PIAT.[12] Meanwhile, McElwee's plan was to regain the ground lost by C Company with a two-section counterattack. Crossing back to the west side of the road, in the vicinity of the southern bridge, McElwee chanced upon Hugh Fyfe, C Company commander, grimly holding on to his reduced perimeter. *'There was a lot of confused fighting just ahead and I gathered that his C Coy were holding a small quarter circle from the road to the river... with covering fire from him my counter attack still seemed feasible.'* McElwee's plan was undone by a sudden eruption of heavy fire from behind their right, apparently coming from the woods above the northern riverbank. Both majors experienced near misses as bullets tore through their personal equipment. To this there could be no satisfactory answer, and McElwee reluctantly pulled back into the woods south east of the bridges, behind the shrinking perimeter still held by the remnants of C Company.

With late afternoon turning to evening, Colonel Tweedie experienced mounting frustration. As McElwee had already found, the dense landscape and the intensity of the battle made it hard to gain an overall picture of what was going on. This was a platoon and section leaders' fight, from which Tweedie was excluded. His annoyance was not eased by the lack of direction from above. The ebullient colonel's ire is clear in his own record of events.

The covered lane along which Germans reached the road behind 11 Platoon.

A grenade flung at McElwee 'knocked me down the bank into the road'.

Frundsberg Panzer IV
knocked out by PIATs in
Gavrus, probably on 29
June by Corporal Stewart
(B Coy) and Private Mantz
(A Coy). Note, poles
behind the tank are not
aerials; this is a standard
Panzer IV Ausf. H or J.

Date and location
confirmed by this 3 July
image of Gavrus.
The photograph above
taken from viewpoint
shown.

'Casualties had mounted a bit but everyone was in excellent form and ready for all comers. Orders were asked for. Were we to move on? Were they going to push armour across as they had done in the first crossing? or relieve us or what?' Tweedie was aware of a battle being fought (between the *Hohenstaufen* and the Seaforth) around the crossroads at le Valtru, a mile to the north, across his lines of communication. (In fact, the position at le Valtru was briefly overrun and only with great resolution re-secured; by now the entire length of the road north from Gavrus to le Valtru was under fire.) The Mortar Platoon had run out of ammunition early in the day, with no prospect of resupply. There was no way to evacuate wounded. And, most disturbingly, Tweedie had lost radio contact with C Company.

Surprising though it might seem, given the small distances concerned, contact between C Company and battalion HQ could not be re-established. In actual fact, after his brief encounter with McElwee, Hugh Fyfe had been blown into the river and, still in shock, had wandered off downriver to Tourmauville, followed by some of his own C Company as well as parts of B. Meanwhile, having gathered all the stragglers and wounded that patrols could round up, McElwee contented himself with defence: *'I was forced to realise that for the moment it was rather a question of holding on to the wood than of organising further counter attacks. I therefore ordered MACFARLANE to withdraw his Pl* [the remnants of A Company, note that McElwee was the senior officer

HQ, Support
& D Coy area

Elements
of C Coy
retiring

McElwee's Composite
Coy area

11 Platoon
holding

present] *and sat down to a dogged defence of the wood. I was, of course, still desperately anxious about MACKENZIE & 11 Pl and was indeed certain in my mind that they must have been overrun.'*

Far from it. Mackenzie's 11 Platoon was gallantly resisting. 11 Platoon had observed the failure of McElwee's attempt to lead a counter attack around their right, followed by the withdrawal of all the rest of B and C Companies east of the road. So, by about 16.00 hours Mackenzie found *'Eleven Platoon were now cut off by the enemy who were now all round us. We had a mortar, four Brens and the remainder were riflemen and a Piat team. We kept on firing…'* A direct hit by a mortar bomb knocked out the two-inch mortar and its crew. With machine gun fire coming in from all angles, the 5 Section Bren gunner was hit through the chest, the 4 Section gunner through the neck, and the 6 Section gunner from behind, a fatal back wound. The Platoon was now down to three NCOs and fourteen Other Ranks, riflemen now manning the Brens. Another man was cut down. Still Mackenzie held on. *'The enemy weren't the only ones who were dishing out the punishment, as our fellows were knocking out the enemy as they tried to infiltrate, but we were running out of ammunition.'* As was happening elsewhere on the battlefield, the bandoliers of riflemen both healthy and wounded were emptied to feed the Bren magazines.

With the platoon almost out of ammunition, Mackenzie judged that the strain was becoming too great for some of the men. The withdrawal began, back under cover of buildings, through the woods east of the road, then down towards the river. Two wounded had to be left behind (one was freed later from hospital in Paris); Private Whittle insisted on accompanying the withdrawal even though he had an arm taken off at the elbow four hours previously. At length, they rejoined the main body of the unit. McElwee was understandably delighted to have the men back. When Mackenzie apologized for pulling out, McElwee confessed that, *'I felt that all the apologies were due the other way, for my lamentable failure to get any relief to him.'*

Mackenzie's account gives 'about 22.00 hours' as the time he made the decision to move from the ground he had held for so long; McElwee makes the specific point about Mackenzie's return that: *'This was at 2130 hours – the only other time of which I am certain during that afternoon. The battle now was dying down and S.B's [sic: stretcher bearers] were clearing up. The 2IC [Major Russell "Hank" Morgan] came over with definite orders to hold the wood for the night as a firm base for resuming the offensive the next day and we reorganized for the night.'* Given the confusion of the evening phase of the battle, it is apparent that this reorganization was largely made possible by the stand of 11 Platoon, which for some hours had sheltered the remaining rifle strength of the battalion south of the river as it regrouped.

30 JUNE: ORDERS FOR THE MAJOR

The night of 29-30 June was miserable and wet. Come dawn, the remaining riflemen south of the river stood-to on the steep, wooded slopes. After a night spent on full alert, breakfast was a miserable affair, with little food and only a single, faulty petrol cooker between McElwee's *ad hoc* company. Nevertheless, their sector remained quiet. It was the northern slopes, around the quarry and west of the road at battalion Headquarters, which now became the focus of enemy attention. Tweedie noted that the morning opened *'with a certain increase in sniping and Bn HQ personnel, especially Russell Morgan, had a lot of fun trying to spot these chaps and shoot back.'*

By 11.00 hours, heavy mortaring was taking place. It was about this time that the battalion's transport began to suffer serious losses. Brigade had sent the Argylls' A Echelon vehicles forward to ease congestion further back where the poor dirt roads of the region were grossly overcrowded. Sheer inexperience had led to the vehicles being parked-up in locations where they could be observed by enemy spotters in the woods to the west, and by now escape via le Valtru was out of the question, with the road under enemy

Before the battle: German entrenchments and heavy anti-aircraft gun positions north of the river (circled).

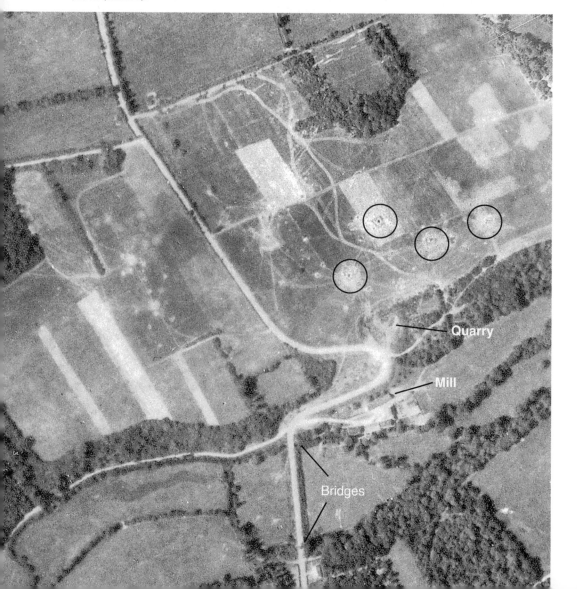

observation and fire. Mortar bombs worked-over the parked soft-skin vehicles. Retaliation was difficult. The distant 495 Battery of 131st Field Regiment responded tirelessly to calls from the battery commander Major Vyvyan Cornwall, acting as Forward Observation Officer at Tweedie's headquarters.[13] But it was next to impossible to identify lone German observers in the woods to the west. The incoming fire increased; the acting Adjutant, John Graham, recalled that 'It really became quite tiresome.' At one point, Colonel Tweedie convinced himself that the immediate area of his HQ must have been infiltrated by the enemy. He instructed the FOO to bring down fire on his own position. The field regiment responded with alacrity. As the battalion HQ personnel huddled deep in their slit trenches, they marvelled at the intensity of their own artillery. 'We thought the RA were magnificent,' Graham recalled, even though one red hot shard came to rest spanning the rim of his trench and his tin hat. But when the fire mission ended and they emerged, 'We didn't find any dead Germans. Perhaps there weren't any there.'

Around 15.00 hours the German mortaring reached a new level of intensity, again appearing deliberately to target the area of battalion headquarters close to the quarry. In hindsight, and with growing battle experience, it was recognised that the quarry was an obvious feature for the German artillery to have pre-registered. On the other hand, most of the battalion's remaining rifle strength was now on the steep southern side of the Odon valley, a reverse slope against most of the incoming artillery fire and harder for spotters guiding mortar fire to observe. Lack of direct lines of sight into these positions no doubt made it harder to coordinate artillery support with advances by the German infantry. Also making life difficult for the *Panzergrenadiere*, on 30 June most if not all the 10. *Panzerregiment* armour had been withdrawn for use elsewhere.

A fallback location for battalion headquarters had already been identified, and at length Tweedie gave the order to move out, up the slope on to the plateau north of the river where a cluster of large gun emplacements had once housed a German antiaircraft battery. But the move was observed. Incoming artillery followed the move remorselessly. The HQ was now out of any visual contact with the main body of riflemen gathered around McElwee on the wooded slopes south of the river. And about this time all radio contact was lost. Having already lost the rear link to Brigade and the 18 Set to the rifle

After the battle: the mill burnt out, the quarry cratered, entrenchments modified by the British.

companies, now the artillery set was hit and Vyvyan Cornwall wounded.

Tweedie's personal record of events repeatedly stressed that as late as 17.00 hours, 'the bridge was perfectly firmly held' and 'the situation on the south bank completely under control'. It is tempting to wonder how accurately these comments reflected his true feelings at the time, or whether they were the wisdom of hindsight (or wishful thinking). The loss of the battalion soft-skin vehicles, with so much kit and essential ammunition evidently troubled the colonel.[14] Just before the Rear Link to Brigade was knocked out, a message had been sent back (by Russell Morgan, not Tweedie himself) making it clear that assistance was absolutely necessary. Tweedie's later actions suggest that he harboured real concerns as to the situation at the bridges, a situation which by now was barely under his control or indeed known to him. The divisional history is in no doubt that, following the move of HQ, 'Casualties were very high; there was some confusion; contact with forward companies was lost.'[15]

The new headquarters position proved a disappointment, turning out to be even more exposed to enemy fire. Shortly after the move, Tweedie recognised that his 'new and very skeleton HQ' had become impossible to maintain and his officers dispersed to find alternative cover. From this point, the story of events north of the river becomes confused as organization broke down.

For his part, the acting Adjutant returned to the original HQ position, but found himself alone there. Picking his way back up the slope, he found no sign of the now-dispersed regimental headquarters. Following the direction of this supposed withdrawal, Graham approached the woods north and east of the le Valtru road. As he neared the point where today power lines cross the road, a Churchill tank appeared around a hedge. 'I ran to it with my helmet in my hand (you couldn't run with it on, it was like a dinner plate). A Royal Tanks sergeant popped up and said something like: "Are you the Herefords? What is the situation?" He went inside and got on the radio – I don't know what he said but it must have worked. He reversed away and I never saw him again.' In fact, the Churchill was one of a half dozen sent to find the Argylls. At 227 Brigade, Mackintosh-Walker had reached the conclusion that no useful purpose was being served by leaving the Argylls out on a limb in Gavrus; and since no armour was planning to cross the bridges there, the infantry should abandon the position. Two troops of C Squadron, 7th RTR were sent forward to make contact. But amid the general confusion, the order was not yet passed on.

After the brief encounter with the tank, 'Nothing much happened for some time.' But as Lieutenant Graham continued his search for fellow officers, his eyes lit on a familiar object. 'I saw Hank Morgan's silver penknife near the road glinting in the sun. I thought, "Thank heavens, he has pulled out OK", assuming this meant he had not gone back to the bridge but had gone north.' The conclusion was mistaken, but the idea of withdrawal to the north was about to be reinforced.[16] At a time estimated by Graham as about five or six p.m., 'A scout car appeared with a RTR subaltern telling us to pull out. I was only a subaltern, but Captain Muirhead [commanding the Antitank Platoon] was close by and we conferred.' The two officers agreed that the order should be carried forward to the men still defending the bridges. So, Willie Muirhead and John Graham moved

Ron Lomas drove the carrier from his gun position (above) to McElwee's command post. (below)

back south. Still they could find no trace of the Commanding Officer or his deputy. About this time the remains D Company and many of the headquarters personnel pulled back north and east into the woods, and played no further part in the action. Whether or not they had received the tank subaltern's withdrawal order is uncertain. In any case, they continued back to Tourmauville.

At length, dodging the small arms fire that periodically swept the road, Muirhead and Graham made their way down to the sharp bend above the mill where Lance-Sergeant David Morris's Number Six gun was covering the northern bridge. With bullets and mortar bombs still in the air, any protection was better than none, even the thin skin of a Loyd carrier. Unfortunately, the carrier's driver had been wounded early in the battle. Pressed into service,

Lance-Corporal Ron Lomas took the driver's position and, keeping his head as far down as possible, drove the two officers the short distance. Down by the north bridge, chaos reigned. Here the Carrier Platoon had lost a number of vehicles; a four-wheeled command truck was blazing; beside it a Vickers machine gun had taken a direct hit.[17] Hauling on the steering sticks, Lomas weaved his way to McElwee's command position just above the southern bridge.

With the colonel and the 2 i.c. both missing, command devolved on Bill McElwee.[18] Even before learning of the disappearance of his superiors, in practice McElwee had been in sole charge of the defence of the Odon bridges throughout the day. By late afternoon, German pressure had increased. Periodically hot fire fights erupted between the northern fringes of Gavrus and the wooded slopes, interspersed with periods of relative calm as the Panzergrenadiere regrouped.

It was in one of those odd periods of quiet in mid-battle that the Loyd carrier arrived at the sunken road that served McElwee as a company headquarters. As his passengers dismounted to find the major, Ron Lomas recalls wandering more-or-less aimlessly up the road towards Gavrus, oblivious of danger. The sun shone and it was deathly quiet: no birds sang in the trees. Meanwhile the officers conferred. Muirhead and Graham found McElwee in confident mood. A replacement artillery officer, Major Gordon Campbell of the 131st Field Regiment, had arrived on foot from the slopes below Tourville where his 320 Battery was supporting the Gordons. Major McElwee flatly refused to leave the position he was holding without proper orders, written and signed, and was certainly not about to pull out on the strength of a reported conversation with a tank subaltern. There were mutterings; McElwee was unmoved.[19] He felt confident that he could continue to hold the crossings. The Germans did not seem to be pressing as hard as the day before, and McElwee had somehow formed the notion that Guards Armoured Division might be seeking to cross the Odon at Gavrus.[20]

The battle rekindled and heavy fighting resumed. Captain Mackenzie, still shaken by events of the day before, was sent back to Brigade for orders.[21] And so, at last, around 21.00 hours a staff officer returned from 227 Brigade, braving the road from le Valtru in an armoured scout car. Charles Alexander was himself an Argyll, and known to the officers of the regiment. He carried the withdrawal order, now properly written and signed by the brigadier.

As Major Campbell called in fire to cover the withdrawal, the remaining riflemen prepared to march away north east through the wooded Odon valley. The guns hooked up and drove off, Ron Lomas's carrier transporting the wounded layer to be treated at the Seaforth's Regimental Aid Post in Mondrainville. Major McElwee departed with the honour of the Argylls intact, insisting then and later that he could have held out another twenty four hours. *'I never lost the Gavrus bridge. I am proud that no one believed my men and I could come alive out of those woods, but we did come out. We withdrew in good order with two hundred and three men and two antitank guns… If I had had a band, they would have played; if I had had the colours I should have paraded them.'*[22]

Contrary to some accounts, few of the men marched by road: the road to le Valtru was still a risky passage. Most made their way back through the woods and the Château avenue via Mondrainville to Colleville, where D Company was already waiting.

The *Panzergrenadiere* came on cautiously to be met by a barrage of fifteen thousand shells of all calibres: field, medium, and even some heavy guns joining in. As the sun finally set on the month of June, Gavrus was left an empty No Man's Land.

References

(1) Much of the Argylls' story recounted in this chapter is based on personal accounts in the author's possession written in the immediate aftermath of the action by (respectively): Lieutenant-Colonel Tweedie (commanding 2nd A&SH), Major McElwee (commanding B Company), and Captain Mackenzie (2 i.c. B Company, whose 11 Platoon he led through much of 29 and 30 June). A summary of McElwee's account later formed part of his history of the battalion, published in 1949. Later, in the 1960s, Normandy historian Albert Grandais corresponded at some length with Tweedie and McElwee in preparation of his history of *La Bataille du Calvados*. Some of the resulting reminiscences are used herein, though where the anecdotes recounted by individuals change over time (as so often happens after many years in the telling) this author gives precedence to the earliest records.
(2) McElwee, 1949, p 29.
(3) This being late June, vegetation was at its densest. However, the trees bordering the river were not quite so high as today. Moreover, as the two-day fight went on and artillery of both sides pounded the terrain, foliage and branches were progressively stripped from the trees, lush orchards becoming reduced to rows of bare stumps.
(4) John Graham, Intelligence Officer and acting Adjutant, recalled being brought a young 'very blond' SS man. Interrogated by Graham whilst lying under one of the Echelon trucks, the man confessed his conviction that Germany had lost the war. The prisoner could not be evacuated and died the next day during German shelling. *Ponder Anew*, J D C Graham, p 64

(5) This flagrant ignoring of strict instructions to preserve scarce APDS rounds for more heavily armoured targets was common practice. Many gunners defined a 'priority' target as any one that was approaching them.

(6) The somewhat confusing order was to take the Monceaux bridge 'at Missy'. Missy itself was a château a good mile further and well to the north of the intended river crossing.

(7) The Scots 'Balmoral' was a flat cap with a bobble, worn at an angle. Officially it was a 'TOS' or 'Tam-o'-Shanter'. Some officers wore the Balmoral out of bravado, others have claimed that it was hard to run wearing the clumsy British helmet.

(8) Corporal James Campbell, interviews with the author.

(9) As previously noted, standard Army abbreviations (as well as non-standard punctuation!) are retained in all direct quotes. Hence: 'Pl and Sec Comd' for 'platoon and section commanders'.

(10) By this stage of the Normandy campaign, the *Panzer* forces had learned that the machine gun was the principal offensive weapon against infantry in close country, recommending the issue of at least 5,500 machine gun rounds per tank in action.

(11) In his unpublished personal account, McElwee does make brief reference to 'A gunner who had mysteriously appeared in our midst' in the C Company area and 'was knocked out'.

(12) The first hit, which clearly failed to penetrate, may well have been responsible for stripping its protective *Schürzen*, enabling a successive PIAT bomb to impact the actual armour of the tank. From the position of the knocked-out tank, it seems highly likely that Mantz fired from within an adjacent building, since unlike the American and German rocket launchers, the PIAT produced no backblast.

(13) Unlike the American and German armies, senior British artillery officers accompanied the forward units and were authorized to command – rather than merely request – fire tasks.

(14) Up to their first action, the Argylls considered loss of kit a serious offence. Jim Ross (Signals Platoon) recalled that, *'Many found themselves on charges after a "scheme" in Yorkshire. I had lost my entrenching tool and was up before John Kenneth. The officer was angry: "We should have lost the desert war if all the men had been so careless losing equipment!" Then we arrived in Normandy, and soon equipment was being discarded everywhere!'* Attitudes changed after Gavrus. Not only did the harsh realities of war become better understood, but for the rest of the campaign in Europe, any man threatened with a charge for being without an item of kit could claim that it was lost at Gavrus! Nevertheless, as one Argylls officer confided to the author, Tweedie was deeply troubled on 30 June by the responsibility for losing so much valuable equipment.

(15) Martin, p 53

(16) For the whereabouts of the Colonel and his 2 i.c., see Appendix VI.

(17) 6 Platoon, The 1st Middlesex (a machine gun battalion), was giving supporting fire from the northern river bank.

(18) Normally the A Company commander would have been next in the chain of command. But Major Kenneth had, inexplicably and to his great personal regret, been ordered to remain 'LOB'. As was standard British practice, a group was 'Left Out of Battle' as a nucleus around which to re-form the regiment should it suffer catastrophic losses. John Kenneth subsequently argued that it might have been more sensible to 'LOB' the second-in-command than to disrupt the command structure of A Company.

(19) It has been recorded that someone exploded, 'For God's sake get out of this cursed wood and don't be so obstinate!' (quoted in How, p 126; Grandais, p 191 claims that it was Graham or Muirhead.) This outburst is not recalled by John Graham, who was present.

(20) *10. SS-Panzerdivision* had indeed redirected its sole *Panzer* battalion away from the Gavrus sector after 29 June, so German pressure on Gavrus through 30 June lacked armour support. The rumours McElwee had picked up about Guards Armoured entering the fray were baseless.

(21) It is not known how Mackenzie managed to contact Brigade. He deservedly won a Military Cross for his action of 29 June; he later suffered a nervous breakdown, possibly in part a consequence of his ordeal that day.

(22) *La Bataille du Calvados*, Grandais, p 192. Curiously, several accounts, including Martin's history of the 15th Scottish, refer to Gavrus being 'lost'. Gavrus was not 'lost'. The position was left in accordance with orders after being successfully defended – incidentally, defended through the day following the abandonment of Hill 112 to the east.

Chapter 9

FRIDAY 30 JUNE – SATURDAY 1 JULY: ROLES REVERSED

If the British commanders in Normandy occasionally appeared over-cautious, their German counterparts tended to give hostages to fortune with overly optimistic situation reports. In the afternoon of 29 June, *SS-Gruppenführer Bittrich* reported that his *II. SS-Panzerkorps* was holding firm on a line from Evrecy to Gavrus south of the Odon, through Grainville and Rauray to the north. Hausser responded with a direct telephone call urging the corps to press on to more distant goals. *'The II. SS-Panzerkorps counter-attack presents the big opportunity. The Schwerpunkt is to be kept on the left with Cheux as the main objective.'*[1] (Note that a drive on Cheux necessarily went through Dempsey's 'Rauray gap'.) But by evening, far from improving on the earlier report, Bittrich had to eat his words. Far from Gavrus and Grainville being springboards for his two divisions' further advances, neither place remained in German hands.

30 JUNE: PRESSURE RENEWED

With some degree of desperation, a late assault on the night of 29-30 June had been planned by the *Hohenstaufen*, using its two best-equipped units: the *Panther*-tank and the armoured-infantry battalions.[2] This came to little. The defenders of the western flank of the Scottish Corridor were tired and depleted, but their Forward Observers were alert. Target coordinates for defensive fire tasks were identified and noted; artillery regiments in the rear, field and medium, were supplied and ready. Confusion was further increased by a concerted night attack on the German rear areas by medium bombers. Seventy-seven Mosquitoes and eleven B25 Mitchells supported 2nd Army with raids during the night, with special emphasis on Villers-Bocage and Thury-Harcourt.[3] Dismounted grenadiers of *20. SS-PzGrRgt.* pressed forward as far as the south west of Grainville, where they screamed for armour support to shoot them into the place. But tactical coordination broke down. The darkness, the haste of the attack, and the limited pre-battle reconnaissance that had been possible all contributed to confusion which was compounded by the constant *'Trommelfeuer'* – artillery bursting so densely that the sound resembled a drum roll. Come the dawn, the attack was called off.

Through 30 June on the *Hohenstaufen* front, attempts to rekindle the offensive continued. By early afternoon, the *20. SS-Panzergrenadierregiment*

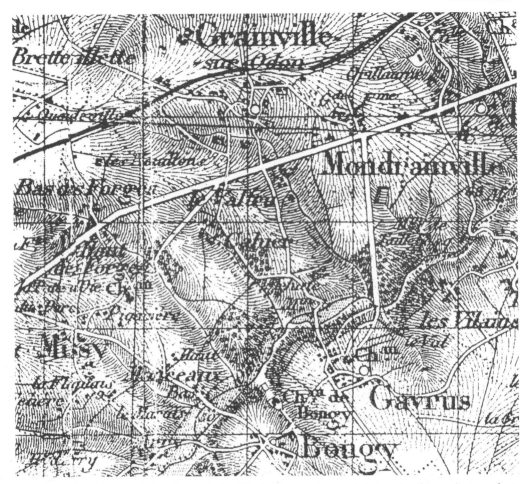

With the British holding from Grainville to Gavrus, Harmel determined to swing south to Hill 112.

had been effectively halted in front of Grainville. Further north, in mid-afternoon the *19. SS-PzGrRgt.* attacked on a north-westwards axis, throwing all three grenadier battalions at the Rauray gap, preceded by the best barrage its remaining artillery could provide. Their right wing, the *III. Abteilung* penetrated as far as Brettevillette and Queudeville; to the left the *II. Abteilung* got within two hundred metres of Rauray. But the British artillery response was pulverizing. Losses were great. Even the regimental commander *Obersturmbannführer* Woith was killed by an artillery shell. *Standartenführer* Müller had to concede that more than twenty four hours of desperate assaults by his division had failed.

South of the Odon, even by the evening of 29 June, it had become clear to *Oberführer* Hans Harmel that the *Frundsberg* tactics were not working. 'We won't get any further like this!' His staff conferred in the divisional command post at St Honorine, concluding that satisfactory progress directly up the Odon valley was unlikely, and that the right flank of the battlefield offered better prospects for the next day, especially with the opening up of vehicle crossings over the valley of the Guigne. (Ironically, this ran counter to Hausser's directive to Bittrich to make Cheux the main axis of the corps advance; staff work and communications were clearly not improved by all the recent changes of senior personnel.) While infantry pressure on Gavrus would be maintained, all the division's scarce tanks and *Sturmgeschütze* were redirected to support the *21. Panzergrenadierregiment* drive eastwards to Hill 112.

Here too, the risks inherent in a night advance were accepted in order to get some momentum into the advance. (Also, it was hoped that by night the British artillery observers would be blind to the changed axis of advance.) So, abandoning the direct road to Hill 112, the reinforced grenadier regiment looped south of Evrecy, securing the Guigne crossings at Avenay and Vieux in order to pass the armour across. By dawn, armour and infantry were ready for the assault on Hill 112. All the divisional and corps artillery, plus the artillery of the *Hitlerjugend* and two independent *Nebelwerfer* brigades swept the crest of 112 as the ground forces stormed the hill.

Hill 112 was taken. Unsurprisingly; since (although German records are

Hill 112 was re-taken.

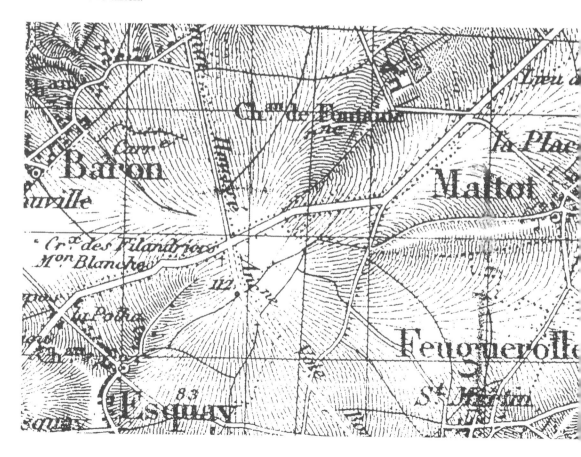

silent on the point) the hill was virtually undefended following the departure of 8th Rifle Brigade during the night. But as ever, taking the hill itself was only a means to an end. The day's objective lay north of the Odon, and with daylight the new occupants of Hill 112 were exposed to pounding by the British artillery. Try as the regiment might, the grenadiers could not progress across the hill into the wooded valley beyond.

On the *Frundsberg* left, contact was re-established with the *Hohenstaufen* north of the Odon, and pressure was maintained on the British pocket still holding around the bridges of Gavrus. But with the divisional *Panzer* battalion now withdrawn for the assault on Hill 112, the priority of 22. *PzGrRgt.* was not so much to reduce the knot of defenders there, as to work around them, eastward towards Baron. Here as elsewhere, small groups of men managed to infiltrate the Herefords' positions around les Vilains, but attempts to exploit these penetrations in any sort of strength were driven back

SS troops in the streets of Villers-Bocage watchful for Allied aircraft.

Villers-Bocage after the RAF bombing raid of 30 June in which 1,100 tons of bombs were dropped on the small town.

by torrential artillery fire.

So, by the end of the second day of its offensive, the *II. SS-Panzerkorps* line had tightened around the stub of the British salient (no longer truly 'Scottish', being now defended on its southern extremity by Welsh border country battalions of 159 Brigade, held on its east by the 43rd Wessex Division, and being reinforced by the 53rd Welsh). The Germans' only significant territorial gains had been to drive the British off Hill 113, and to take Hill 112, though the latter gain was the result of British withdrawal rather than German conquest. And if any further evidence was needed of the Allies' enormous material superiority, this came on the evening of 30 June. Now confident of the air supremacy achieved in the skies over Normandy, RAF Bomber Command put in its first daylight raid in support of the ground campaign. Escorted by fighter squadrons, 266 heavy bombers – Lancasters and Halifaxes, supplemented for this relatively 'safe' operation by obsolescent Wellingtons and Stirlings – dropped 1,100 tons of bombs on the little town of Villers-Bocage. The town was obliterated. Bomber crews noted clouds of red smoke as the brick dust from smashed buildings was hurled thousands of feet into the air. The use of heavy bombers over the battlefield was a science in its infancy. Even allowing for German understatement, the effect of the raid on their offensive operations was not great. The sacrifice of Villers-Bocage was to all intents and purposes unnecessary. The raid was intended to disrupt German communications through the road junctions in the little town, but the truly crippling impact of Allied airpower on German communications and supplies had already been inflicted, extending far back from the battlefield. *II. SS-Panzerkorps* halted offensive operations for the night in order to prepare for a renewed onslaught come the morning.

30 JUNE: DIGGING IN AND HOLDING ON

After four long days of action, 15th Scottish Division was badly bruised. By 30 June losses of men and equipment were heavy; many familiar faces would not be seen again. As ever, the rifle companies suffered most. Platoons that had begun the battle at or near the War Establishment of thirty six men now were much reduced – few would see that level again in the course of the war. Already, battalions were merging rifle companies whose numbers had fallen below effective levels. And as ever it was among the company and platoon leaders that the highest loss rates of all were experienced.[4] So, among the

harsh lessons of war being hastily learned (and drills hastily unlearned), men had to come to terms with operating in smaller groups and under new leadership.

By the morning of 30 June, Mackintosh-Walker's 227 Brigade had regained the two battalions diverted to understudy 46 Brigade's defence the previous day. The first news the 2nd Gordon Highlanders received of their reversion to the brigade came in the form of a curious order. They were to cross the Odon at Tourmauville preparatory to advancing south west to Monceaux, a mile beyond Gavrus. The order was imbecilic. It proposed a move south on a narrow track against the northward flow of 11th Armoured Division, followed by an unsupported advance west over open country held by a full enemy armoured division. Had the order been capable of execution it might have resulted in a 1944 version of the Charge of the Light Brigade. As it was, the battalion suffered an advance down the road from Tourville as far as the Odon, under heavy fire, only to seek what cover could be found until an hour and a half later they were ordered back to their starting position, *'back in their old haunt among the orchards where they were obliged to remain inactive under a hail of fire.'*[5] The 10th Highland Light Infantry fared no better. Having the previous day lost both their Colonel Young and his 2 i.c., the battalion was under the temporary command of the 2nd Gordons' Major Sinclair as they occupied a wood south of Mondrainville. *'Not an ideal place for a Battalion, we did our best and in true 1815 style formed hollow square around a rather disgusting marsh.'*[6] Here the HLI continued to suffer the ill-fortune that dogged them throughout EPSOM. As the rifle companies formed up in a large orchard for a renewed attempt to break through to the Argylls at Gavrus, the bagpipes intended to lift spirits instead brought down a devastating enemy bombardment, made all the worse by rounds bursting overhead in the trees.

The depleted ranks of Barber's 46 Brigade dug deeper into their positions: the 7th Seaforth in le Valtru, the 9th Cameronians in Grainville, the 2nd Glasgow Highlanders behind in Mondrainville. All expected a renewal of the previous day's assault, in all probability on an even greater scale. Although shelling and mortaring were suffered all day long, with losses mounting, nevertheless the three battalions recorded the day as 'quiet'. (A vivid illustration of the change in attitudes wrought by combat experience!) At midday, with no enemy assault forthcoming, a Seaforth patrol pushed west up the high road to 'see what could be seen' in the direction of Cahiers and Missy. With caution born of recent experience, the patrol moved in armoured carriers, their objective barely four hundred yards west of the Valtru crossroads. Half-way there, an unseen enemy gun disposed of one carrier and the expedition was abandoned. Later in the day, as a few surviving Argylls vehicles returned up the road from Gavrus, one of their weary carrier drivers mistakenly turned left at le Valtru instead of right, pressing on westward until it was noted that the soldiers on the roadside were wearing field-grey. A rapid about-turn was executed. The carrier sped back to le Valtru to report the enemy around le Bas des Forges in merely platoon strength. The only other incident worthy of record was a German section infiltrating D Company on the right, killing a corporal and four Other Ranks. An avenging group under D Company's Lieutenant Ewart killed eight Germans and drove the rest off. To the north, in Grainville, the Cameronians' main activity that day was directing counter-battery fire against persistent enemy mortaring.

Come evening, all three battalions of the brigade were to be relieved by the newly arrived 160 Brigade, of 53rd (Welsh) Division. Still the enemy artillery continued. Having agreed preparations for his battalion to relieve the Seaforth at le Valtru, the 1/5th Welch Regiment's Lieutenant-Colonel Ripley was killed shortly before his unit began to arrive. Some confusion followed as Ripley's 2 i.c. had to organize the relief on ground he had not previously seen.[7]

Fortunately the handover was not troubled by enemy fire, though the approach march of the Welshmen was disrupted and delayed by night shelling of the rear areas. In its turn, the relief of the Glasgow Highlanders' by the 2nd Monmouths was troubled by heavy shelling. And like their sister battalions, the Cameronians were delighted to be able to pull out of the battle during the night, to rest, re-form, and come to terms with the loss of twelve officers and 262 Other Ranks.

Further north, 30 June found Money's 44 Brigade still clustered between le Haut-du-Bosq and Belleval. After their battering the previous day, 6th Royal Scots Fusiliers were content to sit in le Haut du Bosq, only in the afternoon advancing to an orchard west of the road to form an 'anti-Panzer hedgehog'. 8th Royal Scots began the day still further

44 Brigade positions at end of 30 June.

north, behind 6th RSF. During the afternoon they were moved forward to positions just behind the 6th King's Own Scottish Borderers, and by midnight split into two groups, either side of the Borderers' position. As for 6th KOSB themselves, they were now to occupy centre stage for the finale of 15th Scottish Division's first battle.

1 JULY: PREPARING THE LAST PUSH

As planned, the *Frundsberg* renewed their assault on the small British bridgehead that remained south of the Odon. Though now able to focus both infantry regiments on the same goal, the division was unable to make progress. A frontal attack over open ground against prepared enemy positions supported by overwhelming artillery assets required more strength than was available. As usual for the British, if the battle was decided by artillery, nevertheless it was the infantry that held the ground. And the

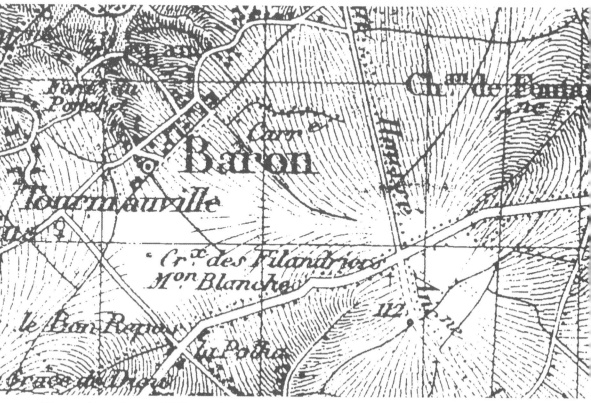

The northern slopes of Hill 112, abandoned by the British, became a killing ground for the Germans.

infantry battle was a nightmare. Defenders dared not leave their entrenchments during the hours of daylight; tactical command and control extended only as far as a leader could shout, unless he took his life in his hands to risk moving from one slit trench to another. Company radios went out of action. As the 4th KSLI's D Company signallers worked on in the radio lorry, 'it was shaking like a blasted boat from the explosions.' When the inevitable happened and the truck went up in flames, *'Even this could not destroy Corporal Ralph's unfailing urbanity as he very politely approached his Company Commander's trench and said, "Excuse me, Sir, may I come in for a moment"* – punctuated by two more shell bursts – *"the wireless is out of action."'*[8]

The German attack was no less deprived of communications. Radio transmissions were quickly located and smashed by fire. Transmitters had to be located remotely at a distance from headquarters, and signallers at their posts were no less exposed to danger when sending as were riflemen in sight of the enemy. Field telephone signals all went undetected, but the general bombardment as well as the chewing up of the ground by tracked vehicles played havoc with field telephone lines. Losses to German despatch riders, runners, and linemen were particularly heavy as their vital specialist jobs had to be performed largely in the open.

While German propaganda celebrated the 'reconquest' of Hill 112, the benefit gained proved mainly defensive, establishing a buffer in front of the Orne crossings, rather than a springboard for further advance. Over the coming fortnight, as the German stance changed from attack to defence, some of the most bitter fighting experienced in Normandy would ensue in this area. Ironically, the outcome of the battle here would have little strategic value, save for the 'writing down' of the German defenders; Hill 112 was not destined to be held again by the British until it ceased to play a part in the Germans' defence west of the Orne River and was abandoned by them.

Meanwhile, north of the Odon, *Hohenstaufen* hopes of using the night of 30 June to regroup had been disappointed. Even when British artillery observers were blind during the brief hours of darkness, predicted fire on known routes and junctions effectively disrupted German movements and added to the day's losses. *20. SS-Panzergrenadierregiment* counted 284 men lost during the day's actions, including the *I. Abteilung* commander, *Sturmbannführer* Lederer.

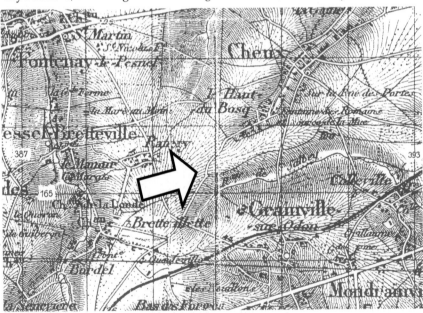

The main axis was to run through the 'Rauray gap'.

The regiment struggled to prepare for a renewal of the offensive, re-forming disrupted and depleted companies, re-equipping with arms and ammunition, while holding the front line against any British night moves, and grabbing any opportunity for sleep. Some confusion resulted. In the small hours of 1 July, the regiment briefly lost contact with *19. SS-PzGrRgt.* to the left, as British bombarded Queudeville and there was some fear of a local counter-attack. Grenadiers of the Nineteenth struggled to close the gap. All too soon came the dawn, and at 06.15 hours the infantry moved up to their start lines.

On a front from Rauray in the west to Grainville in the east, the remaining strength of *Kampfgruppe Weidinger* and the two *Hohenstaufen* grenadier regiments were supported by the first, *Panther*-equipped *Abteilung* of *9. SS-Panzerregiment* and its sister second battalion's *Panzer IV* and *Sturmgeschütze*. This still constituted a formidable offensive force, focused on a relatively narrow sector of the British line, at the junction of two corps. Its axis of attack ran squarely into the 'Rauray gap'.

1 JULY: THE DEFENDERS

The little dirt road leading from Noyers to Cheux indicated the general direction of the German advance; it also marked the boundary between the British XXX Corps and VIII Corps. To the north of the road was 49th (West Riding) Division, whose 11th Durham Light Infantry held the stone buildings of the tiny hamlet of Rauray, with the 1st Tyneside Scottish occupying a five-sided field alongside the boundary road, and the open ground in between.[9] South of the road, and at right angles to it, the 6th King's Own Scottish Borderers were dug in along tall hedgerows on stout earth banks – examples of true Normandy bocage – which lined the large open fields of the Belleval estate. The Belleval château itself, at the heart of the position and some hundreds of yards behind the front line, comprised a substantial group of stone buildings. Around it the Borderers spent the day of 30 June improving their entrenchments in the orchards and hedgerows while remaining vigilant. Apart from sporadic shelling and sniping, the day remained 'suspiciously quiet... a lull between storms'.[10]

6 KOSB company positions. On flanks, carrier platoon (east) and 1st Tyneside Scottish A Company in five-sided field to west.

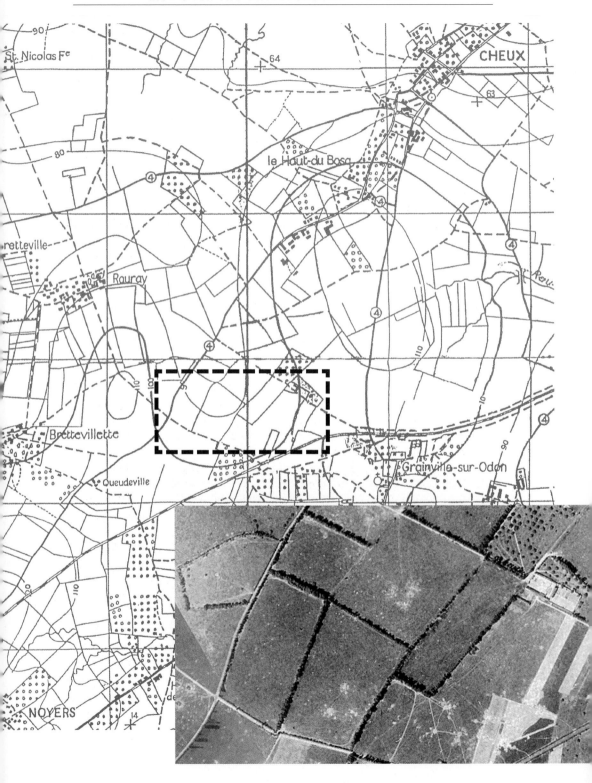

Furthest forward was the Borderers' C Company. Its two forward rifle platoons and supporting six-pounder antitank guns of the KOSB Antitank Platoon were deployed along a substantial hedgerow, facing south west. The company right flank rested on the corps boundary. (On the other side of the road, A Company of the Tyneside Scottish and its own antitank guns likewise fortified the five-sided field, their front line 150 yards further forward than the Borderers'.) Now commanding C Company following the death of Major Going on 26 June, Captain N C Rollo remained alert through the night. Shortly after midnight, a patrol reported to him that the enemy was forming up in strength under cover of darkness a short way down the road. Rollo investigated, and soon after, about 01.30 hours, he transmitted his warning over the company wireless: *'Hello Jig Able Baker* [the battalion call sign] *There is a good deal of enemy movement in front of me. Over.'* Battalion HQ could barely make out his hushed words. *'Can you speak up? I can hardly hear.'* To which Rollo's hoarse response, *'I don't want to talk too loudly. They are too close.'* Understanding the predicament, HQ asked, *'Would you like a Defensive Fire task?'* *'Yes. D.F. 109.'* Very soon after, the gunners of 178 Battery rained 25-pounder shells on the suspected German assembly area, the first of many DF tasks delivered on this climactic day of battle.

Some casualties were suffered from short rounds. One such shell burst in a slit trench of the Intelligence Section by the château, killing its two occupants. The bombardment did its job and a period of quiet ensued, but suspicions had been aroused. Some men were able to rest, but many remained alert, imagining enemy forces forming up in the dark night. Shortly after dawn, imaginings became reality as distinct sounds of tanks were heard to the front. On both sides of the road, the companies stood-to. About 06.45 hours, a sharp enemy bombardment came down: artillery and the inevitable mortars. Behind came tanks and infantry. By 07.00 hours, the battle was raging.

The *Hohenstaufen* wave rolled north-east, its *Schwerpunkt* directed at Cheux. Leaving behind the close fields, orchards, and narrow sunken roads that surrounded Noyers, the assault moved into open ground, rising to the misleadingly named 'Rauray spur', a very gentle rise to a 110 metre ring-contour, beyond which stood the front line of British defences. A tactical pattern had previously emerged on this battleground. As a British antitank commander noted, the enemy tanks were *'V. cleverly handled in small numbers with or without inf. They lie up in or infiltrated into posns from which they can engage our defensive posns by fire.'*[11] The major concluded, as did others on 1 July, that the German armour was reluctant to close over open ground, and that the best defence was therefore to engage with antitank guns from carefully concealed positions. Unfortunately for C Company, however well concealed were their supporting guns, they had to be emplaced close-up to the hedgerow to obtain a field of fire, and so their approximate position was obvious to the enemy, whose fire became progressively more accurate as the morning wore on. As before, the German tanks lay back, seeking hull-down positions, picking off the antitank guns one by one as they were identified.

German artillery laid down a preparatory barrage, changing from High Explosive to smoke to cover the initial advance of the armour. Then from four hundred yards or less range, the tanks emerged from the smoke to spray fire over suspected British positions. Once satisfied that the British antitank screen was suppressed, the tanks rolled on still further in support of the attacking infantry, only to be stopped by repeated defensive fire tasks. The German infantry then went to ground and the tanks pulled back under what cover their own artillery and mortars could provide, to regroup and repeat the process. A rhythm began. Each successive wave inflicted further losses on the rapidly thinning defence line; each wave rolled further forward.

The Borderers held their positions. Antitank guns engaged targets at close range. Bren gunners and riflemen balanced the need to put out defensive fire with the need to shelter in slit trenches, balanced the need to stop the enemy with the need to conserve ammunition whose resupply was far from certain. And for the lonely foot soldiers, fighting two to a slit trench, usually out of contact with their leaders, the greatest encouragement was their own artillery support. Like other Scots units during EPSOM, the Borderers were beginning to appreciate a relationship between infantry battalion and artillery battery which would soon become intimate. As the divisional history was later to reflect, this was *'the system which was to shoot the infantry on to their objectives and hold their front in countless critical situations all the way from Normandy to the Elbe…The regimental commanders* [Royal Artillery] *lived and worked in the pockets of their respective* [infantry] *brigade commanders, the battery commanders in the pockets of their respective battalion commanders, while an F.O.O. and O.P. party went forward with every forward company.'*[12] After the war, it was not unusual for

The Corps boundary: left of the road, the five-sided field held by the Tyneside Scottish of 49th Division, right of the road the hedgerow held by the 6 King's Own Scottish Borderers of 15th Division.

infantry officers to recount, only half in jest, that their companies' role in the campaign had been principally to escort the FOOs across Europe. As for the Borderers, *'afterward, the men of the 178th Field Battery, Royal Artillery, were in the habit of talking about "our infantry" in exactly the same way as we spoke about "our gunners".'*[13]

Nevertheless, the sheer weight and persistence of the assault gradually wore down the defenders. By 11.00 hours, C Company's 13 and 14 Platoons were sadly depleted. The last of the forward antitank guns was knocked out. With two of the crew killed and two wounded, the Borderers' Captain Elliot had continued to fire the gun single-handed until he was blown out of the gun pit. When he recovered consciousness, he reported back to the colonel before continuing back to seek treatment at the Regimental Aid Post. Realising the plight of C Company, and with no alternative communication available, Lieutenant-Colonel Shillington ventured forward into the maelstrom to confer with Captain Rollo. With six more German tanks appearing through the dust and smoke to the C Company front, Rollo informed his commander that the company risked being outflanked and destroyed. Shillington gave the order for the survivors to fall back a hundred yards to the next hedgerow, there to re-form around Rollo's company headquarters and his reserve 15 Platoon.

On both sides of the road, the attack overran the British front line. In the confusion of battle, in the noise and dust and smoke, with individual soldiers becoming isolated and retiring to make contact with their unit, both the 6th KOSB and the 1st Tyneside Scottish suspected that their neighbour might be abandoning the fight. Some men had indeed reached the limits of their endurance; others were simply reacting to the utter confusion of close combat, in search of companions or of leadership. Lieutenant Woolcombe of A Company witnessed both phenomena: *'A single figure appeared, running*

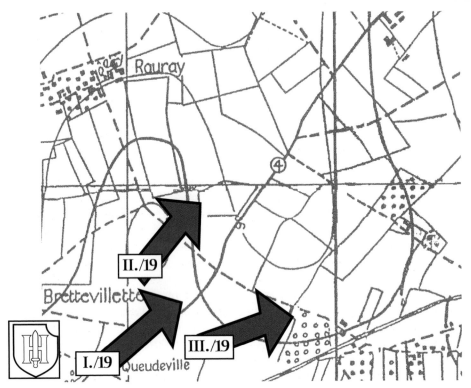

The three-pronged attack of the battalions of *19.SS-Panzergrenadierregiment*.

towards us without a rifle... a Jock from some other company... he was out of his wits... And we saw two or three figures in khaki moving back in disorder... Then two men with a different badge on their shoulders arrived among us, who came from the battalion across the road. Quietly the refugees stayed to fight with us.'[14]

Their attention focused on this key part of the battlefield, Brigade now stepped in. Shillington was passed orders to reinforce C Company's renewed stand with two A Company platoons, and re-establish links with XXX Corps across the road (once again, an instance of higher command responding to pressure by thinking 'two levels down'!). The colonel resented the intrusion into 'his' battle, and Major Gilbertson of A Company concurred that the order was misguided. Quite what was the outcome of these officers' discussion is not known, since the well-respected Gilbertson was struck down by mortar fire as he returned to A Company. By the time Lieutenant Woolcombe became aware that he was the senior surviving A Company officer, the battle had died down, so the reinforcement never took place. [15]

Lieutenant-Colonel Shillington's confidence in holding his battalion position was boosted not only by the eight 25 pounder field guns of 178 Field Battery, but also by the presence nearby of a dozen seventeen pounders of 344 Antitank Battery, R.A. Indeed, in the midst of C Company's new line after its short withdrawal was Bombardier Fox's K Troop gun. Having been positioned for rear-area defence, Fox's detachment 'thus became startlingly farther forward than was intended when it was sited.'[16] The gun soon proved its worth as a German mortar crew emerged from the opposite hedgerow and began to assemble their weapon: they were despatched with a single round of 76mm High Explosive. Fox's gun continued to hold the position through the ensuing six hours, until knocked out by a direct hit which fortuitously left the entire crew uninjured; leaving the wrecked gun, they exited the battle riding on their Crusader tractor.

The rest of 344 Battery had begun 1 July between the Borderers' position and le Haut-du-Bosq, K Troop right, L left, and J in reserve. For long-range defensive antitank fire, the ground was far from ideal: *'positions were for the most part hopeless as far as 17-pdrs were concerned. The arcs were short and the country densely wooded.'*[17] In the course of the day, individual gun detachments went forward to meet the tank threat on the Borderers' front. One L Troop gun under Sergeant McGilvray fired at a *Panzer IV* hull-down behind the opposite hedgerow. Hitting squarely on its mantlet, the enormous impact of the high velocity shell spun the tank's turret through 180 degrees. A KOSB patrol later confirmed the tank knocked out. First Shillington and later the Brigadier ordered further guns forward. One such detachment, Sergeant Orr's of L Troop, showed remarkable energy when the cumbersome seventeen pounder they were manhandling poked its barrel into a field only to find it already occupied by a *Panzer IV*. The crew performed a hasty 'crash action'. Orr leapt onto the layer's seat, and he got off the first round of the duel. This took off the tank's turret and Orr proceeded to 'enjoy a little target practice' until the rest of the wreck was well ablaze.

The afternoon wore on. The *Panzergrenadiere* continued struggling to batter a way forward. The infantry continued sitting out the storm as the two 178 Battery FOOs, Captains Shaw and Meredith, continued to call in Defensive Fire tasks, all of them variations on DF109. At great risk to himself, Lieutenant-Colonel Shillington circulated around the companies, *'walking calmly about the battlefield, a great inspiration to his men in this difficult battle.'* While maintaining a studied calm, the colonel was concerned enough to report to brigade that, *'the right hand position is partially knocked out and any help would be welcome'*. Brigade responded with orders to the rearward battalions to support the Borderers. But before help arrived, the battle took a decisive turn. High in the ruins of the Belleval château, Captain John Shaw perched between rafters to observe the battlefield, calling in fire from his battery. Through the afternoon haze of dust and smoke, he discerned German armour forming up in the triangular wood from which previous attacks had been launched[18] – nine or ten tanks visible and doubtless more in the vicinity. Yet again, he called in the defensive fire task, 'D.F. 109 south

Captain Shaw was perched in the rafters of the heavily damaged Belleval château.

'Give us all you've got!'

The "smashers" of the Medium artillery: loading a 5.5 inch gun.

west 400', emphasizing the urgency with the call to 'Give us all you've got!' In return, Shaw got more than he expected.

The Royal Artillery of 1944 was superbly efficient at co-ordinated and rapid delivery of firepower to a vital spot, and at this moment the most important target was clearly the expected *Hohenstaufen* assault. Captain Shaw had counted on receiving a battery 'Stonk': 'linear, predicted target' fire by eight guns. That is, fire on a given range and bearing as opposed to using ranging shots; and with shells landing in a line, each gun firing on its own allotted part of the line. Unbeknown to Shaw, his request was promoted to a 'Mike Target', for a full field regiment of twenty-four guns, further promoted to a divisional 'Uncle Target' of seventy-two, and on up to become a 'Victor Target' involving all the guns of VIII Corps, mediums and heavies as well as field regiments. A similar call went to XXX Corps, whose guns joined in.[19]

VIII Corps alone had 240 field guns, plus 16 mediums and 16 heavies; XXX Corps had available (respectively) 96, 64, and 16.[20] With an almighty crash, a torrent of High Explosive descended on the Germans' forming-up area. This 'biggest bang of the day' effectively halted the threat to the British defence. A depleted company of 6th Royal Scots came to shore-up the KOSB right flank, and as the fight died down, patrols of Borderers venturing forward met little resistance. Regaining the line originally held by C Company, they found enemy dead and three wrecked *Panzer IV* in the company position. Before dusk, an armoured sweep along the Noyers road confirmed that no active enemies remained within five hundred yards of the front line.

References

(1) *Panzergruppe West* War Diary, quoted in How, p 120

(2) Respectively: the *I. Abteilung, 9. SS-PzRgt.*, and the *III.(gp) Abteilung, 20. SS-PzGrRgt*. From *9. SS-Panzerdivision*, H. Fürbringer, 1984, ISBN 2 902 171 17X, p 280-283.

(3) 2nd Army intelligence report. Both German and British accounts claim that some of this disruption was caused by heavy bombers of RAF Bomber Command. These are mistaken. Of the eight such occasions when the RAF 'heavies' bombed the Normandy battleground, the closest to 29 June was the Villers-Bocage raid on the evening of 30 June.

(4) See Appendix II, especially footnote (11)

(5) *The Life of a Regiment*, Wilfred Miles, 1961, ISBN 0 7232 2785 3, p 270

(6) *Story of 10th HLI*, p. 14

(7) The Seaforth War Diary states that they were relived by 4th Welch. Given the confusion of the handover, recorded some time later in the absence of the dead Intelligence Officer, this author gives preference to the considered judgement of the *History of the 53rd (Welsh) Division*, C N Barclay, p 61.

(8) Recorded by company commander Ned Thornburn, p 46

(9) The story of the defence of Rauray by 1st Tyneside Scottish has been so well told by Kevin Baverstock (in his *Breaking the Panzers*) that this author sees no need to duplicate his efforts, and will instead continue the saga of 15th Scottish in their first battle.

(10) *The 6th (Border) Battalion, The King's Own Scottish Borderers*, Baggaley, p 22

(11) Major Sallis, commanding 346 Antitank Battery, Royal Artillery

(12) Martin, p 31-32. Note that the 'Forward Observation Officer' worked from his 'Observation Post', that term applying equally to a hole in the ground, a tank, or a light aircraft.

(13) Baggaley, p 24

(14) Woolcombe, p 73

(15) Woolcombe's lightly fictionalized account presented in his superb 1955 book *Lion Rampant*

Aftermath at Rauray: crushed despatch rider and crippled *Tiger* tank.

generally remains close to the actual events, to the extent that real personalities can easily be identified behind the fictional names attributed. Nevertheless, in this instance Woolcombe's account of the fate of his company commander differs from the reality. And Gilbertson (unlike 'Gavin' in the book) happily did recover in time to achieve a well-deserved colonelcy in his former regiment, the 8th Royal Scots, before the war's end.

(16) Flower, p 123. Note that the 91st Antitank Regiment history confuses the date, citing these events as occurring on 30 June. Fortunately the battery War Diary survives to resolve any doubt.

(17) 344 Battery War Diary

(18) Many accounts give Queudeville as Shaw's target. While this hamlet was indeed enemy held, attacks on Belleval clearly originated from the wood, which from Shaw's perspective was halfway to Queudeville.

(19) Whether this was by arrangement between the two corps or co-incidence is uncertain. In Rauray, the 185th Field Regiment commander Lieutenant-Colonel Mackay-Lewis had come forward at a critical moment and it is quite possible that, unlike Shaw, he personally called for the XXX Corps Victor Target. The story of 'Squirrel' Mackay-Lewis is recounted in Baverstock, p 107 & 117.

(20) Jackson, p 30-31

Chapter 10

SATURDAY, 1 JULY AND BEYOND: THE RECKONING

At the close of 1 July, the defenders of the 'Scottish corridor' remained grimly defiant. They were unaware that the enemy counter-offensive had failed. Montgomery's report referring to the Germans' 'last and strongest attempt against the salient' was written only later, with benefit of the hindsight which informed so much of his record of events.

TOO GOOD TO BE TRUE

The VIII Corps intelligence summary composed on the evening of 1 July reveals both the seriousness of the Germans' plight and the British failure to recognise that this battle was effectively over. *'The exact purpose of these attacks is not clear, though from prisoners' statements it would appear that they were intended to be on a much larger scale, but that concentration had been prevented by our bombing and artillery fire. As it was, the enemy achieved nothing and suffered heavy casualties both in men and tanks.'*[1] Similarly, the 11th Armoured Division Intelligence Summary for that day related, *'Today has not so far seen the launching of the hy enemy counter attack which the impressive display of SS Pz Divs now grouped around our bridgehead would have seemed to warrant. It is quite possible that after their very hasty journey and recent arrival these fmns have been glad to collect themselves before getting down seriously to the job in hand.'* The combined assault of two *SS-Panzerkorps* was assessed by 11th Armoured staff as no more than 'a series of attempts to gauge the strength of our posns.'[2]

British intelligence reports on the 1 July fighting noted that in the 'fog of war' it had been difficult precisely to identify the enemy units engaged. This was no doubt due to a combination of the defenders being too busy to record events, a paucity of prisoners, and possibly some intermingling of German formations towards the end of the struggle. Gradually, as Sunday 2 July passed without any more than pinprick enemy attacks, in company strength or less, it became clear that the German forces had withdrawn from some of their forward positions. Even then, the extent of the reverse was not appreciated. 11th Armoured Division's assessment was that, *'In view of the fact that the SS Divs undoubtedly form the backbone of the German strategic reserve, it is unlikely that their commitment piecemeal will be allowed to continue, particularly if ROMMEL is now in direct control.'*[3] The field marshal might have permitted himself a wry smile had he seen this neat encapsulation of the very strategy he had earlier advocated.

GOALS UNACHIEVED
Prior to June, the British had rightly feared that the invasion would be met by a spirited German armoured counter-offensive. Several factors conspired to prevent such a decisive counterblow from being struck. On 6 June, Hitler's standing orders froze much of the armoured force. On 11 June, an air strike against la Caine destroyed *General der Panzertruppen* Freiherr Geyr von Schweppenburg's *Panzer Gruppe West* headquarters and along with it General Geyr's counter-attack plan. While storms in the channel slowed the Allied build up, the Germans' preparation of a strategic offensive was slowed by the success of Operation FORTITUDE SOUTH in convincing the Nazi hierarchy that the defence of the sector between Calais and the River Somme should not be weakened. So it was only by early July that the assembly of *Panzer* divisions was expected to be complete for a drive to the beaches.

This drive was pre-empted by Montgomery. But, whatever it finally achieved, Operation EPSOM had not been conceived as a spoiling attack. Montgomery had a real hope of securing the Orne River bridges and outflanking Caen. *'8 Corps was to be launched through the front of 3 Canadian Division, with a view to forcing crossing over the Rivers Odon and Orne and gaining a position on the high ground north-east of Bretteville-sur-Laize, dominating the exits from Caen to the south.'*[4] These objectives were echoed in Operational Orders, and allowed to be communicated to the troops.

So, in its original conception, EPSOM failed. The strategic goal was not achieved, and tactical failings were all too evident. Not for the last time, the flexibility and tenacity of German defences were underestimated. And major shortcomings in British inter-unit co-ordination were exposed. By good fortune, the failure of armour and infantry to work effectively together proved less important than the notable success of cooperation between the infantry and the Royal Artillery.

In their turn, the Germans also failed. Strategically, an absence of clear-thinking generalship allowed the master plan to be abandoned in favour of a reaction to the British initiative. Operationally, the principal German offensive force in the theatre of operations was cast into battle prematurely, with inadequate preparation, against an enemy whose own offensive had already been rebuffed. Tactically, hindsight suggests that the renewed German attack of 1 July had little chance of prevailing against a defence in great depth, including well supplied field and medium artillery and even more tank and antitank assets than could usefully be deployed. (Though this knowledge should not belittle the defenders' significant achievement in stopping the attackers on the very first of the multiple defence lines.)

THE OUTCOME
As he observed the results of loosing *II. SS-Panzerkorps* against the British salient, Geyr von Schweppenburg recognised the effectiveness of the British

battle tactics. By provoking German counter-attacks, they were drawing key German formations onto killing fields where the offensive capability of the German armies in Normandy would be fatally blunted. He realised that the 'drive to the beaches' was no longer an option. Better by far, he reasoned, to suspend such self-defeating attacks and pull back from the area, drawing the Allies on to battlegrounds of his own choosing. He recommended screening Paris with a line further back, out of range of Allied naval gunnery. Straightening the front might allow disengaging the vital armoured divisions. An 'elastic defence' might allow them the time and manoeuvrability to regain a degree of initiative; might give the *Panzertruppen* a chance once again to exploit their superior tactics and equipment in an offensive role. The chance was slim, but General Geyr was willing to risk his career on the gamble.

Von Rundstedt was similarly minded yet more outspoken. Aggrieved by the fruitless journey to Berchtesgaden and back, he was in no mood to be conciliatory. When Keitel called from the *Führerhauptquartier* to demand what could be done after the defeat of *II. SS-Panzerkorps* the old warhorse spoke his mind. To the plea, 'What shall we do? What shall we do?' von Rundstedt famously, and to his lasting credit, responded, 'Make peace you fools!' Of course, both Geyr and Rundstedt were sacked.

In rejecting Geyr's 'elastic defence', Hitler may for once in the campaign have been right. A fighting retreat across France might ultimately have proved as disastrous as a last-ditch stand in the close country of Normandy. Certainly, American advances through the dense bocage of western Normandy were to be painfully slow through the month of July. Nor would repeated British attempts achieve a substantial breakthrough until the end of the month. During that time, the frightful losses suffered by the Germans in Normandy were less evident to the Allies than their own failure to make progress. Real fears arose that the campaign might bog down. *'It wasn't like this in Sicily or Italy,'* some old soldiers present complained, *'There we fought a battle and the Germans pulled out. But here you fight a battle and nothing happens, except you fight another one later on, and nothing happens then either.'*[5] With casualty rates equal to the worst of the First World War, the prospect of prolonged trench warfare in Normandy loomed ominously. And as July wore on, nowhere was the fight more bitter than south of the Odon valley, on the slopes of Hill 112 so briefly held and abandoned by the Rifle Brigade. That bloody battleground would reflect in microcosm the British campaign in Normandy: a battle of attrition forcing the German army to commit force it could not afford to a locality it did not dare to give up.

FORCE APPRAISAL

A key theme of the story of EPSOM is the clash of two very different forces: one highly trained but inexperienced and with much to learn; the other already steeped in the harsh realities of the battlefield. Both sides had their strengths and weaknesses. In the post-war years, the British Army tended to regard the tactics of the Germans in Normandy as exemplary. More recently, the defenders of Normandy have been criticised for some significant failings, including logistics and staff work. For their part, the British in Normandy clearly had significant areas of weakness, key examples being cooperation between infantry and armour, and inconsistencies in training.

No attempt is made here to suggest that either army was 'better'. The opposed forces are simply too different for comparison to be meaningful. On the one hand, a conscript citizen army whose soldiers' attitudes ranged from enthusiasm to resigned apathy, yet which was backed by considerable levels of equipment and supply. British awareness of an impending shortage of manpower ensured that the leadership were at least conscious of the value of men's lives, even though tactical situations did arise in which degrees of ruthlessness were called for. It is noteworthy that, although the typical British infantry or tank battalion was to suffer heavy cumulative losses in the course of the campaign for North-West Europe, nevertheless it was usual for front-line units to experience significant periods of rest and recuperation in between battles. In the course of EPSOM, 15th Scottish Division suffered extremely high casualties. But after 'only' five days of battle, it was relieved, its battered battalions able to escape the dangers and discomforts of the front line, to replenish their depleted ranks and replace lost equipment. And even within those five days, there were opportunities for respite from battle. One battalion's experience may serve as an illustration. After their first day of real action, having lost 143 men, 6th Royal Scots Fusiliers were utterly exhausted. They were withdrawn into reserve to spend two full days behind the lines around le Mesnil-Patry. Only two miles from the fighting, but nevertheless able to 'clean up and reorganize.' Rested, and wiser in the ways of battle, they returned to the fray on 29 June. After three more full days in or near the front line, they were again relieved in the course of 2 July and allowed several days' rest.

By contrast, *21. Panzerdivision* had been continually in action since 6 June, and was to remain actively engaged in the battle until August, with little rest, infrequent and low-quality reinforcement, and scant replacement of lost equipment. *12. SS-Panzerdivision* had suffered similarly for almost as long, and was only fully disengaged from action on 12 July. Later-arriving German formations had similar experiences. Prisoners taken from *9. SS-Panzerdivision* told of their long overdue relief (by *277. Infanteriedivision*) at 03.00 hours on 10 July, only to be thrown back into action against 43rd Division on Hill 112 on the evening of 11 July. (A story described by the historian of VIII Corps as 'extraordinary', though all too common in the Germans' experience.)[6] Such endurance could only be achieved by exceptional measures. The German army encompassed wide ranges of motivation: from virtual slave labourers to individuals fanatically devoted to their nation's cause. In consequence, rigid and ruthless discipline was an essential factor. It should always be remembered that the successes of the German ground forces were based not only on weapons, tactics, and training, but also discipline of a harshness inconceivable in a western, citizen army aspiring to uphold the principles of democracy. While German generals failing to meet impossible demands contemplated suicide, German soldiers (including a host of conscripts from a

The *Versorgenstruppen* had to make up for the shortcomings of a ravaged rail network.

variety of subject nations) were liable to summary capital punishment for a wide range of offences. And the ethos of harsh discipline was if anything strengthened in formations that had suffered the brutalizing experience of the Russian front.

Nor were German sufferings limited to the front line. Merely to reach the Normandy battlefield, units had to undergo air and artillery bombardment of a nature and scale not previously experienced. Far behind the lines, supplying the lifeblood of mechanized divisions was a nightmare. The *Versorgenstruppen* worked around the clock, their trucks braving air attack by day and partisan activity by night. German logistics, dependent on an internal European rail network, were crippled as the French railway system was systematically dismantled by air attack. The *Panzer* divisions became responsible for conveying their own ammunition and fuel from dumps far behind the lines. *9. SS-Panzerdivision* was drawing fuel from Tours, involving a nightly round trip via Le Mans; *10. SS-Panzerdivision* fuel trucks actually had to undergo the return journey to the fuel dump at Sens, on the far side of Paris. And this was just fuel for vehicles: a division's manpower required daily sustenance by 20,000 litres of water, flour for 12,000 loaves, and meat for three tons of sausages.[7]

A British soldier taken prisoner by the Germans had first-hand experience of what they suffered behind the battle zone. He reflected, 'One wonders what we would have been like faced with that kind of air domination.'[8] Conversely, a *Leibstandarte* NCO wrote home, 'If it had not been for their artillery, we should have taught the "Tommies" how to swim.' Once again, the two armies were dissimilar: in weaponry, in composition, in motivation, and in the nature of their suffering. The British forces committed to Operation EPSOM had been largely unaware of the experience that awaited them. In part, they were unprepared. But they learned, and in learning, they prevailed.

'And so this "green" division, whose men wore the Lion Rampant of Scotland upon their shoulders, withstood for its hour the brunt of the German Panzer strength in the West.'[9]

References

(1) Recorded in Jackson, p 58
(2) 11th Armoured Division Intelligence Summary No. 13, 1 July 1944
(3) 11th Armoured Division Intelligence Summary No. 14, 3 July 1944
(4) Montgomery, p 63
(5) Picot, p 116
(6) Jackson, p 65
(7) Tieke, p 100; also Fürbringer, p 305-306
(8) Anonymous, quoted in How, p 105
(9) Woollcombe, p 68

ARMY MAPS AND MAP REFERENCES

The Germans conducted the Normandy campaign using maps developed from pre-war French examples, which used hachure (shading) to give an impression of elevations. The British used much better, contour maps of France. These were prepared using a combination of earlier French cartography and aerial photographs interpreted with stereoscopic viewers. This was quite a remarkable achievement, considering that the first contour maps of the land were produced without access to the territory being mapped; the British Army Geographical Section coyly printed on their maps of enemy-occupied Normandy, 'not been checked on the ground'.

All map references given in this text refer to the standard British Army 1:25,000 tactical map. British map references were generally given in six figures, to indicate a precise location, or in four figures indicating a map square (measuring 4cm, representing a square kilometre).

In a four-figure reference, the first two digits indicate the longitude, and so correspond with the matching pair of digits on the horizontal edges of the map. The third and fourth digits are latitude, matched with a pair on the vertical map edges. Tracing the indicated lines of longitude and latitude to their intersection, the crossing point is the south-west corner of the indicated map square. Thus, '9161' indicates the map square containing the village of Gavrus.

In a six-figure reference, the first two digits similarly indicate the line of longitude (as numbered along the horizontal edges of the map). The third digit indicates the precise 'easting', the distance in hundreds of metres to the east ('right') of the ruled line. Likewise, the fourth and fifth digits indicate the line of latitude

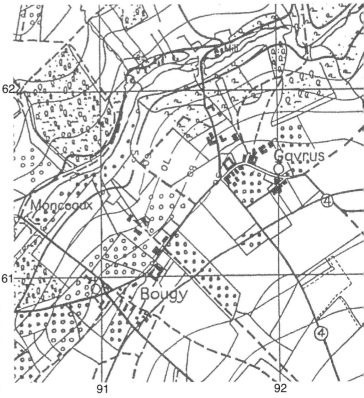

(as numbered along the vertical edges of the map), and the sixth digit the precise 'northing' in hundreds of metres to the north ('above' the ruled line). Having plotted the coordinates, the point at which they intersect is the map reference. So, '920615' approximates the location of Gavrus church, and '912636' the crossroads at le Valtru. Estimating hundreds of metres (or tenths of a kilometre 'box') comes quite easily with a little practice: until familiar with the system, it may help to start by using the master four digits to locate the map square, then work out which quarter of the square the reference falls into, remembering that a third digit of '5' indicates half way along a side of the square.

Lastly, the author points out that some map references in the text appear to contradict references given in original documents. This may occur as a result of (fairly frequent) errors in War Diary entries. For example, 44th RTR War Diary records its C Squadron as leaguering over the night of 28-29 June at '928627'. This appears suspicious, since the rest of the regiment is recorded on the other side of the Odon River. Sure enough, a detailed report appended to the War Diary gives '928617' which makes perfect sense. The meticulously drawn map of Hill 112 on page 136 gives map references as 859620 and 862616; these should have been 959620 and 962616. Pity the poor Intelligence Officer transcribing rough notes, gritty-eyed and tired after a long day's action.

An VIII Corps officer plots locations on the Cheux map (reproduced on pages 10-11).

THE INFANTRY EXPERIENCE: LIFE (AND DEATH) IN A SCOTTISH BATTALION

The British infantry battalion of 1944 was a self-contained, mobile 'family' of something under a thousand men. Though usually part of a three-battalion brigade, which in turn was part of a three-brigade infantry division, the individual battalion typically set itself apart from the other eight in the division. With its own proud traditions, its own 'way of doing things', while acknowledging the chain of command coming down from Brigade or Division, in spirit it 'belonged' to its regimental headquarters back in Britain. Thus, in clear contrast to both German and American armies: when a British infantry battalion (confusingly) spoke of its 'Regiment', this term had no necessary relevance to the larger formation of which it formed a part (or was 'brigaded') for fighting. Sister battalions of the same regiment might be found brigaded together, but this was by no means the 'norm'.

HOUSEKEEPING
The battalion was 'self contained' in most respects other than regular supplies of food, of POL (petrol, oil, and lubricants to 'feed' the motor vehicles), and resupply of ammunition. As well as the chain of command, the unit looked after its own needs medical (M.O.), spiritual (Padre), and sanitary (sanitation team). On strength were such vital services as regimental police, stores men, clerks, cooks, butcher, barber, cobbler (Royal Army Ordnance Corps), and of course in a Scots regiment a quota of trained pipers. (These were supposed to double as stretcher bearers in action; as the campaign wore on, many units quietly relieved them of such hazardous occupation in order to preserve their morale-boosting skills.)

After years of embodiment in Britain, the Scots regiments of 15th Division faced being 'cut loose' from the mother country to travel abroad. Many aspects of mobility had been tested, notably in the great exercises conducted in 1943 and 1944, some of these the largest military manoeuvres ever to take place in Britain. Whatever such exercises as BLACKCOCK and EAGLE might have lacked in terms of realistic combat training, they introduced officers and Other Ranks alike to the realities of living rough, and preparing to fight, quite literally, 'in the field'. Men died of exposure to the elements. Others returned to barracks dirty and exhausted, and hardened. Hardened further still by the issue in May to each soldier of two identity disks: the red to be sent back for Records; the green for burial with the man.

With fastidious attention to detail, battalions prepared for the move overseas. Individual soldiers would carry their razor blades, toothbrush, and book ('issued free, it being the man's responsibility NOT to throw it away'). With the Company truck came 'Housewife' refills (kit for sowing and darning), games ('Housie', obtained by officers, 'it does not matter if not new'), and playing cards (one pack per platoon). The Quartermaster's Stores lorry carried shaving soap, toothpaste, and song sheets; while HQ transport would carry the battalion allocation of communion vessels, hymn sheets, and contraceptives (these divided between the MO's two trucks to reduce the risk of total loss). Amongst all this the Pipe Band drums, pipes, and kilts, officially frowned upon but under no circumstances to be left behind. Officers were encouraged to scrounge, salvage, and save boxes large and small to transport kit, while being solemnly reminded of their personal liability for items in their care: 'to insure uniform, eqpt, and effects against all risks, even in operational areas'. And the final imperative for life 'in the field': '*At times when latrines have not been dug, every offr and man will be taught to go off with a spade.*'[1]

Regiments had their own priorities. The 2nd Argylls made 'quite illegal arrangements' to ensure that officers' kilts were carried across to Europe, hidden in the cooks' lorries, and they smuggled into the concentration area 'the Battalion's secret weapon, the paint sprayer [which] the commanding officer was determined to keep for a final brush-up of the transport before crossing the Channel.'[2] At last came signs that Embarkation would soon be a reality. 'Mae West' life preservers and 'Bags-Vomit' were issued, and finally, 'As a parting gift from Blighty, in each man's possession was a tin of foot powder.'[3] Thus the battalions went to war.

THE SHOCK OF WAR

Though the life of a serving British soldier in wartime Britain could hardly have been considered 'cosy', most came to resign themselves to the routine. The food was not bad; for some urban Scots the combination of exercise and diet proved positively beneficial. One Argylls recruit was to recall '*how much I owed to my Mother for the sensible way she had fed me – good food and few cigarettes, a diet markedly different from that which my fellow recruits had been brought up on.*'[4] Only with the coming of the Americans to Britain had awareness – and resentment – of their superior nourishment and much greater pay become a matter for concern.

Over years of training, officers had time to learn their business. In a society much more accepting of authority than today's, many officers with managerial and even aristocratic backgrounds succeeded in adapting their influence in civil life to suit their Army role. With varying degrees of respect, tolerance, and cynicism, the different social strata within the untried battalions accustomed themselves to military life. And overlaid on social ties, the daily round of Army discipline proved capable of bonding civilians into potentially effective fighting units. The Argylls' acting Adjutant at Gavrus, from a sheltered Cheltenham background, later reflected on how '*those fellows, varied rough diamonds all, soon developed, thanks to Army discipline and a healthy routine, into good soldiers and comrades.*'[5]

Considering the Jocks who made this transition from civilian to military life, an experienced British officer observed that, '*In each generation the British soldier has shown the same dispassionate approach to warfare... a long suffering but slightly contemptuous attitude to war... The soldier in all probability was nagged by Queen Boadicea. He was harangued by Henry V; he was romanticised in his clansmen companies by Bonnie Prince Charlie; he was exhorted by Wellington; inspired by Gordon, and "put in the picture" by Montgomery, and in each generation down the centuries he is the same man; not an unusual man, in fact a very usual man.*'[6] A usual man called upon to experience very unusual events. As another historian described him, 'a civilian trained to do things that no one in his right mind would do, were it not for a war.'[7]

15th Scottish Division began Operation EPSOM with extensive experience of military training, and very little experience of war. 'As for our own Division, hardly an individual except for the Commanders and a sprinkling of senior ranks had seen action before.'[8] Their opponents throughout that operation were highly motivated and highly experienced warriors. The officers and young men of the *Hitlerjugend, Hohenstaufen,* and *Frundsberg* divisions were typically steeped in realistic military training and political indoctrination. They had been tested in combat. Crucially, they had been though the experience of suffering heavy losses, regrouping, and fighting on. The infantry battalions of 15th Scottish had yet to face this epiphany. As one Scot commented following his first days in action, *'We found that our task in a real battle was so different from training that we had to start and re-learn our functions under fire.'*[9]

From battalion to battalion, much depended on the first shock of battle. Inevitably, there were lessons that no amount of training could convey. Instead, 'the battlefield became our teacher and, inevitably, it exacted a grim price.'[10] How each unit stood the test was in large part dependent on luck. Individual units in the inexperienced 'follow-up' (or 'build-up') divisions would encounter the wide range of outcomes fate could bestow. If the realities of war could be learned without undue casualties, a unit might be well placed to continue performing well. If its first brush with the enemy could be accounted a success, so much the better for all concerned. But in some instances the first encounter could have disastrous consequences. If high casualties were experienced, especially among junior leaders, recovery might be difficult. And it was characteristic of the British infantry that officers and NCOs, leading from the front, circulating around entrenchments during bombardments, and clustering for 'O' (orders) Groups, were particularly vulnerable, their losses disproportionately higher than the Other Ranks'.[11] On their first day in action, A Company of the 1st Battalion, the Worcestershire Regiment (with 43rd Wessex Division, moving up to relieve elements of 15th Scottish and hold the eastern side of the Scottish Corridor) lost all its officers to a single mortar bomb during one such conference.

Leaders with whom men had trained, sometimes for years, were not easily replaced. One extreme case was the 6th Battalion Duke of Wellington's regiment (in 49th West Riding Division), which in two weeks of Normandy combat lost 23 officers and 350 Other Ranks. In that time, all company commanders and all officers in battalion headquarters above Second Lieutenant had gone. For this unit there could be no way back. It was recommended that the surviving men be disbanded and dispersed.

THE BUTCHER'S BILL

According to its historian, 15th (Scottish) Infantry Division lost in Operation EPSOM: 31 officers and 257 Other Ranks killed; 91 officers and 1,547 other ranks wounded; plus 8 officers and 786 Other Ranks missing. Casualties were highest on the division's first day of battle, 26 June, its highest daily loss of the entire campaign. In the course of the five days of EPSOM, the division suffered fully one quarter of all the losses it was to experience in the Second World War.

The 6th Kings Own Scottish Borderers were not untypical in losing nearly 150 men in a single day during EPSOM, with C Company reduced to below platoon strength. Just a few days later, in an assault on Hill 113, 6th KOSB's A Company went up the hill with about seventy-five riflemen (or in their terms, 'bayonets'). Only thirty-two returned. After the action, A Company's 7 Platoon was largest with fourteen men, 8 Platoon had eight, and 9 Platoon was reduced to a strength of just six. It was later calculated that in the course of the campaign for North West Europe, the men of 6th KOSB each had a 63.9 per cent chance of becoming a casualty (vs. 58.4 per cent for 15th Scottish overall).

227 Brigade Record of Killed / Wounded / Missing in Action to 1 July

	OFFICERS				OTHER RANKS				TOTALS
	K	W	M	all offr	K	W	M	all OR	
227 Bd	1	1	-	2	-	1	-	1	3
10HLI	3	8	1	12	48	168	17	233	245
2GH	3	7	2	12	46	175	31	252	264
2A&SH	1	11	-	12	21	130	24	175	187
Totals	8	27	3	**38**	115	474	72	**661**	699

The 10th Highland Light Infantry had had a dispiriting start to their war. Officers lost included the Commanding Officer and the 2 i.c. The wounded CO returned – briefly – to reprimand the surviving Non Commissioned Officers for their poor performance: if they had done their jobs properly, fewer of them ought to have survived! One of their number recorded 'The NCOs began to murmur ominously... they knew that this would inevitably reach the ears of the private soldiers and still further lower their confidence in their commanders.'[12] And so it did. As one of those private soldiers confided in this author, 'We did not think highly of the CO. He had us formed up under the trees as if we were on parade. The pipes were playing saying to the Germans "here we are!"'[13] The depressing truth was that throughout their first experience of battle few men of the regiment had even seen a German, far less achieved anything that seemed of importance, and yet losses had been heavy. The colonel's harangue proved counter-productive. 'His battalion had achieved nothing - all their attacks had failed - nothing had succeeded – yet he destroyed any confidence that the battalion had in his ability to lead – known as a man who bluffed his seniors and bullied his juniors, he expected the orders to be carried out in 1914-18 style and success measured by casualties.'[14] These were not the men of 1914-18. The lieutenant-colonel had been wounded and the opportunity was taken to relieve him. Under an able successor the battalion went on to achieve great success in the campaign.

The 2nd Gordon Highlanders had likewise suffered disillusionment as well as casualties. Whatever they had expected war to be like, few had anticipated that their first battle would consist largely of sitting-out German bombardment on open, south-facing slopes opposite enemy observers on the far side of the Odon valley, while taking losses that obliged the battalion to reorganize after the battle with only three, depleted rifle companies. The regimental historian reflects their disappointment: *'It is true to say that this offensive… had not accomplished all that had been hoped of it… The 2nd Gordons had found war, in the words of Montgomery, "a rough and dirty business".'*[15] The Gordons too had been forming up for attack on 30 June with pipes playing, when the rousing effect of the pibroch was shattered by a mortar bombardment. The men's introduction to this 'rough and dirty business' was one of those lessons that only battle could teach. Their commander put a brave face on the experience: 'The one thing we can say is that the battalion did all they were told to do.'

Lastly, the junior battalion of the brigade, the 2nd Argyll & Sutherland Highlanders, experienced heavy casualties in its first battle yet preserved unit cohesion and regimental pride. In spite of losing just short of two hundred men (and a large proportion of vehicles and equipment besides), the survivors could look back on taking important objectives and on returning undefeated from the field of battle. Their success had been the talk not only of 15th Scottish Division and VIII Corps, but the London newspapers had quickly latched on to the story of the 'Crossing Sweepers'. Key officers had survived; the colonel and 2 i.c. were feared lost but soon returned. The battalion was quickly brought up to strength in materials and men. The new drafts were hardly highlanders: most were from the King's Regiment, with a smaller draft from the Oxfordshire and Buckinghamshire Light Infantry, Englishmen almost all. Yet the regiment had long attracted volunteers from outside Scotland,[16] and it was recognised that Englishmen drafted into 15th Scottish soon became 'as Scottish as the Scots'. The divisional history records an argument between two Lancashire lads being settled by one declaring, 'Ah've been a Jock longer than thee!'[17]

References

(1) Extracts from War Diaries including: 227 Brigade, 6th King's Own Scottish Borderers, 2nd Glasgow Highlanders

(2) McElwee, p 7

(3) Woolcombe, p 32

(4) Graham, 'Ponder Anew', p 34

(5) Graham, 'Ponder Anew', p 32

(6) Gunning, p ii of Author's Introduction

(7) Graham, 'Against Odds', p 110

(8) Woolcombe, p 39

(9) Sergeant Hugh Green memoirs

(10) Jary, p 18

(11) Analysis of British officer losses between June and October revealed differences between formations, but an overall average of 30% of company commanders per month had been lost, one third of these killed, and 70% of these officers lost while attacking. *The British Army Manpower Crisis 1944*, Dr John R Peaty, unpublished PhD thesis, King's College, University of London, 2000, p 245

(12) Sergeant Hugh Green memoirs

(13) Private correspondence with 10th HLI soldier

(14) Sergeant Hugh Green memoirs

(15) Miles, p 270-271

(16) Men volunteering before they became liable for conscription were offered (and often received) the opportunity to choose their arm of service and even regiment: the prestige of a Highland regiment was attractive to many an English seventeen year-old.

(17) Martin, p 2

APPENDIX III

BRITISH ANTITANK FORCES

The British in Normandy had three main, dedicated antitank weapons, each with its distinct strengths and weaknesses. Lightest, at just twenty-four pounds, firing a 3 pound hollow-charge bomb, was the 'PIAT'.[1] Next up, the 'Ordnance, QF, Six-Pounder' gun weighed just over a ton. And last, the 'Ordnance, QF, Seventeen-Pounder' gun, weighing in at just under three tons.[2] As a broad generalization: by mid-1944, the PIAT was widely distributed among foot soldiers; the six-pounder equipped the antitank platoons of infantry battalions; while the seventeen-pounder was the principal gun of the antitank regiments of the Royal Artillery.

Intentionally excluded from this list is the most common main armament of British tanks: the dual-purpose, medium-velocity 75mm gun. While this gun had a very good High Explosive shell, its design had not envisaged penetrating enemy armour as its primary role; indeed, its armour piercing capability was somewhat inferior to that of the six-pounder tank gun which it widely replaced. The different subject of tank-vs.-tank combat is not covered here, but can be found in Appendix IV to 'Above the Battlefield: Operation GOODWOOD' by this author.

THE EQUIPMENT

The PIAT, a spring-loaded spigot mortar, demanded of its users skill, daring, and luck in equal measure. Its short range[3] required either waiting until the target approached to point-blank range or else using terrain and the tank's restricted vision to 'stalk' the prey. Hitting the target was not enough. Even if it hit, there were good chances of the bomb either failing to detonate, impacting at the wrong angle for the shaped charge to penetrate, or being detonated prematurely by metal sheets suspended before the main armour for that very purpose (*Schürzen*, sometimes translated as 'skirts' but more accurately 'aprons'). And hit or miss, destroy or fail, the firer was then likely to have attracted attention and become himself a target. Reloading a PIAT could take time, especially when firing failed to re-cock the spring and this had to be done manually, against its two hundred pound pull.

Nevertheless, odd weapon though it was, the PIAT did put into the hands of the infantryman the possibility of knocking out an enemy tank. Like the infantry hollow-charge weapons of the Americans and Germans (the Bazooka and *Panzerfaust*), the PIAT induced fear of close country among tank crews. Now that a lone foot soldier could knock out a tank, the tank more than ever needed accompanying infantry for protection. All the more so in close country. For the British infantry, with a PIAT in every rifle platoon headquarters, the knowledge that they were not entirely defenceless against German armour was a boost to morale.

In general terms,[4] if its bomb impacted squarely on the target, and if it detonated correctly, the PIAT had a good chance of knocking out the most commonly encountered German armour: up to and including the *Panzer IV* and *Sturmgeschütz III* or *IV*. A well placed hit against the side or rear of a *Panther* could often cause it to blow up. Ironically, the more heavy armour of the turret side might be more vulnerable to a PIAT than the weaker side armour of the hull, since the latter was often protected against hollow-charge weapons by *Schürzen*. A PIAT bomb hitting certain parts of a Tiger might immobilize or even destroy, though accounts of this happening are rare, largely anecdotal, and generally unsubstantiated.

The rapid increases in tank armour in the years 1939 to 1945 were followed (though sometimes after disquieting delays) by increases in the calibre of antitank guns. In 1938, the Army received its first dedicated antitank ordnance.[5] At that time, both the infantry and the Royal Artillery were content with the two-pounder antitank gun, which against most German armour of the day performed most acceptably. (Unlike the much less effective French Hotchkiss 25mm gun with which many infantry units went to war in 1940.) As the war progressed, the six-pounder antitank gun likewise suited both the infantry and the artillery. Only slightly heavier than its predecessor, it was handy to move, small enough to camouflage, and capable of rapid laying and firing. The six-pounder proved its worth in the desert war, and continued into 1944 as a reasonably effective antitank weapon, especially at the generally short ranges involved in Normandy armoured combat. Still, it still could not be expected to penetrate the thickest armour of a German *Tiger*,[6] and had virtually no chance against the frontal armour of a *Panther*.

Successor to the six-pounder, the seventeen-pounder was an altogether different matter. To keep up with the development of German armour, this heavy gun was truly an artillery piece, unsuitable for use by the infantry. The size of the gun made emplacing and camouflaging it a difficult job, if done properly taking twelve to fifteen hours.[7] As the Training Manuals made clear, *'Owing to its lack of manoeuvrability, the towed 17-pdr. should not be used in support of units in an advanced guard.'* And if, *'a circular emplacement is not practicable owing to the amount of digging involved… it must be decided whether to prepare an emplacement giving a limited arc of fire, or not to dig in at all.'*[8] Fortunately, where fields of fire permitted, its long range permitted effective deployment some distance behind the front lines.

The weight of the seventeen-pounder gun exceeded the towing capacity of most of the vehicles originally assigned to the role (such four-wheel-drive Field Artillery Tractors as the Guy 'Quad' and the Morris Commercial C8). A typical Normandy comment ran, *'The F. A. Tractor is considered hopeless by all A. tk. gunners. Apparently no one has taken the slightest interest in a suitable tower for the 17 pdr, and consequently we are suffering with a slow, overloaded, and cumbersome vehicle.'*[9] Yet another regiment trying to tow seventeen-pounders noted *'The unsuitability of the Tractor Fld Arty was demonstrated in an accident which occurred.'* (The weight of the gun had overcome the brakes of the tractor on a hill.) (10) Some batteries acquired American half-tracks. A handful of lucky units were issued turretless Crusader tanks as purpose-built tractors: the two towed seventeen-pounder batteries of the VIII Corps' antitank regiment, the 91st, received a full complement of twenty-four Crusader tractors during the month of May before their voyage to Normandy. In mid-July, 65th Antitank Regiment (the Norfolk Yeomanry, with 7th Armoured Division) actually received Crusader anti-aircraft tanks to tow their seventeen-pounders, discarded by the tank regiments and still complete with Oerlikon guns in their turrets. Less fortunate regiments sometimes persuaded accompanying tank squadrons to haul their guns into battle, with varying degrees of success.

And there was an even better way to move the seventeen-pounder. Recognising the need to have heavy antitank support rapidly deployed after the initial landings, the Royal Artillery implemented a plan to issue self-propelled M10s. These were modified Sherman tank chassis with open turrets mounting heavy antitank guns (either American three-inch or British seventeen-pounders). So successful did this expedient prove that the batteries so equipped retained their 'SP' mounts for the duration of the campaign. Typically, an antitank regiment working with an armoured formation had two of its four batteries equipped as SPs.

Ironically, it was the appearance in the desert of early models of the long-ranged seventeen-pounder which had earlier led the Royal Artillery to abandon the concept of self-propelled antitank artillery![11] The Americans had reached similar conclusions and misguidedly prepared for the invasion of Normandy by converting M10 battalions to the unwieldy and mediocre towed 76mm gun. Though the folly of their policy was soon exposed in Normandy, it was doggedly maintained until the end of 1944.[12]

In terms of effectiveness, the seventeen-pounder was a major advance. In range and penetration, it was roughly on a par with the long 7.5cm gun of the German *Panther*. It was generally assured of destroying or disabling any *Panzer IV* it hit, and had a good chance against the front of a mark one *Tiger* or the front turret of an early model (Porsche-built) *Königstiger*. Only the frontal armour of *Panther* and later (Henschel-built) *Königstiger* tanks presented serious problems to the seventeen-pounder.

Lastly, a new form of ammunition, hitherto top secret, became available at the time of the Normandy invasion. The 'discarding sabot' principle involves jacketing a thin, heavy metal 'dart' with a lightweight 'shoe' or sabot. This enables a small-calibre projectile to benefit from the superior velocity imparted by the charge of a larger-calibre gun, combining high muzzle velocity with low 'drag' after firing. As the jacket is discarded after firing, the dart retains its enhanced kinetic energy. The claims made for this 'super velocity' ammunition certainly impressed its users. Both for the 57mm six-pounder and the 76mm seventeen-pounder, the increase in armour penetration was welcomed. It was not without its problems. Accuracy was affected by the unusual ballistic characteristics of the ammunition. The rounds relied for their effect entirely on kinetic energy, lacking explosive capability after penetrating. The unpredictable trajectory of bits of discarded 'sabot' could endanger friendly troops within the arc of fire. The rounds were found to cause rapid wear to gun barrels, few of which would be replaced during the campaign, and were particularly damaging to the seventeen-pounder's muzzle brake. And they were in short supply. Many gunners privileged to receive SABOT rounds in June had never fired one in training and had to get used to their peculiar trajectory 'on the job'.

Whether SABOT lived up to the hopes it raised is questionable.[13] Nevertheless, the special rounds gave the six-pounder at least a statistical possibility of defeating the front of a *Tiger*, and the seventeen-pounder a rather better than fifty-fifty chance of success in a medium range frontal engagement with a *Panther* tank. And as with the PIAT, anything which boosted the confidence of soldiers confronting German armour was to be welcomed. Throughout the summer of 1944, this rare ammunition was in great demand.

TACTICS: INFANTRY ANTITANK PLATOONS

The PIAT was intended to supplement, rather than underpin, the antitank tactics of the British infantry. (Although in the close country of Normandy, 'It was increasingly difficult to get anti-tank guns far enough forward to be effective without exposing the crews to very heavy casualties from small arms fire, and the infantry were obliged to rely more and more on their own platoon anti-tank weapon.') (14) It was the six-pounder which was intended to be the infantry's primary defence against armour. Each infantry battalion had its own Antitank Platoon with six six-pounder guns. In defence, the guns' chief protection was concealment. Ideally they would be sited to achieve overlapping and enfilading (i.e., permitting flank shots) fields of fire. (The Argylls' guns covering the Gavrus bridges were widely separated to ensure that at least one would have a line of fire to the side armour of any approaching tank.) Fire was to be withheld until the enemy came close, which in Normandy could be as little as fifty yards, and then maintained at a rapid rate. Officially this was six rounds per minute, aimed; in practice even higher rates could be achieved over short periods. In theory, alternative defensive positions were to be created to facilitate redeployment. In practice, redeployment under fire rarely happened, especially when engagements opened at short range. It was not uncommon for an infantry antitank platoon relieving another to exchange six-pounders, to avoid disturbing carefully emplaced guns.

In the advance, the intention was to get antitank platoon guns established on a captured position within fifteen minutes, in the expectation of armoured counter-attack within thirty. In Normandy, this was a tall order. The light Loyd carrier benefited from better ground clearance than the Universal (or Bren) of the Carrier Platoon. But it was underpowered for any sort of cross-country towing. Frequently, rifle companies had to depend on their own PIATS and on supporting tanks or 'sp's while waiting for the guns to struggle forward up clogged country lanes.

There was a procedure for emergencies. On arrival in their gun position, the six-pounder crews could execute a 'crash action'. Within moments of the carrier stopping, the gun would be unhooked and turned, with the Numbers 2 and 3 on the trails and the Number 4 (the 'spare' or 'link' man) acting as counterweight on the barrel. The trails were split, spread, and locked; the gun shoved into position; the wheel brakes applied; and ammunition brought forward before the towing carrier pulled back (its driver returning as an ammunition number) and the second Loyd carrier returned to fulfil other duties with Echelon. The gun commander (or Number 1),[15] standing some distance away from the gun to observe and watch the fall of shot, would identify the target and shout the general order, e.g., 'Tank, ten o'clock, four hundred yards, moving left!' The Number 4, senior man on the gun, would grab the rubber-coated Traversing Shoulder Piece protruding under the right shoulder of the layer (Number 2), and swing the barrel to the indicated direction, and shout 'On!' (On level ground, the six-pounder barrel could traverse up to 45 degrees without moving the carriage.) Having set the range and offset required, the layer would engage the gearing for fine control of traverse, acquire the target in his telescope, and shout 'On!' Only then, to avoid a premature, would the loader (Number 3) thump in a round, and shout 'In!' Following this ritual 'On! On! In!' the layer would fire and the process would repeat. (Though as one Argyll gunner told this author, 'In action we soon abandoned the training drill!' In desperate situations, the loader might slam in rounds as soon as the breech was clear, and the layer fire over open sights.) With the first shot, the gun would jump up and the trail spades dig firmly into soft ground.[16] And, according to legend, any inexperienced layer would get a black eye.

TACTICS: ROYAL ARTILLERY TOWED GUNS

As a general rule, every British division and corps in Normandy would have a Royal Artillery antitank regiment on strength. Each antitank regiment had forty-eight guns: four batteries of twelve guns, each battery having three four-gun troops, each troop two two-gun sections. For EPSOM, the 15th (Scottish) Division's own 97th Antitank Regiment allocated a battery to each of the three infantry brigades, each infantry battalion typically receiving a troop of four extra guns (the fourth battery held in reserve).

Within the Battalion Area, the infantry's own Antitank Platoon commander generally took charge of siting all guns (overall responsibility for ensuring coordination with the artillerymen resting with the battalion commander). Conversely, in the Brigade Area the battery commander would advise the infantry brigadier on antitank defences; and the colonel of the Antitank Regiment would advise the divisional CRA. These arrangements did not always run smoothly. Once detected, antitank guns had little defence against enemy infantry and were dependent on their own infantry for support. Artillerymen complained of the infantry 'milling around' and giving away gun positions. Emplaced guns, even six-pounders, could rarely follow the ebb and flow of battle, and needed time to evacuate before the tide turned. Bitter were the recriminations of Royal Artillery commanders whose guns were left exposed by retreating riflemen. In the immediate aftermath of the battle for Gavrus, a battery commander of the 97th Antitank Regiment angrily noted: 'If ATk guns are to be emplaced far fwd it must be made clear to the fwd inf that they must hold their ground at all costs.'[17] A battery engaged elsewhere during EPSOM recorded on 30 June, 'Germans launched heavy infantry attack against 'J' Tp Area. Own Inf were forced back leaving one gun without protection. Owing to confused nature of fighting the detachment could not get away and were pinned down by automatic fire. Finally Germans over-ran the position but most of the detachment escaped by feigning dead.'[18]

Where seventeen-pounders were concerned, artillerymen became especially uneasy under the command of infantry officers. Their manuals specified that the heavy antitank guns should be deployed as backstops, with long fields of fire. One antitank regiment complained that during EPSOM, 'Gun positions were for the most part hopeless as far as 17-pdrs were concerned. The arcs were short and the country densely wooded.'[19] And another that, 'My guns… are bundled into very forward localities by day, and consequently see no tanks but suffer heavily from shelling. I consider the 6 inf 6 pdrs WITH SABOT as being entirely suitable for a Bn. frontal area and that 17 pdrs should be commanded and sited at all times by the Regimental A.tk. Commander and their chief task is in depth.'[20]

TACTICS: ROYAL ARTILLERY SP GUNS

As noted above, the adoption of self-propelled M10 gun carriages with American three-inch antitank guns was a temporary expedient whose success led to its permanent acceptance by the Royal Artillery. Hasty moves were made during April and May to convert M10 batteries to the more powerful seventeen-pounder in time for the invasion.[21] Originally planned to resist expected German armoured counter attacks against the invasion beaches, the wider benefits of highly mobile antitank guns were quickly appreciated by their users. That this was a surprise to the planners is evident. As late as August 1944, the Artillery Training manual was still declaring that 'Until further experience of handling self-propelled anti-tank artillery has been gained, it is only possible to lay *down certain principles governing its deployment.'* Even in 1945, the Manual still maintained that *'Until more experience with S.P. equipments has been gained in battle, no tactical doctrine can be regarded as completely firm.'*[22] Reality outpaced War Office platitudes as artillery officers developed tactics in the field.

The general idea in Normandy came to be that tanks would support infantry onto the objective, remaining to defend against armoured counterattack only as long as it took specialist antitank forces to come forward and get into position. However, if enemy armour was expected in strength, then towed seventeen-pounders would be required. And to hold the ground during the lengthy period of their emplacement would be the job of the M10 batteries. Such was the theory. As usual in the British Army, specialist units often found themselves operating under commanders who did not appreciate their specialism. *'Most of the Battalion Commanders in 15 Scottish Division, for instance, had never seen an M10 before they met them in Normandy: or if they had seen them they had no idea what they could do or could not do... they either forgot about them altogether... or by way of sudden variety whistled them forward and demanded some quite unsuitable action because no-one else would do it.'*[23] While infantry officers siting firing positions might neglect the inability of guns to fall back under enemy pressure, so might officers in armoured regiments mistake M10s for tanks.

Antitank regiments typically operated with their batteries dispersed among different commands, battery commanders out of touch with their parent headquarters. If a battery was acting 'In Support', its commander had some degree of independence. If the battery was 'Under Command' the situation was different, and its commander might find himself in an invidious position. The author has found numerous instances of Royal Artillery antitank battery commanders in Normandy and elsewhere flatly refusing to obey orders which they felt inappropriate to their role. Sometimes the problem was that infantry officers could not distinguish an M10 from a tank, and expected it to fulfil a similar role. And even commanders of tank units might fail to recognise the difference.

A typical example concerns a British battery 'Under Command' of a Yeomanry tank regiment. *'It was quite plain to me that the commanding officer had no knowledge at all about the deployment of SPs... I said my role was to follow the armour.'* When the tank regiment offered to shoot the SPs onto the target, *'I said that if his tanks could not get there, neither could I... I had learnt enough in Normandy not to risk my men's lives unnecessarily, and I would stand up to anyone on this point.'* (The tanks subsequently led the charge and were massacred.)[24]

Nevertheless, armoured regiments with only a fraction of their Sherman or Cromwell tanks carrying seventeen-pounder guns were bound to look enviously at batteries of seventeen-pounder M10s. Acquiring a troop of four M10s would after all double the seventeen-pounder complement of a Sherman squadron (of fifteen 75mm and four seventeen-pounder gun tanks). And some British armoured regiments had no seventeen-pounders at all. In June, the Armoured Divisions' Reconnaissance Regiments with their Cromwell tanks had only 75mm gun- and 95mm howitzer-armed tanks. The 'infantry tank' battalions with their Churchills had only six-pounder and 75mm gun tanks and 95mm howitzer 'close support' tanks. In both cases, M10 batteries might be attached for particular battles; in the case of the Churchill units, the assignment of a Royal Artillery seventeen-pounder M10 battery to the battalion often became a permanent feature.

M10s were not tanks. In Normandy, where seventy per cent of British casualties were attributed to mortar fire, their open-topped turrets left the crews terribly exposed to airburst fragments. Their mobile role frequently denied them the luxury of 'digging in'. And while the SPs outwardly resembled turreted gun tanks, their lack of a power traverse reduced the value of a rotating turret. But it was not only the tank regiments who misunderstood the M10s' true function. Some of the M10 batteries engaged during EPSOM appear to have performed a 'classic' SP antitank role of long-range fire interspersed with rapid redeployment; nevertheless there were occasions where they were handled as if they were indeed tanks.

During 25 June, the 21st Antitank Regiment (of the still-arriving Guards Armoured Division) placed its Q ('Sanna's Post') Battery of seventeen-pounder M10s under command of the 91st Antitank Regiment. On the afternoon of 29 June, the battery was engaged in heavy fighting against the *Hohenstaufen* around Cheux. Around 18.00 hours, '*Q Bty gave infantry support accounting for many Germans who were held up and turned back by fire from Q Bty Browning guns on the SPs and HE fire from the S.P. guns.*' Hardly the tactics expected of an antitank battery, nor the ideal use of the seventeen-pounder gun. Nevertheless, Sergeant Wooley's M10 was credited that afternoon with destroying a '*Mk VI*' (more likely a *Mk IV* since no *Tiger* were present, but he was promoted all the same).

Also on the afternoon of 29 June, south of the Odon, 119 Battery with its seventeen-pounder M10s had been detached from 75th Antitank Regiment in support of 44th RTR and B Company, 2nd KRRC. The armour battle for Hill 113 was raging between Gavrus and Evrecy. The eight M10s were assigned the classic antitank role of using their long-range guns to cover the right flank, between the open slopes and the wooded river valley. Enemy attack was not expected in this area, as elements of 15th Scottish were understood to be holding Gavrus to the north-west, so the move was precautionary. However, during the afternoon German infantry and assault guns did put in a concerted counter attack from that unexpected direction, without any warning from friends in Gavrus. 44th RTR recorded that '*The 17 pdr SP guns withdrew and by their withdrawal not only uncovered B Coy, who were without their own anti-tank guns, but also exposed the flank of C Squadron who again bore the brunt of the attack.*' For his part, the commander of B Company, 2nd KRRC concluded that, '*Bty S.P. 17 Pdr did not succeed in protecting flank of 44 RTR. They were in posn against just such an eventuality as that which occurred, i.e., counter-attack by armoured cars and tanks… They did not fulfil their role because they tried to act as tanks and not anti-tank guns. When A.P. fire was directed against them they withdrew turrett [sic] down. Instead of lining a ridge, they should have been placed in trees and hedges and camouflaged so as to prevent enemy seeing them before they opened up.*' Two 119 Battery M10s and two officers were lost in this action, claiming in return 'three *Panthers*, one *Tiger*, and one unidentified tank', although sad to relate there were no *Panther* or *Tiger* in that engagement.[25]

Ironically, within a year of the British introduction of M10 batteries as dedicated, self-propelled tank destroyers, the successful experiment was to become largely redundant due to the diminishing numbers of enemy tanks encountered. By 1945, some of the antitank regiments were reorganized to meet changing needs. Towed batteries became lorried infantry companies, while the M10s increased their proportion of HE to AP rounds, as appropriate for an infantry support role. The Americans too by this time were commonly assigning M10 battalions to infantry divisions in lieu of tanks. Such flexibility was standard practice for the German *Sturmgeschütz* battalions. These had evolved into *Panzerjäger* (tank hunters) but still retained some proficiency in their earlier assault-gun role. Though lacking turrets and deficient in machine guns, they were nevertheless fully armoured. With effective 7.5cm High Explosive ammunition and a proportion of the vehicles equipped with 10.5cm howitzers, they retained the capability of offering effective infantry support.

One last point should be made relating to the Royal Artillery M10 batteries. They had not only superior mobility but also superior communications. Towed antitank guns, dispersed around the battlefield, were rarely in radio contact. (18 Set wireless equipments were not only rare but at this time rarely reliable.) The M10s' 19 Sets (or 22 Sets) allowed battery commanders to communicate with individual guns, which in turn gave them enhanced manoeuvrability since movement orders could quickly be passed to detachments out of the commander's line of sight. On occasion, the SPs' superior communications could even be used to direct artillery fire from supporting Field Regiments.

The PIAT: twenty-four pounds.

The six-pounder: over a ton.

The seventeen-pounder: almost three tons.

References

(1) Officially, the 'Projector, Infantry, Anti-Tank'

(2) The designation 'QF' or 'quick-firing' indicated that a single-piece round was loaded, incorporating both propellant and projectile.

(3) Officially, up to 100 yards, though its true effective range against armour was less. It could reach out further in its secondary role as an impromptu mortar, utilizing the bomb's blast effect rather than its penetrative capability.

(4) The author is reluctant to appear to be 'fudging' these issues, but believes that precise figures for range and penetration give a misleading impression. There are simply too many variables, and the human factor must always be considered as well as the hardware. As the fighting men knew, antitank fire was an imprecise science.

(5) *The Development of Artillery Tactics and Equipment,* A L Pemberton, The War Office, 1951, p 327 also p 16-17

(6) The author admits the *Tiger* tank in The Tank Museum, Bovington, disabled by a six-pounder firing at its front, as the exception which proves this general rule. Further, this tank was not penetrated; its commander was killed outside the protection of its armour, whereupon the crew panicked.

(7) Pemberton, p 223

(8) 'Artillery Training Vol. I, Pamphlet No. 9, July 1943 and Vol II, Pamphlet No. 5, August 1944, The War Office

(9) July 1944 War Diary of 21st Antitank Regiment

(10) March 1944 War Diary, 257 Battery of 65th Antitank Regiment, the Norfolk Yeomanry

(11) Pemberton, p 150

(12) This sad tale is well recounted in 'US Antitank Artillery 1941-45', Steven A Zaloga.

(13) The debate between proponents of 'large holes' and 'small holes' continued to rage long after the war.

(14) Experience of 2nd Argylls. McElwee, p 39

(15) Numbers are given as in the 1944 official drill. The allocation of Numbers differed between British artillery schools, with possible confusion when newcomers joined a crew.

(16) Photographs showing six-pounder guns in firing position on metalled and cobbled roads can be assumed to have been posed for the camera; no six-pounder gun could safely be fired on a surface too hard for the trail spades without the whole equipment disappearing some considerable distance rearwards!

(17) June War Diary of 346 Battery, 97th Antitank Regiment, RA, attached to 15th (Scottish) Division

(18) June War Diary of 75th Antitank Regiment, attached to 11th Armoured Division

(19) June War Diary of 344 Battery, 91st Antitank Regiment, RA, attached to VIII Corps

(20) July War Diary, 2 Battery, 21st Antitank Regiment (with Guards Armoured Division but supporting VIII Corps during EPSOM)

(21) Many supposed authorities have claimed that seventeen-pounder M10s were introduced only later in the Northwest Europe campaign. Let there be no doubt that a number of batteries were so equipped in Normandy from early June. At the time of writing, there is debate over whether the terms 'Wolverine' for three-inch M10s, and 'Achilles' for seventeen-pounders were actually post-war nomenclatures. Accordingly these terms are not used herein. A number of antitank regiments certainly did refer to their seventeen-pounder M10s as 'Fireflies'.

(22) 'Artillery Training', Vol II, Pamphlet No. 5, August 1944 and Pamphlet No. 9, February 1945

(23) Flower, p 4

(24) During Operation CHARNWOOD, *A Soldier in World War Two*, John Hall (62nd Antitank Regiment), p 54-55

(25) Extracts from 44th RTR; B Company, 2nd KRRC; and 75th Antitank Regiment War Diaries

10. SS-PANZERDIVISION EPSOM ORDER OF BATTLE

INTRODUCTION

10. SS-Panzerdivision, initially named *Karl der Große* (i.e., Charlemagne) but later *Frundsberg* returned to Normandy in June 1944 in great haste. It is difficult to determine exactly which of its elements were available and, more to the point, operational when the division was flung into combat on the afternoon of 29 June.[1]

In theory, the division followed the standard 1943 SS pattern of a two-battalion tank regiment and two three-battalion grenadier regiments, each infantry battalion having four companies and one of the six being equipped with armoured half-track personnel carriers. (The other five in theory had organic motor transport.)

Headquarters

commander: *SS-Oberführer* Heinz Harmel

> Ia (Operations)
> Ib (Logistics)
> Ic (Communications)

Heinz Harmel came from a military family, but was invalided out of the army after an eye injury caused by a training accident in 1928. Harmel was not an active Nazi. Nevertheless, as the *Wehrmacht* reconstructed in the 1930s, it was only the SS that would overlook his handicap and admit Harmel to active service. In January 1938 he achieved the rank of *SS-Obersturmführer*. Winning the Iron Cross in the 1940 Netherlands campaign, he went on to distinguish himself in the Balkans and Russia. Injured again in 1943, he recovered in time to take command of the *Frundsberg* division on 18 May, 1944.

10. SS-Panzerregiment:

SS-Sturmbannführer Leo Reinhold

> I./SS-Pz-Rgt 10
> II./SS-Pz-Rgt 10

In terms of tanks, the *Frundsberg* was the weakest of the *SS-Panzer* divisions in Normandy. Its first *Abteilung*, nominally the stronger, *Panther* tank-equipped half of the regiment, was not present in Normandy and would not join the division before 1945. The standard organization of an *SS Panzer* division did not include an assault gun unit (though *Sturmgeschütze* sometimes served as self-propelled antitank guns in divisional antitank battalions). Nevertheless, due to shortages, both the *Frundsberg* and its sister *Hohenstaufen* division had to make do with half of their second-battalion tank companies being equipped with turretless assault guns in place of *Panzer IV*.

Photographic as well as documentary evidence suggests that many, perhaps all, of the battalion's tanks and assault guns returned with the division from Russia (this was by no means always the case). As recounted in Chapter 7, reports made on 1 June give the second battalion's *Kompanien 5 & 6* between them 32 combat-ready *Panzer IV* and *Kompanien 7 & 8* a total of 34 *Sturmgeschütze III*. In battalion headquarters there were three Mark III command tanks, *Befehlspanzer III*, with 5cm main gun but reduced ammunition to allow for extra radio equipment; and three half-track mounted quadruple 2cm anti-aircraft guns, *Flakvierling (Sf.) Sd.Kfz. 7/1*.

It has been suggested that some elements of the division lacked sufficient fuel for combat on the afternoon of 29 June. The author can only speculate that the few tanks and assault guns of this unit would in all likelihood have enjoyed absolute priority for whatever fuel was available on the day.

10. SS-Panzer-Jäger-Abteilung:
An important adjunct to the combat strength of a Panzer division, supposedly equipped with *Jagdpanzer IV*, this divisional antitank battalion did not take part in EPSOM (though some of its officers are believed to have been present).

21. SS-Panzergrenadierregiment (gp.):
SS-Standartenführer Doktor Eduard Deisenhofer
Even before the start of combat, the division's six grenadier regiments were already under strength, having been unable to make up losses suffered in Russia. Effective manpower percentages shown are as at 1 June, but it is unlikely that any substantial gains were made before seeing action in Normandy.

> I./SS-Pz-Gr-Rgt 21: 83% manpower
> II./SS-Pz-Gr-Rgt 21: 75%
> III./SS-Pz-Gr-Rgt 21: 73%

Nominally the 'armoured' regiment, *21. SS-Pz.Gr. Rgt*. did actually possess a variety of armour, mostly based on the medium *Sd.Kfz. 251* half-track. In regimental headquarters were held twelve *Sd.Kfz.251/16* (flame-throwing) and two *Sd.Kfz. 251/22* (long 7.5cm antitank).

In addition the first grenadier battalion was supposed to have a total of ninety-eight armoured half-tracks. As well as *Sd.Kfz. 251/1* (each carrying three light machine guns, including the LMG of its transported infantry squad), companies 1 to 3 each had two *Sd.Kfz. 251/2* (8.14cm mortar), one command *Sd.Kfz. 251/11* (with 2.8cm antitank gun), two *Sd.Kfz. 251/16*, and two *Sd.Kfz. 251/9* (short 7.5cm howitzer). The fourth (heavy weapons) company had six *Sd.Kfz. 251/16*, six *Sd.Kfz. 251/9*, two towed short 7.5cm and three towed long 7.5cm guns. Once again, how many of these vehicles were actually operational on 29 June can only be guessed at.

The other companies lacked armour, and were not so well equipped with heavy weapons.

22. SS-Panzergrenadierregiment (mot.):
SS-Sturmbannführer Wilhelm Schulze

> I./SS-Pz-Gr-Rgt 22: 76% manpower
> II./SS-Pz-Gr-Rgt 22: 76%
> III./SS-Pz-Gr-Rgt 22: 72%

10. SS-Panzer-Aufklärungsabteilung:

SS-Sturmbannführer Heinz Brinkmann

This unit appears to have been very well equipped, with manpower at full strength. Its variety of equipment reflects the wide range of tasks it was accustomed to being given; nevertheless, for all the unit's impressive array of vehicles, its members were no strangers to holding the line as infantry.

The headquarters possessed thirteen light half-tracks (*Sd.Kfz. 250/1*) and one medium (*Sd.Kfz. 251/1*).

1. Panzerspähkompanie had eighteen light armoured cars (four-wheel, type unknown) and six heavy armoured cars (believed to be *Sd.Kfz.234/1*: eight-wheeler with turreted 2cm gun).

2. Panzerspähkompanie had twenty-five light half-tracks, of which sixteen were *Sd.Kfz. 250/9*, with turreted 2cm gun.

3. Panzeraufklärungskompanie auf Schützenpanzerwagen (gp.) had twenty-three light halftracks, of which three were *Sd.Kfz. 250/7* (8.14cm mortar) and two *Sd.Kfz. 250/10* (with light antitank gun, 2.8 or 3.7cm).

4. Panzeraufklärungskompanie auf Schützenpanzerwagen (gp.) had twenty-three light half-tracks, including three *Sd.Kfz. 250/7*, two *Sd.Kfz. 250/9* , and *three Sd.Kfz. 250/11*.

5. schwere Kompanie had twenty three medium half-tracks including three *Sd.Kfz. 250/9*, with a variety of towed antitank guns (3.7cm, 5cm, and 7.5cm) and two towed short 7.5cm howitzers.

10. SS-Panzer-Pionier-Bataillon:

SS-Sturmbannführer Leopold Tröbinger

The battalion was at 88% of strength. As noted in the text, German pioneers were frequently employed as front-line assault engineers. British observers who took this as evidence of desperation were mistaken.

10. SS-Panzer-Artillerie-Regiment:

SS-Standartenführer Hans Sander

The regiment was well equipped. Its armoured battalion had eleven of its allocated twelve *Wespe* 10.5cm self-propelled guns and all six of its *Hummel* 15cm pieces. In addition, the regiment possessed twelve each towed 10.5cm and 15cm guns and four of the longer-range 10cm pieces.

10. SS-Flak-Artillerie-Abteilung:

SS-Hauptsturmführer Rudolf Schrembs

1. Batterie (mot.) held four 2cm and three 8.8cm Flak (model unknown)

2. Batterie (mot.) held four 2cm and two 8.8cm Flak

3. Batterie (mot.) held four 2cm and three 8.8cm Flak

4. Batterie (Sf.) held nine 3.7cm Flak on half-track Sd.Kfz. 7/2 mounts

Reference

(1) The author acknowledges the valuable work on German archives conducted by Niklas Zetterling (*Normandy 1944: German Military Organization, Combat Power, and Organizational Effectiveness*) and Alain Verwicht (publisher of the French periodical *Panzer Voran*).

15TH (SCOTTISH) DIVISION EPSOM ORDER OF BATTLE

OVERALL DIVISIONAL STRUCTURE

Divisional troops
15th Reconnaissance Regiment, RAC
131st, 181st, and 190th Field Regiments, RA
97th Antitank Regiment, RA
119th Light Anti-Aircraft Regiment, RA
1st Battalion The Middlesex Regiment (Machine Gun)
15th Divisional Engineers
15th Divisional Signals

46 (Highland) Brigade:
9th Battalion The Cameronians (Scottish Rifles)
2nd Battalion The Glasgow Highlanders
7th Battalion The Seaforth Highlanders

44 (Lowland) Brigade:
8th Battalion The Royal Scots
6th Battalion The Royal Scots Fusiliers
6th Battalion The King's Own Scottish Borderers

227 (Highland) Brigade:
10th Battalion The Highland Light Infantry
2nd Battalion The Gordon Highlanders
2nd Battalion The Argyll & Sutherland Highlanders

In Support:
31st Tank Brigade:
7th Battalion Royal Tank Regiment
9th Battalion Royal Tank Regiment
A Squadron, 141st Royal Armoured Corps (The Buffs)
        (equipped with Churchill 'Crocodile' flame-thrower tanks)
with (under command) Sherman 'Crab' mine-clearing 'flail' tanks of
6 Squadron, Westminster Dragoons
B Squadron, 22nd Dragoons

THE TYPICAL INFANTRY BATTALION

Numbers
The numbers of men of a typical Scots infantry battalion going into its first action are well illustrated by the census taken by 7th Seaforth Highlanders before 26 June.

Battalion HQ & HQ Company:	12 officers, 162 other ranks
Support Company:	7 officers, 214 other ranks
A Company:	5 officers, 109 other ranks
B Company:	5 officers, 111 other ranks
C Company:	4 officers, 111 other ranks
D Company:	5 officers, 108 other ranks

total roll: 38 officers, 815 other ranks = 853 men overall

Notes on Manpower
1. by far the largest company is Support
2. the four 'rifle' companies have 19 officers and 439 other ranks, 458 men, accounting for just over half the total manpower
3. Of the total 853 men, 203 were lost during EPSOM (24%):
    34 killed (including 5 officers); 147 wounded (7 officers); and 22 missing (2 officers)

Origins
1. 18 officers and 240 Other Ranks (30% of the battalion) were listed as 'highlanders' (one of whom born in Argentina to parents from Lewis)
2. 11 officers and 409 other ranks (49%) were 'lowland Scots'
3. 9 officers and 166 other ranks (21%) were from outside Scotland, including 2 officers and 1 ranker from Canada, also 6 Irishmen and 1 Channel Islander

Battalion HQ
Commander's carrier and jeep
Command half-track
Scout car
Half-track ambulance

HQ Company
Transport 'Echelons'
    F Echelon = first line transport, organic to sub unit as shown below
    A1 Echelon = immediate resupply
    A2 Echelon = daily/nightly resupply
    B Echelon = backup supply, bulk broken into company/squadron packets
    Second line = not integral to unit, manned by Royal Army Service Corps
1 (Administrative) Platoon
2 (Signals) Platoon

S (Support) Company

3 (Mortar) Platoon

>Seven Universal Carriers, six of these Carrier, Mortar Mk II
>Six 'three inch' mortars (although referred to as 'three inch', this mortar actually had a 3.2 inch tube, and with a modified firing pin proved capable of firing German and Italian 8.1cm rounds). Mortars were carried on the back of their carriers, to be emplaced and fired separately from the vehicle.

4 (Carrier) Platoon

>Thirteen Universal Carriers (see below)

5 (Antitank) Platoon

>Six six-pounder antitank guns, each with a Loyd Carrier to tow the gun and carry the crew of four (plus driver), and a second Loyd carrier and driver for stores and extra ammunition

6 (Pioneer) Platoon

>One half-track and three jeeps. Principal role was clearing and laying mines, also constructing and clearing obstacles

The role of the Carrier Platoon deserves special mention. While the 1944 British infantry battalion had no heavy automatic weapons, it did enjoy the advantage of the Carrier Platoon, its very own inherent armoured unit, small but potentially effective. At full strength the platoon had two officers and fifty-six other ranks. A single Motorcycle Section accounted for fourteen of these men, equipped with eight motorcycles and four motorcycle combinations (i.e., with sidecars). The four Carrier Sections each had nine men in three Universal Carriers each with one Bren, the four section leaders' carriers also with a two-inch mortar capable of firing from the bracket on the left of the gunner's position. The remaining men and the officers with one carrier and a lorry formed Platoon HQ.

The Carrier Platoons rarely fought as a single unit. Detachments were intended to fight dismounted, the Universal Carrier officially being a transport, not a fighting vehicle. With only nine or ten men, Carrier Sections were fragile, but with their machine guns and light armour gave the battalion commander a flexible source of firepower for covering flanks and withdrawals, or simply augmenting the fire of a rifle company. When the Bren detachments were in defensive positions, the carriers would frequently be used as battlefield 'taxis', bringing up ammunition and taking back wounded.

In longer-serving battalions, there was a tendency for older men to gravitate to the Support Company with its more technically demanding roles. Sceptics might add that loss rates were sometimes not so high in Support as in the rifle companies.

A Company

>Company HQ
>One jeep, one carrier, three 15cwt trucks
>7, 8, 9 Platoons
>>Before first action, each platoon approximately thirty men.
>>Platoon HQ with one Bren, one PIAT, and one two-inch mortar
>>Three rifle sections each with one Bren Light Machine Gun.

B Company
> 10, 11, 12 Platoons

C Company
> 13, 14, 15 Platoons

D Company
> 16, 17, 18 Platoons

Platoon strengths generally diminished as the campaign progressed. Companies reduced to half strength or below were customarily amalgamated.

Note that the 1944 British infantry battalion (in an infantry division; armoured divisions were different) was equipped with no automatic weapon heavier than the Bren, the standard British light machine gun. Possessed of many excellent qualities, the Bren differed from 'general purpose' machine guns such as the German MG 34 and 42 in being strictly magazine-fed. Thus any sort of sustained fire required exceptional alacrity on the part of the number two, who would be continually changing magazines, and the gun risked overheating until the trigger was almost too hot to touch. Bren tripods were available on Carrier Platoon vehicles, but due to the difficulty of sustaining fire on fixed lines these were rarely used. Heavier machine guns (typically the belt-fed, water-cooled Vickers) were manned and directed by specialist units, trained in indirect fire and only exceptionally in the front line.

The two-inch mortar was a handy, light weapon, especially useful for laying light smoke screens and for searching-out enemy trenches. It could be fired horizontally, shotgun-like, which proved useful for fighting in built-up areas. It was capable of using German 5cm rounds with some loss of range (though the reverse was not possible: captured German 5cm mortars would not take British two-inch bombs).

THE MYSTERY OF THE MISSING COLONEL

The jigsaw pieces which make up the story of the Argylls at Gavrus come from a wide variety of sources. Together, the pieces form a reasonably coherent picture of the action – certainly a clearer picture than anyone present could have formed during the battle. However, one mystery endures.

**Lieutenant-Colonel
John W Tweedie.**

THE COLONEL

Lieutenant-Colonel John W Tweedie took command of the 2nd Argyll & Sutherland Highlanders on 31 December, 1942. Shortly after, his cousin Major D Russell Morgan joined the unit as second in command (2 i.c.).[1] Tweedie was a career soldier, his arrival something of a shock to the officers of the battalion who came from civilian professions. In the eighteen months prior to Normandy, Tweedie transformed the inexperienced Argylls into a unit capable of giving a good account of itself in combat. After leading the Argylls through their first two months of action, Tweedie went on to command another Argylls battalion, the 5th (the 91st Antitank Regiment, Royal Artillery); later in the war he was promoted Brigadier.

Tweedie's style was judged 'sound but orthodox'. As one informant put it to the author, 'He wasn't the brightest but we liked him.' In particular, he was known for his quick temper and purple complexion on the occasions when his wrath erupted. One of Tweedie's officers who, as a regular soldier, perhaps had a deeper insight into

Major D Russell Morgan.

the military psyche recalls that, *'his explosions of wrath, like squalls of rain, soon blew over. A devout Catholic, he was in fact a sensitive and very kind-hearted man… a worrier, prone to periods of self-doubt.'*[2]

QUESTIONS

By late afternoon on 30 June, the colonel found himself in an unenviable situation. Engaged in its first major battle, his unit had become cut off from outside support, effectively surrounded. His command was separated: bisected by a river gorge, obscured by woods, and in the heat of battle now lacking all radio communication. He had already lost a good proportion of his transport (in itself a potentially serious offence) and with it a quantity of supplies and ammunition (a more immediate concern). The one consolation was that the last word from south of the river, before the 18 Set failed, had indicated that Bill McElwee had the situation there 'completely under control'.

Under these circumstances, with his own position under enemy observation and almost constant fire, the commanding officer's radius of influence over events was dwindling almost to zero. And following the dispersal of his battalion headquarters from its second position, on the plateau north of the river, Tweedie disappears from the story altogether. Nor did he disappear alone. Also removed from the picture was the regimental 2 i.c.

Some time after, following a lull in the incoming fire, the young acting Adjutant John Graham gathered a small band of Jocks and returned to the first headquarters location. *'We crept back to the shambles of our former position in the cornfield, extremely thirsty, knackered and mentally confused. Of John Tweedie and Russell Morgan there was now no sign.'*[3] D Company men were in the area, some of them wounded, at least one dead. A Support Company corporal recalled the total confusion that had reigned around the HQ position. *'There was muck of all sorts coming in. The CO told us all to burn everything as we had been surrounded: pay books, personal letters, everything. We could see the carriers blazing.'*[4] One man told Graham he had heard that Tweedie had gone off to find a radio set. Another thought the CO was dead. (Hence Graham's great relief later on when he found Russell's silver penknife by the Valtru road, wrongly deducing from the find that Russell and Tweedie had already escaped to the north.) One D Company survivor frankly told the author that he had no recollection whatever of how he got away from the scene, so great was the confusion there.

The two officers had gone south. Precisely why, where, or when they disappeared may never be known for certain. As to intentions, in his account written shortly after the battle, Tweedie indicated that he and Russell were still unaware of any withdrawal order. They had observed friendly tanks in the distance but 'We didn't know at this time that the tanks had come to take us out.' McElwee reinforces this in the regimental history: the CO and 2 i.c. were 'still ignorant of these withdrawal orders'.[5] Some years later, in correspondence with historian Albert Grandais, Tweedie had changed his story, claiming to have gone south because, 'I was not sure that the withdrawal order had reached the forward companies.'[6] This interpretation is not convincing, perhaps a lapse of memory by an elderly soldier not in the best of health. Lastly, it is curious that the two senior officers of the battalion should have gone off together, effectively halving the chances of one of them finding friends, and decapitating at a stroke the top two tiers of battalion command.

As to direction, it seems inconceivable that Tweedie's route could have led him to the Gavrus bridges, since these were guarded right up to the final departure of McElwee's two hundred. Besides, McElwee's command post was not far from the southern bridge. Tweedie and Russell could hardly have failed to locate McElwee's force had they passed anywhere in its vicinity. Yet Tweedie's after-action report is emphatic that he did cross to the south side of the Odon. If the party crossed upstream of the bridges, even disregarding the proximity of the enemy front line, it seems unlikely that Tweedie would have failed to recall and record a most difficult and wet wade.

As to timing, Tweedie and Russell appear to have been pinned down by fire for some time before making their move. But how long? Could Tweedie have remained in hiding until after McElwee's departure, and only then crossed by the bridges? Tweedie claimed that it was getting dark by the time they left the shelter of their shared slit trench. If he and Russell only began their 'recce' during twilight, that would have been some time after sunset at approximately 22.15 hours (allowing for Army time being Double British Summer Time, Greenwich Mean Time plus two hours).[7] However, Tweedie's account appears to indicate that his first view of the destruction and burning vehicles around the bridges occurred the following morning. This author feels it unlikely that Tweedie was pinned down in his slit trench for so long. Crucially, had he remained that long, he could hardly have missed the sight and sound of carriers towing guns northwards out of Gavrus, up the Valtru road.

EXPLANATIONS

The options facing the colonel and his second in command were either to fall back, away from the enemy, or to locate and rejoin the largest body of their regiment still in action. Clearly, there could be no doubt that the responsible option was to move south towards the Odon valley, much of which the Germans had now conveniently shrouded in smoke. So Tweedie and Russell set off, into the murk. Accompanying them were the only Jocks they could find, two Signals Despatch Riders, Privates Chapman and Watson, who had been sheltering in a slit trench adjacent to the colonel's.

But in which direction did they go? Having ruled-out the Gavrus bridges, the single most likely scenario has been constructed in discussion with surviving Argylls.[8] The starting point of the move was somewhat to the east of the Gavrus-le Valtru road. The nearest cover was to be found in the woods to the east, which also had the advantage of leading away from the incoming bombardment. Any move in this direction would eventually encounter a small stream, flowing down to join the river where the two branches of the Odon rejoin. A short way further east from this junction, the river passes under the ornamental stone bridge linking the Gavrus chateau with its formal approach, a mile-long, straight avenue running north from the river to Mondrainville and the Caen road. This is the only place where Tweedie could have crossed the Odon dry-shod other than at Gavrus. Also, should any of the main force have been moving back from Gavrus towards Tourmauville, Tweedie would have expected to encounter them along this route.

With hindsight, any move further south from the bridge reduced the chances of encountering McElwee's force. But clearly the colonel was determined to make contact, so on he went. In the gloom of twilight and the confusion of battle, avoiding a German machine gun firing on fixed lines[9] the small band became lost. The evening wore on. At some point, as McElwee received and executed the written order to withdraw, the covering artillery fire called in by Gordon Campbell further disoriented the four men. At length, past midnight and weary after several nights on semi-permanent alert with practically no sleep, 'We bedded down in the woods and hoped for the best.' At some time before dawn, Tweedie's patience was sorely tried as Russell's alarm clock in his small pack, set to wake him for morning stand-to, began to ring its bell. Fortunately no Germans were alerted.

As 1 July dawned, the colonel pressed on, still intent on contacting the forward

Suggested route of Tweedie and Morgan on the night of 30 June.

companies for which he felt so heavy a responsibility. He searched in vain. *'We heard a few "Ja! Ja!s" in the most NORTHERN cottage of GAVRUS but no sign of the fwd coys. It was all very worrying.'* After returning to the night position, the group decided to split up: Morgan with Chapman to make their way to Tourmauville in search of a radio set to contact Brigade, while Tweedie with Private Watson continued their search. Morgan set off. Tweedie eventually found a vantage point from which he could survey the burning carriers and other vehicles around the bridges and the quarry: 'The whole place was deserted and un-inviting looking.' Later, at an agreed rendezvous, Tweedie was met not by Morgan (who had gone on from Tourmauville to 15th Division HQ) but by Captain Law Moreton, Support Company commander, who led the two through the woods to Tourmauville and safety. Once again, the best fit with Tweedie's tale is the scenario that has him approaching from, and returning to, a hideout in the woods north and east of Gavrus. From here, following any one of a number of paths, Morgan would have been able quickly to reach the château of Tourmauville; and Moreton's return journey, once the route was described, could be speedily accomplished.

As all this was happening, Tweedie and Russell had been reported missing, presumed lost, and the A Company commander Major John Kenneth came up (from his frustrated role as senior officer LOB) to take over the returned battalion from McElwee. On rejoining, Tweedie and Russell briefly resumed their positions. Russell was shortly after promoted to command of 10th HLI. Tweedie was awarded a DSO for his part in EPSOM. But the experience had taken its toll on the sensitive colonel, and he was hospitalized later that month with a severe attack of piles, leaving Major Kenneth to lead the battalion at the outset of Operation BLUECOAT[10] Colonel Tweedie is described by those who knew him as eccentric, irascible, occasionally apoplectic. If anyone ever asked him to explain his Gavrus recce, the answer went unrecorded. A typical response to this author by a brother officer was: 'I don't know. I never asked him. I didn't think it would be proper.'

References

(1) Russell was a handsome and popular officer, known as 'Hank' by all in the regiment, which later in the campaign he rose to command.

(2) Graham, *Ponder Anew*, p 49

(3) Graham, *Ponder Anew*, p 65

(4) Corporal James Campbell, interviews with the author.

(5) McElwee, p 35

(6) Grandais, p 193

(7) *Telling The Time*, Appendix III to *Over the Battlefield: Operation GOODWOOD*, Ian Daglish

(8) For this, as for so much else, the author is particularly indebted to Ron Lomas, Antitank Platoon, 2nd Argylls.

(9) It was common German practice to fire machine gun tracer above head-height at night in the hopes that British soldiers would confidently walk upright, and be cut down by bursts of tracer-less machine gun fire directed along lower, fixed lines.

(10) As related in *Operation BLUECOAT: the British Armoured Breakout*, Ian Daglish, 2004, ISBN 0 85052 912 3

BRITISH TANK-INFANTRY COOPERATION

Much of the Normandy campaign was fought in close country: small fields and orchards bounded by earth banks topped with dense hedgerows. Advance into such country demanded close cooperation between the three arms: artillery, infantry, and armour. But adequate observation posts or fields of fire for the artillery were frequently lacking. Infantry alone could be held up by skilfully concealed machine guns. Tanks without infantry in close support were terribly vulnerable to the new generation of hand-held infantry antitank weapons. For these conditions the British (and the Allies generally) were ill-prepared.

6th GUARDS TANKS

Operation EPSOM was planned to start on 26 June 1944 with the Churchill 'infantry' tanks of 31st Tank Brigade supporting 15th (Scottish) Division, while 11th Armoured Division waited in the wings to exploit the hoped-for breakthrough. The two Churchill regiments of 31st Brigade (7th and 9th RTR) had virtually no previous opportunity to train with the Scottish infantry, and the shock of battle led to some tragic misunderstandings.

The tragedy was all the greater for being entirely unnecessary. 15th Scottish Division had in fact trained extensively with Churchill tank battalions. Indeed, for some time the 6th Guards Tank Brigade had been an integral part of the division. And even after the abandonment of the 'New Model' divisions, with their two brigades of infantry and one of tanks, when 15th Scottish reverted to being a 'pure' infantry formation, relations with 6th Guards Tanks remained close. This mattered. In mid-1944, battlefield communication between tanks and infantry was difficult. *'Perhaps the hardest problem was that of communication between the man in the tank and the man on the ground. The human voice was no good on account of the noise made by the tank engines, and hand or flag signals were unreliable because the various members of the tank crew were more or less blind.'*[1] The noise factor was important. One oddity of the Churchill tank was its lack of 'return rollers': the top run of the metal tracks simply rasped along metal skids. A Scots Guards officer noted that infantry unaccustomed to working with Churchills, *'told us later that one of the things which took them by surprise was the appalling noise of fighting so closely with tanks – the din of the tracks and the engines, and the constant firing of 75 mm guns and BESA machine guns from each tank.'*[2]

Only after a period of familiarization could tank and infantry units begin to understand each other's strengths and weaknesses. By early 1944, close bonds had been formed. Individual Guards tank squadrons became used to working with specific Scots battalions; troop commanders and company commanders knew each other personally.

This relationship is exemplified in a 1944 diary kept by an officer of the 2nd Argylls.

'*Monday 27th March: Coy/Squadron training - a most valuable day. The technique of a combined infantry-tank attack has altered since our last tank training – owing to the implications of reverse slope defence and it was necessary to go over it again.*

Tuesday 28th March: Bn attack supported by the 6 Tks' Scots Guards watched by our own Bn Cmdr went off very successfully. In the evening our Bn football team beat the Scots Guards by 2 goals to 1 and the officers lost on Rugby by 18 points to 8.

Wednesday 29th March: Went back to camp feeling more impressed that ever with what a fine Bn the Scots Guards are – and most happily aware that their opinions of us are not unfavourable.'[3]

This was exactly what the manual required. '*A team, the members of which have by personal experience gained confidence in each other, will generally prove more effective... Successful co-operation between tanks and infantry depends upon officers and NCOs having a thorough understanding of each other's tactics.*'[4]

Then, in April 1944, this relationship was abruptly terminated. The story is long and discreditable. Briefly told: in June 1943, a plan to disband 6th Guards Tank Brigade in order to provide replacements for Guards infantry units in Italy had been rejected. But in April 1944, with the 6th Guards Tanks trained, equipped, and ready for war, Montgomery resurrected the idea, only to be thwarted by the influence of the Brigade of Guards, exercised through Winston Churchill himself. Montgomery's pride was hurt. His reaction was spiteful and irrational in equal measure: '*I have withdrawn 6th Guards Tank Brigade into Army Group Reserve. This means that it is not in the build-up for Operation OVERLORD and will not be called to France for a long time. I must have a tidy set-up... I shall, therefore, not take 6th Guards Tank Brigade to war.*' The Brigade then languished in Britain until the end of July, after which time they were reunited with 15th Scottish to resume a successful partnership which was to endure from Normandy to the Baltic.

31st TANK BRIGADE

So, through no fault of their own, a wholly unfamiliar tank brigade was pitched into battle with the Scots infantry. With the troops about to enter pre-invasion concentration areas, there was virtually no time for inter-unit training. The tankers had their hands full accustoming themselves to the tanks (including the latest, 75mm-equipped Mark VI Churchills) taken-over from 6th Guards Brigade.[5]

As the battle began, the 'infantry' tank units of 31st Brigade advanced in pouring rain (which also meant a total absence of air support). They had difficulty even locating the infantry. As traffic jams began to build up, tanks moving off clogged roads ran onto unreconnoitred minefields and suffered their first vehicle casualties as tracks were blown off. Consequently, many foot soldiers stepped off from their Forming Up Places towards the Start Line with none of the expected tanks in support.

Things were little better on the second day of the battle. The 10th HLI had a particularly bad time south of Cheux. The Brigade War Diary makes dismal reading. Due to move out at 06:30 hours, the HLI were delayed by 'difficulty in contacting their tanks.' Problems with the wireless sets were universal that day. Also two squadrons of 7th RTR Churchills had run into an enemy minefield, and the occasional downpours of rain did not help. Later, '10HLI reached the Start Line only to find it covered with fire from MGs.' (Unbeknown to them at the time, Hans Siegel's section of four *8. Kompanie* tanks and supporting mortars.) 'They suffered casualties and were unable to get forward.' Then the

Jocks had the dispiriting experience of seeing their late-arriving Churchills picked off one by one as they crossed the crest line south of Cheux. As the surviving Churchills fell back, the infantry hugged the ground.

Incidents of what would today be called 'friendly fire' (or 'blue on blue') were not infrequent on the British side during the Battle of EPSOM. Lack of experience combined with poor visibility and unserviceable radios led to accidents. The 15th Division history records of the Seaforth advance on le Valtru that, *'Very confused fighting followed, during which the supporting Churchills* [of A Squadron, 9th RTR] *more than once put down the forward companies by firing their Besas across their front and hitting a number of Jocks.'*[6] The history of 7th Seaforth Highlanders makes it quite clear that the Jocks did not appreciate the tanks' presence: *'The advance to Le Valtru, on 28th June, was complicated by an Armoured battle... Our tanks twice went trigger happy.'*[7]

Not only the infantry suffered friendly fire during EPSOM. During the engagement related above, the 2nd Northants Yeomanry were fired on by friendly tanks, unfamiliar with the appearance of the new Cromwell (even after liaison officers had been despatched to Sherman-equipped units with pictures of Cromwell tanks). And the diary of a tank wireless operator with the 4th/7th Dragoon Guards records of 26 June: *'One of Thompson's crew, Jackie Birch, had been shot through the head by a King's Royal Rifle Corps man who mistook him for a Jerry after he baled out...'* Though not all stories had such tragic ends. A baled-out Churchill crew member recalled an encounter with 53rd (Welsh) Division: *'This Welsh chap called out, "Hande hoch, stick yer hands up," and I said to him, "You get stuffed you Welsh git, I'm English" and they said "Oh alright boyo," and we made our way back.'*[8]

THE BROADER PROBLEM

If 'infantry tanks' and infantry were uncoordinated, then it was hardly surprising that O'Connor's despatch of 11th Armoured Division's tanks to assist the infantry achieved little. As Pip Roberts described events on 26 June, 15th Scottish and 11th Armoured were 'not very close; they rather went their separate ways.'[9] In fact, lacking pre-arranged signals, the tanks and the infantry had no way at all of contacting each other except by direct speech. Having started their battle without the expected tank support, then seeing the late-arriving Churchills routed, the pinned-down Jocks of 10th HLI looked back over their shoulders at Shermans (of the 23rd Hussars), buttoned up and motionless in the fields and blocking the narrow, rubble strewn lanes of Cheux. They had no means of communicating with the tanks, which remained, infuriatingly, 'closed down and deaf to all appeals.'[10]

If the infantry lacked support from the tanks, the armour too suffered from being sent forward alone. 11th Armoured Division's tank and infantry brigades had been deployed separately. As related by Roberts, *'About 12:30 hrs I got orders to send 2nd Northants Yeomanry on their dash for the Odon bridges, to be followed by 23rd Hussars, 2nd Fife and Forfarshire Yeomanry, and supported by 3rd RTR. But unfortunately no close infantry/tank mutual support for which the Division had trained...'* He later reasoned: *'It was thought that being tanks they would have a better chance of breaking out.'* But, *'I never thought much of their luck if they had to make a fight of it.'*[11] Roberts was right. The Northants' Cromwells struggled through Cheux, tank commanders reduced to hurling phosphorous grenades at young Germans, but ran out of steam before reaching the Odon. The Fifes' advance cut across the approach march of Scots infantry battalions, the units obstructing rather than aiding each other. Their Shermans filed unsupported along the narrow lane into le Haut-du-Bosq, where they were ambushed and only an inglorious yet timely withdrawal prevented worse losses. (Ironically, a similar event was to occur the following day in that same location, when unsupported German tanks were driven off by British infantry!) The Hussars were stopped near the railway crossing at Colleville, co-located but hardly in cooperation with the forward B Company of the 2nd Gordons. Their southernmost probe ran into a single *Tiger* tank which, in the words of Kurt Meyer of the *Hitlerjugend* division, 'soon sorted things out.'

Separation of units that had trained together was not restricted to 6th Guards Tanks nor the brigades of 11th Armoured. As recalled by another armoured battalion engaged during EPSOM, *'We* [44th RTR] *started to do joint training schemes with the gunners and infantry of 51st Highland Division who were billed to be our associates in the battle ahead. Looking back now, it is almost sad to think of the good beer we bought for our Highland friends in the interests of "liaison" when in the outcome we never fought with them.'* [12]

Bad feelings between infantry and tankers were perhaps understandable. Norman Smith of 3rd RTR recalled a burly Scottish sergeant saying ('not entirely jokingly'), 'Why don't you tankies piss off and leave us in peace for a bit?' The German shells the tanks always attracted were indeed causing infantry casualties. Geoffrey Picot (Mortar Platoon commander, 1st Hampshires) put this more politely: *'We infantrymen, although very fond of having tanks near us, were always afraid that their noise would draw fire. When this happened the tank crews got inside their tanks and I imagine they were safe. We infantry... dug our slit trenches a bit deeper...'* [13] Perhaps hardest of all for the foot soldier to understand was the tanks' invariable disappearance come nightfall. Of course, the tanks were not only blind and vulnerable during the hours of darkness, but needed to return to their soft-skinned supply vehicles to rearm and refuel. Nor did their crews necessarily have the night to rest: maintenance and guard duties ate into the few hours before dawn. But all this took place far from the eyes of the infantryman left holding the front line in his slit trench.

Difficulties in coordinating infantry and armour were by no means limited to the British. A good example of what could occur when infantry were asked to accompany an unfamiliar tank unit can be found in the American sector on 10 August 1944. *'When the Shermans arrived, there was some confusion regarding which platoon was to mount the leading tanks. Since this was the first time that any of the riflemen had ridden on a tank, many of the men had difficulty in locating somewhere to sit. Lieutenant Hank Morgan, commanding the 1st Platoon of B/320th, had arranged for his men to ride the leading tank platoon. The Shermans designated to carry his men, however, halted in front of Lieutenant Sam Belk's 2nd Platoon, who scrambled aboard. The tanks moved out before the question could be settled.'* [Later, the tanks came under fire.] *'The riflemen, huddling in ditches along the road, were unable to communicate with the tank commanders who refused to open their turret hatches. Prodded by radio calls from Lieutenant Colonel Hamilton, the Shermans began edging forward without waiting for their passengers to remount. When the tanks started moving, the infantry was forced to run after them, hauling themselves onto any available vehicle. The unit integrity of Lieutenant Gardner's B Company was badly mixed up by the uncoordinated departure of the tanks. Many of the infantrymen who succeeded in climbing aboard a vehicle found themselves atop a different tank looking at a mixture of strangers and familiar faces.'* [14] As the British manual pointed out, troops 'should not be having their first ride when moving up to their assembly area for action.' [15]

It is worth pointing out that the later idea of mounting telephones on the back of tanks for use by the infantry was far from being a universal panacea. When this was done by the US Army in 1944 it was most often a field modification, not a standard fitting. In the British, the only known wartime tanks so equipped were the later marks of Churchill (Mk VI onwards). Its usefulness was limited. A tank crew in combat tends to be extremely busy with multiple tasks, and it was frequently found that sparing the time to 'answer the telephone' was a low priority. Peter Beale (Troop commander, 9th RTR during EPSOM) confirmed to the author that he could not remember ever taking a call through the infantry phone mounted on the back of his Churchill. To his knowledge, the infantry were not trained in its use (how to make a call, what procedures to use); nor did the tank crew know how the thing worked, so how could they instruct the infantry? Also, he felt that the infantry would be ill-advised to stand behind a tank in action, which might at any moment reverse back over them.

SOLUTIONS

Many British units were to remain in a similar state of unfamiliarity with armour co-operation. As late as September 1944, in Helchteren, a young Irish Guards officer serving with Guards Armoured Division confessed, '*For the first time, we rode on tanks instead of in TCVs, clinging to the few handholds against the lurches and swaying of the tank. There was inevitably some competition for space behind the protection of the turret... It required two and possibly three tanks to accommodate the average platoon. For most of us, it was out first close-up view of a tank. On reflection, it seems surprising that, for infantry in an armoured division, training in Britain did not include any exercises in company with tanks.*'[16] Surprising indeed. Though in other formations, lessons had by then been learned.

As related in the narrative of EPSOM, the tank battalions of 29th Armoured Brigade were truly grateful for the cover afforded their nightly leaguers by their assigned motor infantry companies. And there were instances in which tanks unfamiliar with accompanying infantry could provide the 'edge', moral as well as physical. On the morning of 28 June, a young lieutenant of the 6th KOSB watched as a troop of '*three British cruiser tanks*' (actually Cromwells of the 2nd Northants Yeomanry) began '*a series of evolutions in front of the Company trenches; racing to and fro to halt, swivel their grim closed-down turrets, and lace the hedges and thickets with long, chattering bursts of Besa... We blessed them.*'[17]

By August, Pip Roberts' 11th Armoured had transformed the division's previous structure of two, separate infantry and armoured brigades into a flexible arrangement of mixed infantry, armour, and artillery battle groups. And another Guards formation came close to perfecting infantry-armour cooperation. After being reunited at the end of July, 6th Guards Tank Brigade and 15th (Scottish) Division continued a successful partnership between Churchills and Jocks which was to endure to the end of the conflict, fostering respect which remains evident amongst surviving tank men and foot soldiers to this day.

The success was achieved less by formal drill than relations of trust. An officer of the 3rd Scots Guards summarized how these were so successfully established. '*The tanks must support the infantry, and not vice versa. This is where everybody else went wrong. Tank crews can easily get into an attitude of mind where they think that, not only does the whole battle depend on them, but that, if they suffer losses, they are so important that they need not go on... If you can once convince the infantry that you will see them onto the objective at any cost, that you will not desert them the moment a German tank appears, and that once you have got them there, that you will stay and see that nobody pushes them off, then the battle is as good as won.'*[18]

References

(1) *6th Guards Tank Brigade, the Story of Guardsmen in Churchill Tanks*, Patrick Forbes, p 6

(2) Farrell, p 92

(3) Handwritten War Diary, A&SH Regimental Archives, Stirling Castle. The tanks involved were actually 'S' Squadron, 3rd Tank Scots Guards, whose Charles Farrell reciprocated the Argylls' good wishes, although he was long to suffer from a shoulder wrenched during the officers' rugby match.

(4) *Military Training Pamphlet No. 63: The Co-Operation of Tanks With Infantry Divisions*, The War Office, 1944, p 28-29

(5) 31st Tank Brigade, April 1944 War Diary:

Re-distribution of tks

23. In view of the new holdings for 7 R. Tks and 9 R. Tks, a re-distribution is necessary as between this fmn and 6 Gds Tk Bde. Taking-over parties from 7 R. Tks and 9 R. Tks will probably be despatched 6 Gds Tk Bde shortly. These will remain with Tks taken-over and will travel direct with Tks from 6 Gds Tk Bde area to conc area. These vehs will be handed over in a thoroughly clean & respectable condition, having been previously passed as fit for transfer by Unit EME. Full details to follow.

FINAL ANTICIPATED HOLDINGS OF TANKS

7 R Tks & 9 R Tks

30 Churchills Mk III		}14 to be converted	
6	"	Mk IV	} to 75mm tks
6	"	Mk V	
16	"	Mk VI or VII	

141 RAC

45 Churchills Mk VII		
6	"	Mk V
7	"	Mk IV (to be converted to 75mm tks)

(6) Martin, p 44

(7) Sym, p 289-290

(8) *Tank Tracks: 9th Battalion RTR at War*, Peter Beale, p 60-61

(9) Roberts, p 164

(10) Martin, p 39

(11) Roberts, quoted in How, p 46

(12) Hopkinson, p 135

(13) Picot, p 216

(14) *Victory at Mortain*, M J Reardon, p 206-210

(15) *Military Training*, p 26

(16) *The Ever Open Eye*, B D Wilson, p 87

(17) Woolcombe, p 66

(18) Quoted in *The Sharp End*, John Ellis, p 141

GAVRUS, THE FRENCH EXPERIENCE

At the time of the invasion, Gavrus was a quiet little Normandy village of eighty-five souls. At the top of the village stood the schoolhouse and church, the oldest part of a settlement which had stood above the river since prehistoric times. At the bottom of the steep-sided valley, two bridges linked by a straight causeway spanned the twin branches of the Odon River, leading to the tall mill building on the north bank. Between church and mill clustered substantial farms, villagers' houses, and the elegant Château de

Gavrus. Apart from church, school, mill and château, most in Gavrus were occupied with work on the three principal farms, which in turn supplied nearby markets, especially the little town of Evrecy, two kilometres to the south over the open crest of Hill 113.

The 6 June invasion was heralded by a night of aerial activity. With the dawn came the bombardment of the beaches, clearly heard from twenty kilometres away. All that day, fighter aircraft swept overhead. The only Germans seen were the odd car or truck speeding past on the road to the bridges, occasionally halting as their occupants spotted aircraft and plunged for cover into the roadside ditches.

The war came steadily closer. On 10 June a company of tanks of the *Hitlerjugend* division arrived, to be hastily camouflaged with branches. For some time to come, this unit would return each evening to be refuelled and rearmed in the village, before again disappearing into action in the pre-dawn. It was noted as time went by that the tanks returning each evening carried casualties. Before long, the SS troopers installed themselves in the villagers' houses, obliging the women to provide hot water for washing, and the men to bury their dead crew members. They took to stealing food; and as the days passed, their demands grew more forceful. Fortunately for Gavrus, a heavy

LES ARMEES DE L'AIR AMERICAINES ADRESSENT CE MESSAGE AU PEUPLE FRANÇAIS

Les bombardements alliés ont atteint ces jours derniers une puissance destructrice accrue.

Nous attaquons l'ennemi partout où il est. En Allemagne d'abord; dans les Balkans, de concert avec l'armée soviétique; en France et en Belgique.

Partout où des voies ferrées servent au transport de troupes allemandes, de munitions allemandes, de ravitaillement allemand, nous frappons.

Nous savons que
vous subissez l'occupation allemande
vous subissez la police de Vichy
vous subissez la milice de Darnand.

Nous savons que depuis quatre ans l'ennemi vous inflige l'oppression morale et physique, le mensonge, la contrainte, la faim.

"Ils savent tout cela," dites-vous, "et ils nous bombardent."

De même qu'en 1914-18 les territoires français occupés étaient inévitablement atteint par des obus français, de même aujourd'hui le sol de France reçoit des bombes alliées.

Nous savons que ces bombardements ajoutent aux souffrances de certains d'entre vous. Nous ne prétendons pas ignorer cela. Il serait impudique de notre part de prétendre alléger ces souffrances en vous affirmant notre sympathie.

Nous vous disons: nous nous fions à votre compréhension pour tout entreprendre afin de vous écarter, dans toute la mesure du possible, des centres ferroviaires, des gares de triage, des embranchements, des dépôts' de locomotives, des ateliers de réparations.

La destruction systématique des voies de communications de l'ennemi est une nécessité militaire.

C'est un gage de votre libération.

U.S.F.107

American leaflets asked the French to accept the bombing of their country as 'the price of your freedom'.

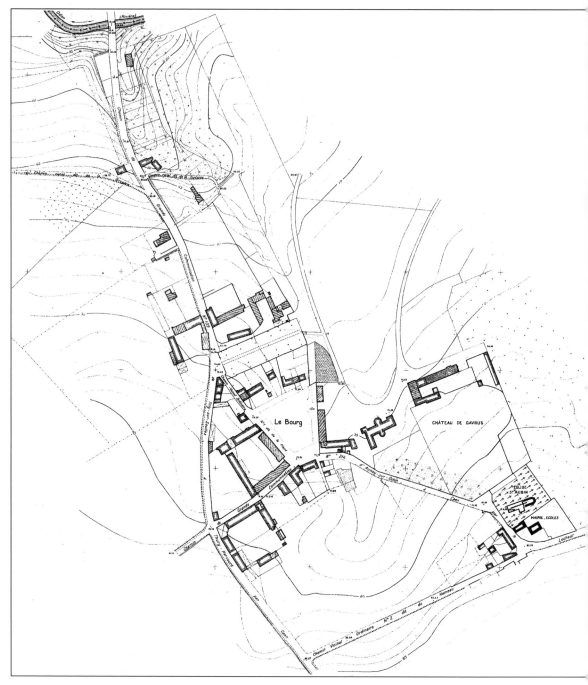

1946 plan of Gavrus for the Ministry of Reconstruction: two thirds of the village buildings (shaded, including the château) were damaged beyond economic repair.

anti-aircraft battery had been established on the south side of the village, whose captain heeded the villagers' pleas for help and intervened, sometimes at gunpoint, to curb the worst excesses of the young SS tank men.[1]

On the night of 14-15 June, three waves of heavy bombers roared over the Gavrus. The target was close by. Huddled in their shelters, the villagers could hear the exploding bombs. Next morning, the men of the village walked over the hill intent on assisting the people of Evrecy, but of the small town and its five hundred inhabitants, they found little but rubble. Evrecy and Aunay had been targeted by RAF Bomber Command as likely forming-up areas for German counter-attacks, and both had been obliterated. In aerial photographs taken ten days later, what at first appears as a length of over-exposed film covering the area south of Hill 113 actually turns out to be an expanse of white dust and rubble where once had stood Evrecy. The next aerial bombardment came in daylight. On 23 June, American medium bombers attacked the *I. SS-Panzerkorps* headquarters in Baron-sur-Odon. Abandoning the funeral of their adjutant in the Gavrus churchyard, German artillerymen ran to their guns and brought down a Marauder in flames. Parachutes were seen, but the villagers only found one survivor, left hanging where his chute had snagged an electricity pylon. (Decades later, in 1986, the remains of five American airmen were discovered while undergrowth was being cleared: these were presumed to have been taken and quietly disposed of by the SS.)

By the last week of June, life was becoming ever more difficult. The village was now subjected to artillery fire, and while the villagers huddled in their bomb shelters, their cows in the fields were exposed and vulnerable. Few survived. While the villagers took shelter, the SS helped themselves to the remaining chickens and the meat of the dead animals. Just a few cows were preserved to give the villagers milk, while a young man of sixteen braved the shelling to return to the village and keep a farmhouse oven alight for baking bread. Soon, the SS ordered the villagers out of their two shelters. A new, larger trench was dug further away from the village, towards Bougy. Many villagers had by this time given up and evacuated to safer areas, but the numbers in Gavrus were maintained by a stream of newcomers, evacuees escaping the fighting around Caen.

Incoming artillery fire reached new levels on 26 June. In the fields around the villagers' shelter, the Germans dug machine gun nests. Tanks forced breaches in the wall around the Bougy château.[2] Finally, an officer of *Kampfgruppe Weidinger*, wearing the armband of the *SS-Panzergrenadierregiment 'Der Führer'*, commandeered the villagers' new trench for military use. As the civilians gathered their remaining possessions, the village schoolmistress, Madame Guillot, sent a messenger to the mayor, le Comte de Guitaut. Taking his life in his hands, de Guitaut gave the German officer assurances that the civilians were authorised by the local commandant to take shelter in the château cellars. The ruse worked, and an unknown number of French civilians endured the ensuing battle under the Château de Gavrus.

When the Argylls arrived and consolidated the south bank of the Odon, late in the afternoon of 28 June, the French were still taking shelter, most in the château cellars. The idea of liberation registered only slowly. First to greet the newcomers were two self-styled 'résistants'. These were surprised by the cool reception they received. B Company commander McElwee himself recalled that *'Various strange Frenchmen, who claimed to be members of the Maquis and to be possessed of vital information, came in and were received at Battalion H.Q. with the deepest mistrust.'*[3] For their part, the French were puzzled to find the Scots officers only interested in knowing if there were any 'Tigers' in the vicinity.

This was not untypical. A young Argylls officer had already observed that the people of Normandy 'did not seem to be all that pleased to have been liberated. We were disappointed and a bit shocked.'[4] The New Zealand observer attached to XXX Corps, Brigadier James Hargest, noted in his report of 1 July that, 'The general attitude of the British Army towards the French people is one of mistrust. The mistrust becomes more pronounced as the rank becomes more exalted. Why, I frankly don't know. Since we arrived here the people have been distinctly friendly. They offer us a welcome, they have acted as guides; they are our best informants. Certainly they are not effusive, but after their gruelling experiences we should not expect effusiveness from them… They must be stunned by the misfortune that singled out their villages for destruction and scattered their life savings. But they are still friendly and glad to be free... Yet for some reason there is among the British army, (sic) a distrust, a lack of sympathy amounting to marked dislike that puzzles me.' Hargest went on to note instances of new graves being decorated with bunches of flowers by French women 'who do this out of love at a time when their own distress must be overpowering.'

Hargest appears to have been unaware of the British Army policy for dealing with French civilians, or as standing orders referred to them, 'refugees'. McElwee would doubtless have been familiar with the order that 'All ranks other than those detailed for Refugee Control will avoid contact with civilians. Civilians will NOT be allowed to hang about bivouacs or billets.' Should a civilian, exceptionally, be allowed vehicular transport, 'No veh normally used for the carrying of, food, clothing or personnel will be used.' And after such use, 'the veh will be decontaminated at the first opportunity.'[5]

On the other hand, one elderly Frenchwoman discovered her doors and furniture being commandeered by men of 10th HLI to provide overhead cover for their slit trenches. Alexander McKee related the abuse hurled at the Jocks by the enraged old crone.

"Worse than the Boche! Worse than the Boche! Worse than the Boche!"

The Scots, sentimental towards a woman old enough to be their mother, rather pitied her, and their replies were consequently of a moderate nature.

"Och away, yer bluidy awd hen. Shoot the old bastard."

"'Worse than the Boche! Worse than the Boche!"

"Think yersen lucky it's still stanning. Allez, yer bluidy awd hag, afore somebody shoots thi."

"'Worse than the Boche! Worse than the Boche!"

"Och awa'."[6]

Even the Comte himself was greeted with some suspicion when he arrived bearing refreshments for the liberators. McElwee recalled the count's arrival, carrying a bottle of brandy and a large jug of milk. "'The milk for the soldiers, cognac for the commander", he said wickedly.'[7] In Gavrus that summer afternoon, the first Jocks to venture up as far as the buildings of the village suddenly fond themselves surrounded. As the cellars rapidly emptied, the street filled with civilians celebrating their liberation. In the spirit of the occasion, the soldiers handed out sweets, chocolate, and cigarettes. But the celebrations were premature. The Scots patrol pulled back and the civilians were stricken with panic by the prospect of the SS returning.

The civilians played little part in the ensuing battle. Those already in the château cellars sat tight; other civilians were summarily directed there by the Germans. Two young men from St-Manvieu, Pascal Martel and (Moroccan) Ben-Laheyn Larbi, paused briefly and fatally to inspect the pockets of a dead Argyll. Caught in the act by a squad of Germans, they were arrested and marched off to Bougy. Martel's body was next seen in a pool of blood in the road opposite the Bougy château; Larbi's turned up four months later. For two days, the fighting continued literally over the heads of those in the cellars. The Comtesse de Guitaut led the prayers as shells exploded and bullets whistled. Even the most basic hygiene was impossible; food ran out, the daily ration reduced to two potatoes. After the departure of the Argylls, the artillery storm overhead redoubled in intensity. The château above was gutted and at length one shell penetrated and burst in the cellars. A nine year old girl and her grandfather were killed outright; her mother, aunt, and grandmother were both wounded (the aunt and grandmother mortally: both died over the next few days, the young aunt leaving five orphans). The position was unsustainable. In a brief lull, the survivors fled. The wounded were evacuated, leaving in a cart pulled by the village's one surviving horse (a second, wounded horse was retained by the Germans, no doubt with an eye to extending their rations).

Gavrus became a no man's land. Ravaged by artillery of both sides, scorched by *Frundsberg* flamethrowers, stone buildings were reduced to rubble, orchards to matchwood. After the Argylls' withdrawal, the Germans occupied the ruins only briefly before realising the hopelessness of the vigil. Even a fortnight later, the place was still deserted as two Royal Engineers made a dawn road reconnaissance south from le Valtru, *'down into the dip through which the River Odon ran, to a masonry bridge which was our front*

line. The village of Gavrus started on the up slope the other side of the river and our destination was the cross roads in the centre of the village… The whole front was eerily silent as we made our way through the heavily shelled village and we heard just two sounds. The first was a cat making its way through the rubble and the second we believed to be a slate falling off a roof. We went as far as the crossroads, turned round and returned to the bridge.'[8]

After the war moved on, the surviving villagers returned to devastation. Before the ruins could be made habitable, wooden huts were erected, both for the French families and also for the large number of enemy captives accommodated in the Gavrus prison camp. Times were hard. Still a prisoner-of-war in Germany, Monsieur Guillot (not directly related to the schoolmistress Madame Guillot) sent a stream of anguished letters enquiring after the fate of his family. Only towards the end of the year did he finally learn of the death of his daughter in the château cellars. His letters remain illustrations of just one among so many family tragedies. They are kept by his daughter Annick, born after the war, who has long welcomed old soldiers revisiting their battlefields.

To this day, the ground around Gavrus is rich in shards of metal. Finding a cartridge

The château before and after the battle.

case in the grass is still an everyday occurrence. Some buildings were rebuilt (not the château, damaged beyond economic repair). Remarkably, the people of Gavrus who had lost homes, possessions, and loved ones never faltered in their gratitude for their costly liberation.

Year after year, Gavrus turns out to honour returning servicemen: the 8th Royal Scots whose arrival on the morning of 16 July marked the final 'liberation' of the rubbled village; the 4th & 6th Royal Welsh Fusiliers of 53rd (Welsh) Division; the 6th Royal Scots Fusiliers of 15th (Scottish). And of course, the 2nd Argylls. In 1955, Bill McElwee returned to Gavrus with the first Staff College tour to study EPSOM. In 2004, this author was

privileged to accompany a dozen veterans of the 2nd Argylls visiting Gavrus on the sixtieth anniversary of their first major battle.[9] Received with due pomp and ceremony at the bridges, they proceeded to a civic reception in the château. There, as the sun shone and the band played, elderly Jocks told their tales to young families from the new housing that has mushroomed around the old village.

On the occasion of the 2nd Battalion Argyll and Sutherland Highlanders return in 2004, Ron Lomas and the Maire of Gavrus lay a wreath watched (far left) by Annick Bittle (née Guillot).

References

(1) Relations between the *Wehrmacht* and the SS were not always easy. In the grounds of the nearby Château of Grainville-sur-Odon, an SS headquarters, the French witnessed a German Army man wired to a tree and machine gunned for some unknown offence.

(2) At the time of writing, these breaches can be clearly seen, both large gaps to accommodate tanks and smaller 'mouseholes' for machine gun emplacements. Whether these were made before or during the Argylls' battle is uncertain.

(3) McElwee, p 29

(4) *Graham, Ponder Anew*, p 56

(5) EPSOM orders, from 8th Royal Scots War Diary

(6) McKee, p 199-200

(7) McElwee, quoted in Grandais, p 160. With hindsight, it is probable that the brandy offered to the major was not Cognac but Calvados.

(8) Sergeant Les Bourne, 244 (Welsh) Field Company, RE, quoted in *Welsh Bridges to the Elbe*, John H Roberts, p 103

(9) Earlier in 2004, a commemorative plaque was erected at the southern end of the Gavrus causeway. Sadly, even after changes made at the suggestion of this author, the present plaque still retains a number of factual errors (which a visitor armed with this volume will be able to detect!).

Gavrus before and
after the fighting.
The above
photograph was
taken on 24 June;
below, 3 July.

APPENDIX IX

CANLOAN

From 1943 onwards, with Britain's manpower reaching full mobilization, the British Army was no longer able to maintain its numbers. During the campaign for north-west Europe, the impact of losses was experienced most keenly by the infantry, and most critically amongst the infantry officers. On average, officers were substantially more likely to be wounded than Other Ranks. Throughout the campaign, rifle platoon commanders were lost at a rate of 31% per month, rifle company commanders 30% per month, one third of these casualties killed and two-thirds incapacitated by wounds. [1]

Nevertheless, the offer of Canadian officers to serve in the British Army was a Canadian initiative, pre-dating the manpower crisis of 1944.

THE SCHEME

By the autumn of 1943, the Canadian authorities foresaw a surplus of Army officers, due partly to the disbandment of home defence divisions and partly to the numbers of junior officers in training. In discussions with the British, the War Office was found to be receptive to the idea of 'borrowing' a number of Canadian subalterns (i.e., officers below the rank of captain). The resulting scheme became known as 'Canloan'. In the early months of 1944, practical considerations such as pay, uniform, and promotion were thrashed out. The first group of Canloan officers arrived in Britain on 7 April; by the time of the invasion many British units had received a quota of Canadians, mostly lieutenants. These were not cast-offs. Before leaving Canada, they had been carefully screened by age, health, and qualifications and given a four-week refresher course to ensure they would be up to the job.

ACTION

In spite of widespread anecdotes depicting rough backwoodsmen of uncouth habits, the Canloan officers were generally very well received. 15th Scottish Division found that *'These Canadians generally were first-class officers, and were to prove welcome reinforcements to their units throughout the campaign.'* [2] The 2nd Argylls went to Normandy with six Canloan lieutenants; more joined later as replacements. These *'were all absorbed into the Argylls remarkably quickly and nearly all proved themselves outstanding junior leaders.'* [3] Of a total of 673 Canloan officers joining the British Army between April and July 1944, 51 were Ordnance Corps and the remaining 622 went to the infantry. Most of these were lieutenants serving as rifle platoon commanders. And in this most dangerous of roles, they suffered accordingly, their losses rightly described by the Canadian official history as 'exceptionally heavy'. [4] Nearly three-quarters were to become casualties: 465 wounded, 127 mortally. Nor were these men mere cannon-fodder. Their losses appear to have resulted largely from their enthusiasm for a dangerous job, as attested by the 41 awarded the Military Cross.

References

(1) *The British Army Manpower Crisis 1944*, Dr John R Peaty, unpublished PhD thesis, King's College, University of London, 2000, p 245
(2) Martin, p 23
(3) McElwee, p 13
(4) *The Victory Campaign*, C P Stacey, p 633-5

APPENDIX X

THE PR SORTIES

The subject of aerial photo reconnaissance is under-represented in the literature of the Second World War. The dramatic breaking of the Enigma codes, the enormously important ULTRA material that resulted, and the no less remarkable security surrounding the Bletchley Park operation, all have tended to eclipse the stories of other intelligence sources. A rule-of-thumb sometimes overheard in the Intelligence community is that something close to eighty per cent of military intelligence is gathered from the air. Photographic Intelligence is generally quick, reliable, and very difficult for an enemy to deceive or 'plant'. Certainly, in the Second World War, aerial photography accounted for much of the raw material of the Allies' intelligence. From almost a standing start at the beginning of hostilities, depending largely on the initiative of Sidney Cotton and a privately owned aircraft, by 1944 British airborne photo reconnaissance was a huge business. [1]

THE PR STORY

Immediately after the Dunkirk evacuation, the immediate priorities for aerial reconnaissance were locating and identifying radar installations, and following the movements of German shipping (especially capital warships). The Blenheim bombers pressed urgently into service were hopelessly inadequate even for relatively short-range tasks. Of a total of forty-two P.R. sorties in the last three months of 1939, no fewer than eight failed to return (and only fourteen brought back photographs). By 1940, with awareness of the importance of P.R. rapidly growing, precious Spitfires were diverted to this specialist work. As high-altitude, high-speed platforms for cameras, they quickly became indispensable. By July of 1940, it was work by Spitfires of the Photo Reconnaissance Unit that first alerted Coastal Command to the accumulation of German invasion barges in the Channel ports.

Later, the RAF bombing campaign required target photography for guidance. Later still (though rather less welcome to Bomber Command) came photographic assessment of bombing accuracy. The Butt report of August 1941 revealed the failure of most of the night bombers to get even close to their targets, findings that would barely have been credited had they not been underpinned by photographic evidence. Bomber Command could not refute 'evidence in camera'. Thereafter, as strenuous efforts were made to improve the situation with various navigation aids, the emphasis gradually shifted from bombing accuracy to target damage assessment.

Suspicions early in 1943 of German secret weapons led to firm evidence of the 'flying bomb' programme. Photo Reconnaissance (PR) and its indispensable partner Photo Interpretation (PI) served as the front line in the fight against the 'V' weapons. In the year from their identification until the ground war swept over the launch areas of northern France, over 3,000 sorties had been flown over V weapon facilities, with over 1,200,000 photos interpreted. Simultaneously, as the resources invested in PR and PI steadily grew, preparation for the coming invasion also gained priority. Surveillance of the proposed Normandy landing beaches (plus diversionary flights over other sectors of the 'Atlantic

Wall') led to extremely detailed foreknowledge of the landing areas. And following the invasion, the work continued. By 1944, experience in North Africa and Italy had confirmed the need of a modern army for constantly updated aerial intelligence. Ground units were increasingly accustomed to receiving the fruits of that intelligence, quite often in the form of detailed photographs of planned battlefields, distributed down through the organization: to battalions, platoons, and even single-squad fighting patrols. Alongside strategic surveillance of German factories and airfields, tactical reconnaissance sorties over the Normandy battlefield monitored enemy defences by day and troop movements by night.

400 SQUADRON OVER NORMANDY

For 5 June 1944, The Operations Record Book of 400 Squadron, RCAF recorded, *'Cloudy and dull all day. A talk given by Group Captain N H C Moncrieff, Commanding Officer, No. 39 Wing, re time-set for invasion. This was a happy moment for everybody. All aircraft painted with black and white stripes on the wings. Nil operations carried out.'*[2]

Three entire 'wings', with a total of thirteen PR squadrons, were devoted to photo reconnaissance over Normandy. 34 Wing, with squadrons of PR Spitfires, Mosquitoes, and Wellingtons, reported directly to the Headquarters section of the Second Tactical Air Force. 35 Wing with three RAF squadrons of Mustangs and Spitfires came under 84 Group, and would support 1st Canadian Army when that formation was created. 39 (RCAF) Wing comprised three Mustang squadrons: 168, 414, and 430; plus 400 (RCAF) Squadron with its Spitfires.

Based at RAF Odiham in Hampshire, 400 Squadron had twenty-five pilot officers, and twenty Spitfire PR XIs. Prior to June, their main task had been preparing for the invasion with 'Popular' missions. This rather misleading code name indicated particularly hazardous tasks: usually aircraft flying singly or in pairs across the Channel to take low-level oblique photographs of the French coast, where they were vulnerable both to light Flak and enemy aircraft.

Though still using the code 'Popular' to describe their missions, by mid June the role had changed to tasks prescribed by British Second Army, or occasionally 21st Army Group. Typically, these involved photographing either specific enemy defences or, more often, 'mosaic' coverage of areas of the Normandy battleground. These were generally less hazardous missions. Enemy aircraft were occasionally sighted, but most sorties were logged as 'uneventful', and as the month wore on, the main difficulty was with the deteriorating weather conditions: eight-tenths and even ten-tenths cloud cover becoming commonplace.

24 JUNE: TASK SA 1066

After a day of cloud too low for operations, 24 June dawned dull and still cloudy. Nevertheless, there appears to have been some urgency in Second Army's request for Task 1066: a photo mosaic of a swathe of the battleground between Caen and Juvigny. By this time, aerial photographs of the coming battleground had long since been distributed to the troops.[3] The interest of Second Army was to update enemy gun positions immediately before the commencement of EPSOM. Flight Lieutenant Morton was airborne from Odiham at 06.36 hours, but returned two hours later to report only limited success due to cloud conditions over Normandy. Due to the urgency of pre-battle cover, and with some improvement in the weather, four Spitfires took off between 15.12 and 15.20. Each pair of aircraft covered half of the designated task area, and all four landed back between 17.16 and 17.31 to report 'Pix taken and believed successful'. It is from this superb set of photographs taken just before the EPSOM offensive that many of the battleground images used in this book have been produced (though note that these mosaics were assembled using sophisticated software unavailable in 1944!).

3 JULY: TASK SA 1084

3 July 1944 was an eventful date for 400 Squadron. The previous day, squadron ground crew and six of the pilots had boarded Dakotas to fly to Normandy. At the squadron's new base, Aerodrome B8 at Sommervieu, east of Bayeux, they were reunited with the 39 Wing Army Photographic Interpretation Section (APIS) which had made the journey from Odiham by sea. Nine pilots remained for the time being at Odiham, recording that the 'Pilots' room looks almost deserted.'

The only PR sortie by 400 Squadron on 2 July had been Squadron Leader Ellis' attempt at Second Army Task 1084: a mosaic of the Odon river line south west of Caen. He was unsuccessful, abandoning the mission due to Flak over the target area. The following day, the weather closed in completely over Odiham, where no operations were possible. However, at Sommervieu there was brisk activity. 'Everybody busy digging slit trenches. Dispersal, Pilots' Room and Orderly Room situated in an apple orchard. Very clean set-up.' Slight rain in the morning gave way to dull overcast, which under the hot Normandy sun burned off by evening to permit flying.

At 18.55 hours, four Spitfires taxied out onto the B8 strip to undertake the Second Army task, and apart from some early-evening cumulus clouds returned with the makings of a complete mosaic, ground features accentuated by the long evening shadows. The CO's flight of 2 July had been the last 'Popular' sortie logged; from 3 July onwards, 400 Squadron operations from Sommervieu were to be logged as 'Photo/R.'

In these images, we have fascinating confirmation of the events of Operation EPSOM. Tracks and wrecks mark the precise locations of armoured battles. New slit trenches are clearly seen, while German gun emplacements of 24 June have in some instances been changed by their new owners into infantry shelters. Before-and-after comparison is especially poignant around the little village of Gavrus where on 3 July, 29,000 feet below the Spitfires, the survivors of the Guillot family are still huddled in the ruins of the chateau cellars.[4]

References

(1) The story of the evolution of the British PR and PI services is told in *Evidence in Camera*, Constance Babington-Smith, 1958; and well summarized in a book of the same name published in 2003 by The GeoInformation Group, ISBN 0-9545270-0-3, available from The Medmenham Club at the Intelligence Museum, Chicksands, Bedfordshire.

(2) This and other details from 400 Squadron Operations Record Book

(3) A typical example of air photos, cut-and-pasted into a crude mosaic, printed to the same scale as the accompanying 1:25,000 Army map, and marked up for the 26 June assault, can be found with the 2nd Glasgow Highlanders' War Diary. These photographs used for EPSOM are from a 20 April 1944 sortie.

(4) Appendix VIII

BIBLIOGRAPHY & A BRIEF NOTE ON SOURCES

Wherever possible, details in published works have been checked against primary sources: contemporary diaries, unit records, photography, etc. Important discrepancies are noted in the text.

Special attention is drawn to Major Joe How's *Hill 112*, one of the first studies to do justice to EPSOM, and to Robert Woollcombe's *Lion Rampant* which so well captures life in a British infantry company.

PUBLISHED SOURCES

Babington-Smith, Constance, *Evidence in Camera*, 1958

Baggaley, J R P, *The 6th (Border) Battalion, The King's Own Scottish Borderers, 1939-1945*, 1945

Barclay, C N, *The History of the Cameronians (Scottish Rifles)*, vol III, 1947

Barclay, C N, *History of the 53rd (Welsh) Division*, 1956

Baverstock, Kevin, *Breaking the Panzers: the Bloody Battle for Rauray*, 2002, ISBN 0 7509 2895 6

Baynes, John, *The Forgotten Victor*, 1989, ISBN 0-08-036269-9

Beale, Peter, *Tank Tracks: 9th Battalion Royal Tank Regiment at War 1940-45*, 1995, ISBN 1-84015-003-3

Bell, Noel, *From the Beaches to the Baltic: The Story of G Company, 8th Rifle Brigade*, 1947

Bennett, Ralph, *Ultra in the West*, 1979, ISBN 0 09 139330 2

Bidwell & Graham, *Firepower*, 1982, ISBN 1 84415 216 2

Bishop, G S C, *The Battle: a Tank Officer Remembers*, (undated)

Bishop, G S C, *The Story of the 23rd Hussars*, 1946

Bradley, Omar *A Soldier's Story*, 1951

Close, Bill, *A View From the Turret*, 1998, ISBN 0-9533359-1-7

Daglish, Ian, *Operation BLUECOAT: the British Armoured Breakout*, 2004, ISBN 0 85052 912 3

Daglish, Ian, *Over the Battlefield: Operation GOODWOOD*, 2005, ISBN 1 84415 153 0

D'Este, Carlo, *Decision in Normandy*, 1983, ISBN 0-141-39056-5

Ellis, John, *The Sharp End*, 1980, ISBN 1-872004-56-3

Ellis, L F, *Victory in the West*, Vol 1, 1962, ISBN 1-870423-07-0

Farrell, Charles *Reflections 1939-1945: A Scots Guards Officer in Training and War*, 2000, ISBN 1 85821 761 X

Flower, Desmond, *The History of the 5th Argylls (91st Anti-Tank Regiment)*, 1950

Forbes, Patrick, *6th Guards Tank Brigade, the Story of Guardsmen in Churchill Tanks*, 1946

French, David, *Raising Churchill's Army*, 2000, ISBN 0-19-924630-0

Fürbringer, Herbert, *9. SS-Panzer-Division*, 1984, ISBN 2-902 171-17-X

Godfrey & Goldsmith, *The History of the Duke of Cornwall's Light Infantry*, 1966

Graham, Dominic, *Against Odds: Reflections on the Experiences of the British Army*, 1999, ISBN 0-333-66858-8

Graham, J D C, *Ponder Anew*, 1999, ISBN 1-86227-068-6 (privately published)

Grandais, Albert, *La Bataille du Calvados*, 1973

Gunning, Hugh, *Borderers in Battle: The War Story of the King's Own Scottish Borderers*, 1948

Hall, John, *A Soldier in World War Two*, privately published

Harrison Place, Timothy, *Military Training in the British Army 1940-44 From Dunkirk to D-Day*, 2000, ISBN 0-7146-5037-4

Hart, Stephen Ashley, *Montgomery and "Colossal Cracks": The 21st Army Group in Northwest Europe*, 2000, ISBN 0-275-96162-1

Hastings, Max, *Overlord*, 1984, ISBN 0 330 28691 9

Hastings, R H W S, *The Rifle Brigade in the Second World War*, 1950

Hopkinson, G C, *A History of the 44th Royal Tank Regiment in the War of 1939-45* Part III, 1965

How, J J, *Hill 112: Cornerstone of the Normandy Campaign*, 1984, ISBN 0-7183-0540-X

Jackson, G S, *Operations of Eighth Corps*, 1948

Jary, Sydney, *18 Platoon*, 1987, ISBN 0 9512978 0 6

Johnston, Steward, & Dunlop, *Campaign in Europe: the Story of the 10th Battalion, The Highland Light Infantry*, published by the regiment

Keegan, John, *Six Armies in Normandy*, 1982, ISBN 0 14 00 5293 3

Kemsley, W, and Riesco, M R, *The Scottish Lion on Patrol: the Story of the 15th Scottish Reconnaissance Regiment 1943-1946*

Leleu, Jean-Luc, *10. SS-Panzer-Division*, 1999, ISBN 2 84048 125 1

McElwee, W L, *History of the Argyll & Sutherland Highlanders, 2nd Battalion (Reconstituted)*, 1949

McKee, Alexander, *Caen, Anvil of Victory*, 1964

Martin, H G, *The Fifteenth Scottish Division*, 1948

Meyer, Hubert, *The History of the 12. SS-Panzerdivision Hitlerjugend*, 1994, ISBN 0-921991-18-5

Miles, Wilfred, *The Life of a Regiment: The History of the Gordon Highlanders, Vol V, 1919-1945*, 1961, ISBN 0 7232 2785 3

Montgomery, Field Marshall B L, *Normandy to the Baltic*, 1946

Moore, William, *Panzer Bait*, 1991, ISBN 0-85052-3281

Oatts, L B, *Proud Heritage: The Story of the Highland Light Infantry, Vol 4, 1919-1959'*, 1963

Palamountain, E W I, *Taurus Pursuant: A History of 11th Armoured Division*, 1945

Pemberton, A L, *The Development of Artillery Tactics and Equipment*, The War Office, 1951

Picot, Geoffrey, *Accidental Warrior*, 1993, ISBN 0-14-017626-8

Reardon, M J, *Victory at Mortain*, 2002, ISBN 0-7006-1295-5

Roberts, G P B, *From the Desert to the Baltic*, 1987, ISBN 0-7183-0639-2

Roberts, John H, *Welsh Bridges to the Elbe*, 1994, ISBN 1-898893-00-4

Rosse & Hill, *The Story of the Guards Armoured Division*, 1956

Sellar, R J B, *The Fife and Forfar Yeomanry*, 1960

Stacey, C P, *The Victory Campaign: The Operations in North-West Europe*, Vol III, 1960

Steel Brownlie, W, *The Proud Trooper*, 1964

Sym, J, *The Seaforth Highlanders*, 1962

Thornburn, Ned, *The 4th KSLI in Normandy*, 1990

Tieke, Wilhelm, *Im Feuersturm Letzter Kriegsjahre*, 1975, ISBN 3-921242-18-5; pages referenced relate to the English-language edition *In the Firestorm of the Last Years of the War*, 1999, ISBN 0-921991-43-6

Weidinger, Otto, *Comrades to the End: The 4th SS-Panzer-Grenadier-Regiment "Der Führer"'*, 1998, ISBN 0-7643-0593-X

Wilson, B D, *The Ever Open Eye*, 1998, ISBN 1 85821 532 3

Wood & Dugdale, *Orders of Battle: Waffen SS Panzer Units in Normandy 1944*, 2000, ISBN 0 9528867 0 7

Woollcombe, Robert, *Lion Rampant*, 1955

Young & Gray, *A Short History of the Ayrshire Yeomanry (Earl of Carrick's Own), 151st Field Regiment, RA*, 1947

Zaloga, Steven A, *US Antitank Artillery 1941-45*, Osprey New Vanguard, 2005, ISBN 1-84176-690-9

Zetterling, Niklas, *Normandy 1944: German Military Organization, Combat Power, and Organizational Effectiveness*, 2000, ISBN 0-921991-56-8

INDEX

Note: to avoid unhelpful repetition places, personalities, units, and weapons which recur constantly throughout the text are not listed, e.g., Gavrus, General Roberts, Argyll & Sutherland Highlanders, Sherman tank